Praise for *Speaking JavaScript*

"A lot of people think JavaScript is simple and in many cases it is. But in its elegant simplicity lies a deeper functionality that if leveraged properly, can produce amazing results. Axel's ability to distill this into an approachable reference will certainly help both aspiring and experienced developers achieve a better understanding of the language."

—*Rey Bango*
Advocate for cross-browser development, proponent of the
open web, and lover of the JavaScript programming language

"Axel's writing style is succinct, to the point, yet at the same time extremely detailed. The many code examples make even the most complex topics in the book easy to understand."

—*Mathias Bynens*
Belgian web standards enthusiast who likes HTML, CSS,
JavaScript, Unicode, performance, and security

"*Speaking JavaScript* is a modern, up to date book perfectly aimed at the existing experienced programmer ready to take a deep dive into JavaScript. Without wasting time on laborious explanations, Dr. Rauschmayer quickly cuts to the core of JavaScript and its various concepts and gets developers up to speed quickly with a language that seems intent on taking over the developer world."

—*Peter Cooper*
Publisher, entrepreneur, and co-organizer of
Fluent Conference

"If you have enjoyed Axel's blog, then you'll love this book. His book is filled with tons of bite-sized code snippets to aid in the learning process. If you want to dive deep and understand the ins and outs of JavaScript, then I highly recommend this book."

—*Elijah Manor*
Christian, family man, and front end web developer for
Dave Ramsey; enjoys speaking, blogging, and tweeting

"This book opens the door into the modern JavaScript community with just enough background and plenty of in-depth introduction to make it seem like you've been with the community from the start."

—*Mitch Pronschinske*
DZone Editor

"After following Dr. Axel Rauschmayer's work for a few years, I was delighted to learn that he was writing a book to share his deep expertise of JavaScript with those getting started with the language. I've read many JavaScript books, but none that show the attention to detail and comprehensiveness of Speaking JS, without being boring or overwhelming. I'll be recommending this book for years to come."

—*Guillermo Rauch*
Speaker, creator of socket.io, mongoose, early Node.js contributor, author of "Smashing Node.js", founder of LearnBoost/Cloudup (acq. by Wordpress in 2013), and Open Academy mentor

Speaking JavaScript

Axel Rauschmayer

Beijing · Cambridge · Farnham · Köln · Sebastopol · Tokyo O'REILLY®

Speaking JavaScript

by Axel Rauschmayer

Printed in the United States of America.

Published by O'Reilly Media, Inc., 1005 Gravenstein Highway North, Sebastopol, CA 95472.

O'Reilly books may be purchased for educational, business, or sales promotional use. Online editions are also available for most titles (*http://my.safaribooksonline.com*). For more information, contact our corporate/institutional sales department: 800-998-9938 or *corporate@oreilly.com*.

Editors: Simon St. Laurent and Amy Jollymore	**Indexer:** Ellen Troutman
Production Editor: Kara Ebrahim	**Cover Designer:** Randy Comer
Copyeditor: Rachel Monaghan	**Interior Designer:** David Futato
Proofreader: Charles Roumeliotis	**Illustrator:** Rebecca Demarest

March 2014:   First Edition

Revision History for the First Edition:

2014-02-20:   First release

See *http://oreilly.com/catalog/errata.csp?isbn=9781449365035* for release details.

ISBN: 978-1-449-36503-5

[LSI]

Table of Contents

Part IV.   Tips, Tools, and Libraries

Preface

Due to its prevalence on the Web and other factors, JavaScript has become hard to avoid. That doesn't mean that it is well liked, though. With this book, I'm hoping to convince you that, while you do have to accept a fair amount of quirks when using it, JavaScript is a decent language that makes you very productive and can be fun to program in.

Even though I have followed its development since its birth, it took me a long time to warm up to JavaScript. However, when I finally did, it turned out that my prior experience had already prepared me well, because I had worked with Scheme, Java (including GWT), Python, Perl, and Self (all of which have influenced JavaScript).

In 2010, I became aware of Node.js, which gave me hope that I'd eventually be able to use JavaScript on both server and client. As a consequence, I switched to JavaScript as my primary programming language. While learning it, I started writing a book chronicling my discoveries. This is the book you are currently reading. On my blog, I published parts of the book and other material on JavaScript. That helped me in several ways: the positive reaction encouraged me to keep going and made writing this book less lonely; comments to blog posts gave me additional information and tips (as acknowledged everywhere in this book); and it made people aware of my work, which eventually led to O'Reilly publishing this book.

Therefore, this book has been over three years in the making. It has profited from this long gestation period, during which I continually refined its contents. I'm glad that the book is finally finished and hope that people will find it useful for learning JavaScript. O'Reilly has agreed to make it available to be read online, for free, which should help make it accessible to a broad audience.

What You Need to Know About This Book

Is this book for you? The following items can help you determine that:

Who this book is for

This book has been written for programmers, by a programmer. So, in order to understand it, you should already know object-oriented programming, for example, via a mainstream programming language such as Java, PHP, C++, Python, Ruby, Objective-C, C#, or Perl.

Thus, the book's target audience is programmers who want to learn JavaScript quickly and properly, and JavaScript programmers who want to deepen their skills and/or look up specific topics.

What's not covered

This book focuses on the JavaScript language proper. For example, you won't find information on programming web browsers (DOM, asynchronous programming, etc.). However, Chapter 33 points to relevant material.

How this book is organized

This book is divided into four parts, but the main two are:

- JavaScript Quick Start
- JavaScript in Depth

These parts are completely independent! You can treat them as if they were separate books: the former is more like a guide, the latter is more like a reference. "The Four Parts of This Book" on page xii tells you more about the structure of this book.

What JavaScript version this book uses

This book teaches ECMAScript 5, the current version of JavaScript that is supported by all modern engines. If you have to work with, say, older web browsers, then Chapter 25 explains what features are exclusive to ECMAScript 5.

Tips for Reading This Book

The most important tip for learning JavaScript is *don't get bogged down by the details*. Yes, there are many details when it comes to the language, and this book covers most of them. But there is also a relatively simple and elegant "big picture" that I will point out to you.

The Four Parts of This Book

This book is organized into four parts:

Part I, JavaScript Quick Start

This part teaches you "Basic JavaScript," a subset of JavaScript that is as small as possible while still enabling you to be productive. The part stands on its own; it doesn't depend on other parts and no other parts depend on it.

Part II, Background
> This part puts JavaScript in historical and technical context: When, why, and how was it created? How is it related to other programming languages? What were the important steps that got us to where we are today?

Part III, JavaScript in Depth
> This part is more of a reference: look for a topic that you are interested in, jump in, and explore. Many short examples should prevent things from becoming too dry.

Part IV, Tips, Tools, and Libraries
> This part gives tips for using JavaScript: best practices, advanced techniques, and learning resources. It also describes a few important tools and libraries.

JavaScript Command Lines

While reading this book, you may want to have a command line ready. That allows you to try out code interactively. The most popular choices are:

Node.js (http://nodejs.org)
> Node.js comes with an interactive command line. You start it by calling the shell command node.

Browsers
> All major browsers have consoles for entering JavaScript that is evaluated in the context of the current page. Simply search online for the name of your browser and "console."

Notational Conventions

The following notational conventions are used throughout the book.

Describing syntax

Question marks (?) are used to mark optional parameters. For example:

```
parseInt(str, radix?)
```

French quotation marks (guillemets) denote metacode. You can think of such metacode as blanks, to be filled in by actual code. For example:

```
try {
    «try_statements»
}
```

"White" square brackets mark optional syntactic elements. For example:

```
break [«label»]
```

In JavaScript comments, I sometimes use backticks to distinguish JavaScript from English:

```
foo(x, y); // calling function `foo` with parameters `x` and `y`
```

Referring to methods

I refer to built-in methods via their full path:

```
«Constructor».prototype.«methodName»()
```

For example, `Array.prototype.join()` refers to the array method `join()`; that is, Java-Script stores the methods of `Array` instances in the object `Array.prototype`. The reason for this is explained in "Layer 3: Constructors—Factories for Instances" on page 231.

Command-line interaction

Whenever I introduce a new concept, I often illustrate it via an interaction in a JavaScript command line. This looks as follows:

```
> 3 + 4
7
```

The text after the greater-than character is the input, typed by a human. Everything else is output by the JavaScript engine. Additionally, I use the method `console.log()` to print data to the console, especially in (non–command-line) source code:

```
var x = 3;
x++;
console.log(x); // 4
```

Tips, notes, and warnings

 This element signifies a tip or suggestion.

 This element signifies a general note.

 This element indicates a warning or caution.

Quickly Finding Documentation

While you can obviously use this book as a reference, sometimes looking up information online is quicker. One resource I recommend is the Mozilla Developer Network (*https://developer.mozilla.org/en-US/*) (MDN). You can search the Web to find documentation on MDN. For example, the following web search finds the documentation for the push() method of arrays:

```
mdn array push
```

Safari® Books Online

 Safari Books Online is an on-demand digital library that delivers expert content in both book and video form from the world's leading authors in technology and business.

Technology professionals, software developers, web designers, and business and creative professionals use Safari Books Online as their primary resource for research, problem solving, learning, and certification training.

Safari Books Online offers a range of product mixes and pricing programs for organizations, government agencies, and individuals. Subscribers have access to thousands of books, training videos, and prepublication manuscripts in one fully searchable database from publishers like O'Reilly Media, Prentice Hall Professional, Addison-Wesley Professional, Microsoft Press, Sams, Que, Peachpit Press, Focal Press, Cisco Press, John Wiley & Sons, Syngress, Morgan Kaufmann, IBM Redbooks, Packt, Adobe Press, FT Press, Apress, Manning, New Riders, McGraw-Hill, Jones & Bartlett, Course Technology, and dozens more. For more information about Safari Books Online, please visit us online.

How to Contact Us

Please address comments and questions concerning this book to the publisher:

O'Reilly Media, Inc.
1005 Gravenstein Highway North
Sebastopol, CA 95472
800-998-9938 (in the United States or Canada)
707-829-0515 (international or local)
707-829-0104 (fax)

We have a web page for this book, where we list errata, examples, and any additional information. You can access this page at *http://oreil.ly/speaking-js*.

To comment or ask technical questions about this book, send email to *bookques tions@oreilly.com*.

For more information about our books, courses, conferences, and news, see our website at *http://www.oreilly.com*.

Find us on Facebook: *http://facebook.com/oreilly*

Follow us on Twitter: *http://twitter.com/oreillymedia*

Watch us on YouTube: *http://www.youtube.com/oreillymedia*

Acknowledgments

I would like to thank the following people, all of whom helped make this book possible.

Preparing for JavaScript

The following people laid the foundations for my understanding of JavaScript (in chronological order):

- Prof. François Bry, Sven Panne, and Tim Geisler (Scheme)
- Prof. Don Batory (technical writing, programming language design)
- Prof. Martin Wirsing, Alexander Knapp, Matthias Hölzl, Hubert Baumeister, and various other former colleagues at the Institute for Informatics of the University of Munich (formal methods, various software engineering topics)

Help with JavaScript

Participants of the es-discuss mailing list
Their answers helped me understand the design of JavaScript. I am deeply thankful for their patience and tirelessness. Four people stood out: Brendan Eich, Allen Wirfs-Brock, Mark Miller, and David Herman.

Readers of my blog 2ality (http://www.2ality.com)
I published bits and pieces of this book on my blog and got an incredible amount of useful feedback. A few names among many: Ben Alman, Brandon Benvie, Mathias Bynens, Andrea Giammarchi, Matthias Reuter, and Rick Waldron.

More sources are acknowledged in the chapters.

Reviewers

I am much obliged to the following people who reviewed this book. They provided important feedback and corrections. In alphabetical order:

- Mathias Bynens
- Raymond Camden
- Cody Lindley
- Shelley Powers
- Andreas Schroeder
- Alex Stangl
- Béla Varga
- Edward Yue Shung Wong

PART I

JavaScript Quick Start

This part is a self-contained quick introduction to JavaScript. You can understand it without reading anything else in this book, and no other part of the book depends on its contents. However, the tips for how to read this book in "Tips for Reading This Book" on page xii do apply.

CHAPTER 1

Basic JavaScript

This chapter is about "Basic JavaScript," a name I chose for a subset of JavaScript that is as concise as possible while still enabling you to be productive. When you are starting to learn JavaScript, I recommend that you program in it for a while before moving on to the rest of the language. That way, you don't have to learn everything at once, which can be confusing.

Background

This section gives a little background on JavaScript to help you understand why it is the way it is.

JavaScript Versus ECMAScript

ECMAScript is the official name for JavaScript. A new name became necessary because there is a trademark on *Java* (held originally by Sun, now by Oracle). At the moment, Mozilla is one of the few companies allowed to officially use the name *JavaScript* because it received a license long ago. For common usage, the following rules apply:

- *JavaScript* means the programming language.
- *ECMAScript* is the name used by the language specification. Therefore, whenever referring to versions of the language, people say *ECMAScript*. The current version of JavaScript is ECMAScript 5; ECMAScript 6 is currently being developed.

Influences and Nature of the Language

JavaScript's creator, Brendan Eich, had no choice but to create the language very quickly (or other, worse technologies would have been adopted by Netscape). He borrowed from several programming languages: Java (syntax, primitive values versus objects), Scheme and AWK (first-class functions), Self (prototypal inheritance), and Perl and Python (strings, arrays, and regular expressions).

JavaScript did not have exception handling until ECMAScript 3, which explains why the language so often automatically converts values and so often fails silently: it initially couldn't throw exceptions.

On one hand, JavaScript has quirks and is missing quite a bit of functionality (block-scoped variables, modules, support for subclassing, etc.). On the other hand, it has several powerful features that allow you to work around these problems. In other languages, you learn language features. In JavaScript, you often learn patterns instead.

Given its influences, it is no surprise that JavaScript enables a programming style that is a mixture of functional programming (higher-order functions; built-in map, reduce, etc.) and object-oriented programming (objects, inheritance).

Syntax

This section explains basic syntactic principles of JavaScript.

An Overview of the Syntax

A few examples of syntax:

```
// Two slashes start single-line comments

var x;  // declaring a variable

x = 3 + y;  // assigning a value to the variable `x`

foo(x, y);  // calling function `foo` with parameters `x` and `y`
obj.bar(3);  // calling method `bar` of object `obj`

// A conditional statement
if (x === 0) {  // Is `x` equal to zero?
    x = 123;
}

// Defining function `baz` with parameters `a` and `b`
function baz(a, b) {
    return a + b;
}
```

Note the two different uses of the equals sign:

- A single equals sign (=) is used to assign a value to a variable.

- A triple equals sign (===) is used to compare two values (see "Equality Operators" on page 14).

Statements Versus Expressions

To understand JavaScript's syntax, you should know that it has two major syntactic categories: statements and expressions:

- Statements "do things." A program is a sequence of statements. Here is an example of a statement, which declares (creates) a variable `foo`:

    ```
    var foo;
    ```

- Expressions produce values. They are function arguments, the right side of an assignment, etc. Here's an example of an expression:

    ```
    3 * 7
    ```

The distinction between statements and expressions is best illustrated by the fact that JavaScript has two different ways to do `if-then-else`—either as a statement:

```
var x;
if (y >= 0) {
    x = y;
} else {
    x = -y;
}
```

or as an expression:

```
var x = y >= 0 ? y : -y;
```

You can use the latter as a function argument (but not the former):

```
myFunction(y >= 0 ? y : -y)
```

Finally, wherever JavaScript expects a statement, you can also use an expression; for example:

```
foo(7, 1);
```

The whole line is a statement (a so-called *expression statement*), but the function call `foo(7, 1)` is an expression.

Semicolons

Semicolons are optional in JavaScript. However, I recommend always including them, because otherwise JavaScript can guess wrong about the end of a statement. The details are explained in "Automatic Semicolon Insertion" on page 59.

Semicolons terminate statements, but not blocks. There is one case where you will see a semicolon after a block: a function expression is an expression that ends with a block. If such an expression comes last in a statement, it is followed by a semicolon:

```
// Pattern: var _ = ___;
var x = 3 * 7;
var f = function () { };  // function expr. inside var decl.
```

Comments

JavaScript has two kinds of comments: single-line comments and multiline comments. Single-line comments start with // and are terminated by the end of the line:

```
x++; // single-line comment
```

Multiline comments are delimited by /* and */:

```
/* This is
   a multiline
   comment.
 */
```

Variables and Assignment

Variables in JavaScript are declared before they are used:

```
var foo;  // declare variable `foo`
```

Assignment

You can declare a variable and assign a value at the same time:

```
var foo = 6;
```

You can also assign a value to an existing variable:

```
foo = 4;  // change variable `foo`
```

Compound Assignment Operators

There are compound assignment operators such as +=. The following two assignments are equivalent:

```
x += 1;
x = x + 1;
```

Identifiers and Variable Names

Identifiers are names that play various syntactic roles in JavaScript. For example, the name of a variable is an identifier. Identifiers are case sensitive.

Roughly, the first character of an identifier can be any Unicode letter, a dollar sign ($), or an underscore (_). Subsequent characters can additionally be any Unicode digit. Thus, the following are all legal identifiers:

```
arg0
_tmp
$elem
 п
```

The following identifiers are *reserved words*—they are part of the syntax and can't be used as variable names (including function names and parameter names):

arguments	break	case	catch
class	const	continue	debugger
default	delete	do	else
enum	export	extends	false
finally	for	function	if
implements	import	in	instanceof
interface	let	new	null
package	private	protected	public
return	static	super	switch
this	throw	true	try
typeof	var	void	while

The following three identifiers are not reserved words, but you should treat them as if they were:

```
Infinity
NaN
undefined
```

Lastly, you should also stay away from the names of standard global variables (see Chapter 23). You can use them for local variables without breaking anything, but your code still becomes confusing.

Values

JavaScript has many values that we have come to expect from programming languages: booleans, numbers, strings, arrays, and so on. All values in JavaScript have *properties*. Each property has a *key* (or *name*) and a *value*. You can think of properties like fields of a record. You use the dot (.) operator to read a property:

```
value.propKey
```

For example, the string 'abc' has the property length:

```
> var str = 'abc';
> str.length
3
```

The preceding can also be written as:

```
> 'abc'.length
3
```

The dot operator is also used to assign a value to a property:

```
> var obj = {};  // empty object
> obj.foo = 123; // create property `foo`, set it to 123
123
> obj.foo
123
```

And you can use it to invoke methods:

```
> 'hello'.toUpperCase()
'HELLO'
```

In the preceding example, we have invoked the method `toUpperCase()` on the value `'hello'`.

Primitive Values Versus Objects

JavaScript makes a somewhat arbitrary distinction between values:

- The *primitive values* are booleans, numbers, strings, `null`, and `undefined`.
- All other values are *objects*.

A major difference between the two is how they are compared; each object has a unique identity and is only (strictly) equal to itself:

```
> var obj1 = {};  // an empty object
> var obj2 = {};  // another empty object
> obj1 === obj2
false
> obj1 === obj1
true
```

In contrast, all primitive values encoding the same value are considered the same:

```
> var prim1 = 123;
> var prim2 = 123;
> prim1 === prim2
true
```

The next two sections explain primitive values and objects in more detail.

Primitive Values

The following are all of the primitive values (or *primitives* for short):

- Booleans: `true`, `false` (see "Booleans" on page 12)
- Numbers: `1736`, `1.351` (see "Numbers" on page 14)
- Strings: `'abc'`, `"abc"` (see "Strings" on page 15)
- Two "nonvalues": `undefined`, `null` (see "undefined and null" on page 10)

Primitives have the following characteristics:

Compared by value
> The "content" is compared:

```
> 3 === 3
true
> 'abc' === 'abc'
true
```

Always immutable
> Properties can't be changed, added, or removed:

```
> var str = 'abc';

> str.length = 1; // try to change property `length`
> str.length      // ⇒ no effect
3

> str.foo = 3; // try to create property `foo`
> str.foo      // ⇒ no effect, unknown property
undefined
```

(Reading an unknown property always returns `undefined`.)

Objects

All nonprimitive values are *objects*. The most common kinds of objects are:

- *Plain objects*, which can be created by *object literals* (see "Single Objects" on page 25):

  ```
  {
      firstName: 'Jane',
      lastName: 'Doe'
  }
  ```

  The preceding object has two properties: the value of property `firstName` is `'Jane'` and the value of property `lastName` is `'Doe'`.

- *Arrays*, which can be created by *array literals* (see "Arrays" on page 28):

```
[ 'apple', 'banana', 'cherry' ]
```

The preceding array has three elements that can be accessed via numeric indices.
For example, the index of 'apple' is 0.

- *Regular expressions*, which can be created by *regular expression literals* (see "Regular
Expressions" on page 31):

```
/^a+b+$/
```

Objects have the following characteristics:

Compared by reference
Identities are compared; every value has its own identity:

```
> {} === {}   // two different empty objects
false

> var obj1 = {};
> var obj2 = obj1;
> obj1 === obj2
true
```

Mutable by default
You can normally freely change, add, and remove properties (see "Single Objects"
on page 25):

```
> var obj = {};
> obj.foo = 123; // add property `foo`
> obj.foo
123
```

undefined and null

Most programming languages have values denoting missing information. JavaScript
has two such "nonvalues," undefined and null:

- undefined means "no value." Uninitialized variables are undefined:

```
> var foo;
> foo
undefined
```

Missing parameters are undefined:

```
> function f(x) { return x }
> f()
undefined
```

If you read a nonexistent property, you get undefined:

```
> var obj = {}; // empty object
> obj.foo
undefined
```

- null means "no object." It is used as a nonvalue whenever an object is expected (parameters, last in a chain of objects, etc.).

undefined and null have no properties, not even standard methods such as toString().

Checking for undefined or null

Functions normally allow you to indicate a missing value via either undefined or null. You can do the same via an explicit check:

```
if (x === undefined || x === null) {
    ...
}
```

You can also exploit the fact that both undefined and null are considered false:

```
if (!x) {
    ...
}
```

false, 0, NaN, and '' are also considered false (see "Truthy and Falsy" on page 13).

Categorizing Values Using typeof and instanceof

There are two operators for categorizing values: typeof is mainly used for primitive values, while instanceof is used for objects.

typeof looks like this:

```
typeof value
```

It returns a string describing the "type" of value. Here are some examples:

```
> typeof true
'boolean'
> typeof 'abc'
'string'
> typeof {} // empty object literal
'object'
> typeof [] // empty array literal
'object'
```

The following table lists all results of `typeof`:

Operand	Result
undefined	'undefined'
null	'object'
Boolean value	'boolean'
Number value	'number'
String value	'string'
Function	'function'
All other normal values	'object'
(Engine-created value)	JavaScript engines are allowed to create values for which `typeof` returns arbitrary strings (different from all results listed in this table).

`typeof null` returning `'object'` is a bug that can't be fixed, because it would break existing code. It does not mean that `null` is an object.

`instanceof` looks like this:

```
value instanceof Constr
```

It returns `true` if `value` is an object that has been created by the constructor `Constr` (see "Constructors: Factories for Objects" on page 28). Here are some examples:

```
> var b = new Bar();  // object created by constructor Bar
> b instanceof Bar
true

> {} instanceof Object
true
> [] instanceof Array
true
> [] instanceof Object  // Array is a subconstructor of Object
true

> undefined instanceof Object
false
> null instanceof Object
false
```

Booleans

The primitive boolean type comprises the values `true` and `false`. The following operators produce booleans:

- Binary logical operators: && (And), || (Or)
- Prefix logical operator: ! (Not)

- Comparison operators:
  - Equality operators: ===, !==, ==, !=
  - Ordering operators (for strings and numbers): >, >=, <, <=

Truthy and Falsy

Whenever JavaScript expects a boolean value (e.g., for the condition of an `if` statement), any value can be used. It will be interpreted as either `true` or `false`. The following values are interpreted as `false`:

- `undefined`, `null`
- Boolean: `false`
- Number: `-0`, `NaN`
- String: `' '`

All other values (including all objects!) are considered `true`. Values interpreted as `false` are called *falsy*, and values interpreted as `true` are called *truthy*. `Boolean()`, called as a function, converts its parameter to a boolean. You can use it to test how a value is interpreted:

```
> Boolean(undefined)
false
> Boolean(0)
false
> Boolean(3)
true
> Boolean({}) // empty object
true
> Boolean([]) // empty array
true
```

Binary Logical Operators

Binary logical operators in JavaScript are *short-circuiting*. That is, if the first operand suffices for determining the result, the second operand is not evaluated. For example, in the following expressions, the function `foo()` is never called:

```
false && foo()
true  || foo()
```

Furthermore, binary logical operators return either one of their operands—which may or may not be a boolean. A check for truthiness is used to determine which one:

And (&&)

If the first operand is falsy, return it. Otherwise, return the second operand:

```
> NaN && 'abc'
NaN
> 123 && 'abc'
'abc'
```

Or (||)

If the first operand is truthy, return it. Otherwise, return the second operand:

```
> 'abc' || 123
'abc'
> '' || 123
123
```

Equality Operators

JavaScript has two kinds of equality:

- Normal, or "lenient," (in)equality: == and !=
- Strict (in)equality: === and !==

Normal equality considers (too) many values to be equal (the details are explained in "Normal (Lenient) Equality (==, !=)" on page 84), which can hide bugs. Therefore, always using strict equality is recommended.

Numbers

All numbers in JavaScript are floating-point:

```
> 1 === 1.0
true
```

Special numbers include the following:

NaN *("not a number")*

An error value:

```
> Number('xyz')  // 'xyz' can't be converted to a number
NaN
```

Infinity

Also mostly an error value:

```
> 3 / 0
Infinity
> Math.pow(2, 1024)  // number too large
Infinity
```

Infinity is larger than any other number (except NaN). Similarly, -Infinity is smaller than any other number (except NaN). That makes these numbers useful as default values (e.g., when you are looking for a minimum or a maximum).

Operators

JavaScript has the following arithmetic operators (see "Arithmetic Operators" on page 122):

- Addition: `number1 + number2`
- Subtraction: `number1 - number2`
- Multiplication: `number1 * number2`
- Division: `number1 / number2`
- Remainder: `number1 % number2`
- Increment: `++variable`, `variable++`
- Decrement: `--variable`, `variable--`
- Negate: `-value`
- Convert to number: `+value`

The global object `Math` (see "Math" on page 31) provides more arithmetic operations, via functions.

JavaScript also has operators for bitwise operations (e.g., bitwise And; see "Bitwise Operators" on page 124).

Strings

Strings can be created directly via string literals. Those literals are delimited by single or double quotes. The backslash (\) escapes characters and produces a few control characters. Here are some examples:

```
'abc'
"abc"

'Did she say "Hello"?'
"Did she say \"Hello\"?"

'That\'s nice!'
"That's nice!"

'Line 1\nLine 2'  // newline
'Backlash: \\'
```

Single characters are accessed via square brackets:

```
> var str = 'abc';
> str[1]
'b'
```

The property `length` counts the number of characters in the string:

```
> 'abc'.length
3
```

Like all primitives, strings are immutable; you need to create a new string if you want to change an existing one.

String Operators

Strings are concatenated via the plus (+) operator, which converts the other operand to a string if one of the operands is a string:

```
> var messageCount = 3;
> 'You have ' + messageCount + ' messages'
'You have 3 messages'
```

To concatenate strings in multiple steps, use the += operator:

```
> var str = '';
> str += 'Multiple ';
> str += 'pieces ';
> str += 'are concatenated.';
> str
'Multiple pieces are concatenated.'
```

String Methods

Strings have many useful methods (see "String Prototype Methods" on page 139). Here are some examples:

```
> 'abc'.slice(1)  // copy a substring
'bc'
> 'abc'.slice(1, 2)
'b'

> '\t xyz  '.trim()  // trim whitespace
'xyz'

> 'mjölnir'.toUpperCase()
'MJÖLNIR'

> 'abc'.indexOf('b')  // find a string
1
> 'abc'.indexOf('x')
-1
```

Statements

Conditionals and loops in JavaScript are introduced in the following sections.

Conditionals

The `if` statement has a `then` clause and an optional `else` clause that are executed depending on a boolean condition:

```
if (myvar === 0) {
    // then
}

if (myvar === 0) {
    // then
} else {
    // else
}

if (myvar === 0) {
    // then
} else if (myvar === 1) {
    // else-if
} else if (myvar === 2) {
    // else-if
} else {
    // else
}
```

I recommend always using braces (they denote blocks of zero or more statements). But you don't have to do so if a clause is only a single statement (the same holds for the control flow statements `for` and `while`):

```
if (x < 0) return -x;
```

The following is a `switch` statement. The value of `fruit` decides which `case` is executed:

```
switch (fruit) {
    case 'banana':
        // ...
        break;
    case 'apple':
        // ...
        break;
    default:  // all other cases
        // ...
}
```

The "operand" after `case` can be any expression; it is compared via `===` with the parameter of `switch`.

Loops

The `for` loop has the following format:

```
for ([«init»]; [«condition»]; [«post_iteration»])
    «statement»
```

`init` is executed at the beginning of the loop. `condition` is checked before each loop iteration; if it becomes `false`, then the loop is terminated. `post_iteration` is executed after each loop iteration.

This example prints all elements of the array `arr` on the console:

```
for (var i=0; i < arr.length; i++) {
    console.log(arr[i]);
}
```

The `while` loop continues looping over its body while its condition holds:

```
// Same as for loop above:
var i = 0;
while (i < arr.length) {
    console.log(arr[i]);
    i++;
}
```

The `do-while` loop continues looping over its body while its condition holds. As the condition follows the body, the body is always executed at least once:

```
do {
    // ...
} while (condition);
```

In all loops:

- `break` leaves the loop.

- `continue` starts a new loop iteration.

Functions

One way of defining a function is via a *function declaration*:

```
function add(param1, param2) {
    return param1 + param2;
}
```

The preceding code defines a function, `add`, that has two parameters, `param1` and `param2`, and returns the sum of both parameters. This is how you call that function:

```
> add(6, 1)
7
> add('a', 'b')
'ab'
```

Another way of defining `add()` is by assigning a *function expression* to a variable `add`:

```
var add = function (param1, param2) {
    return param1 + param2;
};
```

A function expression produces a value and can thus be used to directly pass functions as arguments to other functions:

```
someOtherFunction(function (p1, p2) { ... });
```

Function Declarations Are Hoisted

Function declarations are *hoisted*—moved in their entirety to the beginning of the current scope. That allows you to refer to functions that are declared later:

```
function foo() {
    bar();  // OK, bar is hoisted
    function bar() {
        ...
    }
}
```

Note that while var declarations are also hoisted (see "Variables Are Hoisted" on page 23), assignments performed by them are not:

```
function foo() {
    bar();  // Not OK, bar is still undefined
    var bar = function () {
        // ...
    };
}
```

The Special Variable arguments

You can call any function in JavaScript with an arbitrary amount of arguments; the language will never complain. It will, however, make all parameters available via the special variable arguments. arguments looks like an array, but has none of the array methods:

```
> function f() { return arguments }
> var args = f('a', 'b', 'c');
> args.length
3
> args[0]  // read element at index 0
'a'
```

Too Many or Too Few Arguments

Let's use the following function to explore how too many or too few parameters are handled in JavaScript (the function toArray() is shown in "Converting arguments to an Array" on page 21):

```
function f(x, y) {
    console.log(x, y);
    return toArray(arguments);
}
```

Additional parameters will be ignored (except by `arguments`):

```
> f('a', 'b', 'c')
a b
[ 'a', 'b', 'c' ]
```

Missing parameters will get the value `undefined`:

```
> f('a')
a undefined
[ 'a' ]
> f()
undefined undefined
[]
```

Optional Parameters

The following is a common pattern for assigning default values to parameters:

```
function pair(x, y) {
    x = x || 0;  // (1)
    y = y || 0;
    return [ x, y ];
}
```

In line (1), the || operator returns x if it is truthy (not `null`, `undefined`, etc.). Otherwise, it returns the second operand:

```
> pair()
[ 0, 0 ]
> pair(3)
[ 3, 0 ]
> pair(3, 5)
[ 3, 5 ]
```

Enforcing an Arity

If you want to enforce an *arity* (a specific number of parameters), you can check `arguments.length`:

```
function pair(x, y) {
    if (arguments.length !== 2) {
        throw new Error('Need exactly 2 arguments');
    }
    ...
}
```

Converting arguments to an Array

arguments is not an array, it is only *array-like* (see "Array-Like Objects and Generic Methods" on page 262). It has a property length, and you can access its elements via indices in square brackets. You cannot, however, remove elements or invoke any of the array methods on it. Thus, you sometimes need to convert arguments to an array, which is what the following function does (it is explained in "Array-Like Objects and Generic Methods" on page 262):

```javascript
function toArray(arrayLikeObject) {
    return Array.prototype.slice.call(arrayLikeObject);
}
```

Exception Handling

The most common way to handle exceptions (see Chapter 14) is as follows:

```javascript
function getPerson(id) {
    if (id < 0) {
        throw new Error('ID must not be negative: '+id);
    }
    return { id: id }; // normally: retrieved from database
}

function getPersons(ids) {
    var result = [];
    ids.forEach(function (id) {
        try {
            var person = getPerson(id);
            result.push(person);
        } catch (exception) {
            console.log(exception);
        }
    });
    return result;
}
```

The try clause surrounds critical code, and the catch clause is executed if an exception is thrown inside the try clause. Using the preceding code:

```javascript
> getPersons([2, -5, 137])
[Error: ID must not be negative: -5]
[ { id: 2 }, { id: 137 } ]
```

Strict Mode

Strict mode (see "Strict Mode" on page 62) enables more warnings and makes JavaScript a cleaner language (nonstrict mode is sometimes called "sloppy mode"). To switch it on, type the following line first in a JavaScript file or a <script> tag:

```
'use strict';
```

You can also enable strict mode per function:

```
function functionInStrictMode() {
    'use strict';
}
```

Variable Scoping and Closures

In JavaScript, you declare variables via var before using them:

```
> var x;
> x = 3;
> y = 4;
ReferenceError: y is not defined
```

You can declare and initialize several variables with a single var statement:

```
var x = 1, y = 2, z = 3;
```

But I recommend using one statement per variable (the reason is explained in "Syntax" on page 382). Thus, I would rewrite the previous statement to:

```
var x = 1;
var y = 2;
var z = 3;
```

Because of hoisting (see "Variables Are Hoisted" on page 23), it is usually best to declare variables at the beginning of a function.

Variables Are Function-Scoped

The scope of a variable is always the complete function (as opposed to the current block). For example:

```
function foo() {
    var x = -512;
    if (x < 0) {  // (1)
        var tmp = -x;
        ...
    }
    console.log(tmp);  // 512
}
```

We can see that the variable tmp is not restricted to the block starting in line (1); it exists until the end of the function.

Variables Are Hoisted

Each variable declaration is *hoisted*: the declaration is moved to the beginning of the function, but assignments that it makes stay put. As an example, consider the variable declaration in line (1) in the following function:

```
function foo() {
    console.log(tmp); // undefined
    if (false) {
        var tmp = 3;  // (1)
    }
}
```

Internally, the preceding function is executed like this:

```
function foo() {
    var tmp;  // hoisted declaration
    console.log(tmp);
    if (false) {
        tmp = 3;  // assignment stays put
    }
}
```

Closures

Each function stays connected to the variables of the functions that surround it, even after it leaves the scope in which it was created. For example:

```
function createIncrementor(start) {
    return function () {  // (1)
        start++;
        return start;
    }
}
```

The function starting in line (1) leaves the context in which it was created, but stays connected to a live version of `start`:

```
> var inc = createIncrementor(5);
> inc()
6
> inc()
7
> inc()
8
```

A *closure* is a function plus the connection to the variables of its surrounding scopes. Thus, what `createIncrementor()` returns is a closure.

The IIFE Pattern: Introducing a New Scope

Sometimes you want to introduce a new variable scope—for example, to prevent a variable from becoming global. In JavaScript, you can't use a block to do so; you must use a function. But there is a pattern for using a function in a block-like manner. It is called *IIFE* (immediately invoked function expression (*http://bit.ly/i-ife*), pronounced "iffy"):

```
(function () {  // open IIFE
    var tmp = ...;  // not a global variable
}());  // close IIFE
```

Be sure to type the preceding example exactly as shown (apart from the comments). An IIFE is a function expression that is called immediately after you define it. Inside the function, a new scope exists, preventing tmp from becoming global. Consult "Introducing a New Scope via an IIFE" on page 183 for details on IIFEs.

IIFE use case: inadvertent sharing via closures

Closures keep their connections to outer variables, which is sometimes not what you want:

```
var result = [];
for (var i=0; i < 5; i++) {
    result.push(function () { return i });  // (1)
}
console.log(result[1]()); // 5 (not 1)
console.log(result[3]()); // 5 (not 3)
```

The value returned in line (1) is always the current value of i, not the value it had when the function was created. After the loop is finished, i has the value 5, which is why all functions in the array return that value. If you want the function in line (1) to receive a snapshot of the current value of i, you can use an IIFE:

```
for (var i=0; i < 5; i++) {
    (function () {
        var i2 = i; // copy current i
        result.push(function () { return i2 });
    }());
}
```

Objects and Constructors

This section covers two basic object-oriented mechanisms of JavaScript: single objects and *constructors* (which are factories for objects, similar to classes in other languages).

Single Objects

Like all values, objects have properties. You could, in fact, consider an object to be a set of properties, where each property is a (key, value) pair. The key is a string, and the value is any JavaScript value.

In JavaScript, you can directly create plain objects, via *object literals*:

```
'use strict';
var jane = {
    name: 'Jane',

    describe: function () {
        return 'Person named '+this.name;
    }
};
```

The preceding object has the properties `name` and `describe`. You can read ("get") and write ("set") properties:

```
> jane.name  // get
'Jane'
> jane.name = 'John';  // set
> jane.newProperty = 'abc';  // property created automatically
```

Function-valued properties such as `describe` are called *methods*. They use `this` to refer to the object that was used to call them:

```
> jane.describe()  // call method
'Person named John'
> jane.name = 'Jane';
> jane.describe()
'Person named Jane'
```

The `in` operator checks whether a property exists:

```
> 'newProperty' in jane
true
> 'foo' in jane
false
```

If you read a property that does not exist, you get the value `undefined`. Hence, the previous two checks could also be performed like this:

```
> jane.newProperty !== undefined
true
> jane.foo !== undefined
false
```

The `delete` operator removes a property:

```
> delete jane.newProperty
true
```

```
> 'newProperty' in jane
false
```

Arbitrary Property Keys

A property key can be any string. So far, we have seen property keys in object literals and after the dot operator. However, you can use them that way only if they are identifiers (see "Identifiers and Variable Names" on page 6). If you want to use other strings as keys, you have to quote them in an object literal and use square brackets to get and set the property:

```
> var obj = { 'not an identifier': 123 };
> obj['not an identifier']
123
> obj['not an identifier'] = 456;
```

Square brackets also allow you to compute the key of a property:

```
> var obj = { hello: 'world' };
> var x = 'hello';

> obj[x]
'world'
> obj['hel'+'lo']
'world'
```

Extracting Methods

If you extract a method, it loses its connection with the object. On its own, the function is not a method anymore, and this has the value undefined (in strict mode).

As an example, let's go back to the earlier object jane:

```
'use strict';
var jane = {
    name: 'Jane',

    describe: function () {
        return 'Person named '+this.name;
    }
};
```

We want to extract the method describe from jane, put it into a variable func, and call it. However, that doesn't work:

```
> var func = jane.describe;
> func()
TypeError: Cannot read property 'name' of undefined
```

The solution is to use the method bind() that all functions have. It creates a new function whose this always has the given value:

```
> var func2 = jane.describe.bind(jane);
> func2()
'Person named Jane'
```

Functions Inside a Method

Every function has its own special variable this. This is inconvenient if you nest a function inside a method, because you can't access the method's this from the function. The following is an example where we call forEach with a function to iterate over an array:

```
var jane = {
    name: 'Jane',
    friends: [ 'Tarzan', 'Cheeta' ],
    logHiToFriends: function () {
        'use strict';
        this.friends.forEach(function (friend) {
            // `this` is undefined here
            console.log(this.name+' says hi to '+friend);
        });
    }
}
```

Calling logHiToFriends produces an error:

```
> jane.logHiToFriends()
TypeError: Cannot read property 'name' of undefined
```

Let's look at two ways of fixing this. First, we could store this in a different variable:

```
logHiToFriends: function () {
    'use strict';
    var that = this;
    this.friends.forEach(function (friend) {
        console.log(that.name+' says hi to '+friend);
    });
}
```

Or, forEach has a second parameter that allows you to provide a value for this:

```
logHiToFriends: function () {
    'use strict';
    this.friends.forEach(function (friend) {
        console.log(this.name+' says hi to '+friend);
    }, this);
}
```

Function expressions are often used as arguments in function calls in JavaScript. Always be careful when you refer to this from one of those function expressions.

Constructors: Factories for Objects

Until now, you may think that JavaScript objects are *only* maps from strings to values, a notion suggested by JavaScript's object literals, which look like the map/dictionary literals of other languages. However, JavaScript objects also support a feature that is truly object-oriented: inheritance. This section does not fully explain how JavaScript inheritance works, but it shows you a simple pattern to get you started. Consult Chapter 17 if you want to know more.

In addition to being "real" functions and methods, functions play another role in Java-Script: they become *constructors*—factories for objects—if invoked via the new operator. Constructors are thus a rough analog to classes in other languages. By convention, the names of constructors start with capital letters. For example:

```
// Set up instance data
function Point(x, y) {
    this.x = x;
    this.y = y;
}
// Methods
Point.prototype.dist = function () {
    return Math.sqrt(this.x*this.x + this.y*this.y);
};
```

We can see that a constructor has two parts. First, the function Point sets up the instance data. Second, the property Point.prototype contains an object with the methods. The former data is specific to each instance, while the latter data is shared among all instances.

To use Point, we invoke it via the new operator:

```
> var p = new Point(3, 5);
> p.x
3
> p.dist()
5.830951894845301
```

p is an instance of Point:

```
> p instanceof Point
true
```

Arrays

Arrays are sequences of elements that can be accessed via integer indices starting at zero.

Array Literals

Array literals are handy for creating arrays:

```
> var arr = [ 'a', 'b', 'c' ];
```

The preceding array has three elements: the strings 'a', 'b', and 'c'. You can access them via integer indices:

```
> arr[0]
'a'
> arr[0] = 'x';
> arr
[ 'x', 'b', 'c' ]
```

The length property indicates how many elements an array has. You can use it to append elements and to remove elements:

```
> var arr = ['a', 'b'];
> arr.length
2

> arr[arr.length] = 'c';
> arr
[ 'a', 'b', 'c' ]
> arr.length
3

> arr.length = 1;
> arr
[ 'a' ]
```

The in operator works for arrays, too:

```
> var arr = [ 'a', 'b', 'c' ];
> 1 in arr // is there an element at index 1?
true
> 5 in arr // is there an element at index 5?
false
```

Note that arrays are objects and can thus have object properties:

```
> var arr = [];
> arr.foo = 123;
> arr.foo
123
```

Array Methods

Arrays have many methods (see "Array Prototype Methods" on page 286). Here are a few examples:

```
> var arr = [ 'a', 'b', 'c' ];

> arr.slice(1, 2)  // copy elements
[ 'b' ]
> arr.slice(1)
[ 'b', 'c' ]
```

```
> arr.push('x')  // append an element
4
> arr
[ 'a', 'b', 'c', 'x' ]

> arr.pop()  // remove last element
'x'
> arr
[ 'a', 'b', 'c' ]

> arr.shift()  // remove first element
'a'
> arr
[ 'b', 'c' ]

> arr.unshift('x')  // prepend an element
3
> arr
[ 'x', 'b', 'c' ]

> arr.indexOf('b')  // find the index of an element
1
> arr.indexOf('y')
-1

> arr.join('-')  // all elements in a single string
'x-b-c'
> arr.join('')
'xbc'
> arr.join()
'x,b,c'
```

Iterating over Arrays

There are several array methods for iterating over elements (see "Iteration (Nondestructive)" on page 291). The two most important ones are forEach and map.

forEach iterates over an array and hands the current element and its index to a function:

```
[ 'a', 'b', 'c' ].forEach(
    function (elem, index) {  // (1)
        console.log(index + '. ' + elem);
    });
```

The preceding code produces the following output:

```
0. a
1. b
2. c
```

Note that the function in line (1) is free to ignore arguments. It could, for example, only have the parameter elem.

map creates a new array by applying a function to each element of an existing array:

```
> [1,2,3].map(function (x) { return x*x })
[ 1, 4, 9 ]
```

Regular Expressions

JavaScript has built-in support for regular expressions (Chapter 19 refers to tutorials and explains in more detail how they work). They are delimited by slashes:

```
/^abc$/
/[A-Za-z0-9]+/
```

Method test(): Is There a Match?

```
> /^a+b+$/.test('aaab')
true
> /^a+b+$/.test('aaa')
false
```

Method exec(): Match and Capture Groups

```
> /a(b+)a/.exec('_abbba_aba_')
[ 'abbba', 'bbb' ]
```

The returned array contains the complete match at index 0, the capture of the first group at index 1, and so on. There is a way (discussed in "RegExp.prototype.exec: Capture Groups" on page 305) to invoke this method repeatedly to get all matches.

Method replace(): Search and Replace

```
> '<a> <bbb>'.replace(/<(.*?)>/g, '[$1]')
'[a] [bbb]'
```

The first parameter of replace must be a regular expression with a /g flag; otherwise, only the first occurrence is replaced. There is also a way (as discussed in "String.prototype.replace: Search and Replace" on page 307) to use a function to compute the replacement.

Math

Math (see Chapter 21) is an object with arithmetic functions. Here are some examples:

```
> Math.abs(-2)
2

> Math.pow(3, 2)  // 3 to the power of 2
9
```

```
> Math.max(2, -1, 5)
5

> Math.round(1.9)
2

> Math.PI  // pre-defined constant for π
3.141592653589793

> Math.cos(Math.PI)  // compute the cosine for 180°
-1
```

Other Functionality of the Standard Library

JavaScript's standard library is relatively spartan, but there are more things you can use:

Date *(Chapter 20)*
> A constructor for dates whose main functionality is parsing and creating date strings and accessing the components of a date (year, hour, etc.).

JSON *(Chapter 22)*
> An object with functions for parsing and generating JSON data.

console.* *methods (see "The Console API" on page 351)*
> These browser-specific methods are not part of the language proper, but some of them also work on Node.js.

PART II

Background

This part explains the history and nature of JavaScript. It provides a broad first look at the language and explains the context in which it exists (without going too much into technical details).

This part is not required reading; you will be able to understand the rest of the book without having read it.

CHAPTER 2

Why JavaScript?

There are many programming languages out there. Why should you use JavaScript? This chapter looks at seven aspects that are important when you are choosing a programming language and argues that JavaScript does well overall:

1. Is it freely available?
2. Is it an elegant programming language?
3. Is it useful in practice?
4. Does it have good tools, especially good *integrated development environments* (IDEs)?
5. Is it fast enough for what you want to do?
6. Is it widely used?
7. Does it have a future?

Is JavaScript Freely Available?

JavaScript is arguably the most open programming language there is: ECMA-262, its specification, is an ISO standard. That specification is closely followed by many implementations from independent parties. Some of those implementations are open source. Furthermore, the evolution of the language is handled by TC39, a committee comprising several companies, including all major browser vendors. Many of those companies are normally competitors, but they work together for the benefit of the language.

Is JavaScript Elegant?

Yes and no. I've written fair amounts of code in several programming languages from different paradigms. Therefore, I'm well aware that JavaScript isn't the pinnacle of elegance. However, it is a very flexible language, has a reasonably elegant core, and enables you to use a mixture of object-oriented programming and functional programming.

Language compatibility between JavaScript engines used to be a problem, but isn't anymore, partly thanks to the test262 suite (*https://github.com/tc39/test262*) that checks engines for conformance to the ECMAScript specification. In contrast, browser and DOM differences are still a challenge. That's why it is normally best to rely on frameworks for hiding those differences.

Is JavaScript Useful?

The most beautiful programming language in the world is useless unless it allows you to write the program that you need.

Graphical User Interfaces

In the area of graphical user interfaces, JavaScript benefits from being part of *HTML5*. In this section, I use the term HTML5 for "the browser platform" (HTML, CSS, and browser JavaScript APIs). HTML5 is deployed widely and making constant progress. It is slowly becoming a complete layer for writing full-featured, cross-platform applications; similar to, say, the Java platform, it's almost like an embedded operating system. One of HTML5's selling points is that it lets you write cross-platform graphical user interfaces. Those are always a compromise: you give up some quality in exchange for not being limited to a single operating system. In the past, "cross-platform" meant Windows, Mac OS, or Linux. But we now have two additional interactive platforms: web and mobile. With HTML5, you can target all of these platforms via technologies such as PhoneGap (*http://phonegap.com*), Chrome Apps (*http://developer.chrome.com/apps/*), and TideSDK (*http://www.tidesdk.org/*).

Additionally, several platforms have web apps as native apps or let you install them natively—for example, Chrome OS, Firefox OS, and Android.

Other Technologies Complementing JavaScript

There are more technologies than just HTML5 that complement JavaScript and make the language more useful:

Libraries
> JavaScript has an abundance of libraries, which enable you to complete tasks ranging from parsing JavaScript (via Esprima (*http://esprima.org*)) to processing and displaying PDF files (via PDF.js (*https://github.com/mozilla/pdf.js*)).

Node.js (http://nodejs.org)
> The Node.js platform lets you write server-side code and shell scripts (build tools, test runners, etc.).

JSON (JavaScript Object Notation, covered in Chapter 22)
> JSON is a data format rooted in JavaScript that has become popular for exchanging data on the Web (e.g., the results of web services).

NoSQL databases (such as CouchDB (http://couchdb.apache.org) and MongoDB (http://www.mongodb.org))
> These databases tightly integrate JSON and JavaScript.

Does JavaScript Have Good Tools?

JavaScript is getting better build tools (e.g., Grunt (*http://gruntjs.com*)) and test tools (e.g., mocha (*http://visionmedia.github.io/mocha/*)). Node.js makes it possible to run these kinds of tools via a shell (and not only in the browser). One risk in this area is fragmentation, as we are progressively getting too many of these tools.

The JavaScript IDE space is still nascent, but it's quickly growing up. The complexity and dynamism of web development make this space a fertile ground for innovation. Two open source examples are Brackets (*http://brackets.io*) and Light Table (*http://www.lighttable.com*).

Additionally, browsers are becoming increasingly capable development environments. Chrome, in particular, has made impressive progress recently. It will be interesting to see how much more IDEs and browsers will be integrated in the future.

Is JavaScript Fast Enough?

JavaScript engines have made tremendous progress, evolving from slow interpreters to fast just-in-time compilers. They are now fast enough for most applications. Furthermore, new ideas are already in development to make JavaScript fast enough for the remaining applications:

- asm.js (*http://asmjs.org/*) is a (very static) subset of JavaScript that runs fast on current engines, approximately 70% as fast as compiled C++. It can, for example, be used to implement performance-critical algorithmic parts of web applications. It has also been used to port C++-based games to the web platform.
- ParallelJS (*http://www.2ality.com/2013/12/paralleljs.html*) parallelizes JavaScript code that uses the new array methods `mapPar`, `filterPar`, and `reducePar` (parallelizable versions of the existing array methods `map`, `filter`, and `reduce`). In order

for parallelization to work, callbacks must be written in a special style; the main restriction is that you can't mutate data that hasn't been created inside the callbacks.

Is JavaScript Widely Used?

A language that is widely used normally has two benefits. First, such a language is better documented and supported. Second, more programmers know it, which is important whenever you need to hire someone or are looking for customers for a tool based on the language.

JavaScript is widely used and reaps both of the aforementioned benefits:

- These days, documentation and support for JavaScript comes in all shapes and sizes: books, podcasts, blog posts, email newsletters, forums, and more. Chapter 33 points you toward important resources.
- JavaScript developers are in great demand, but their ranks are also constantly increasing.

Does JavaScript Have a Future?

Several things indicate that JavaScript has a bright future:

- The language is evolving steadily; ECMAScript 6 looks good.
- There is much JavaScript-related innovation (e.g., the aforementioned asm.js and ParallelJS, Microsoft's TypeScript, etc.).
- The web platform of which JavaScript is an integral part is maturing rapidly.
- JavaScript is supported by a broad coalition of companies—no single person or company controls it.

Conclusion

Considering the preceding list of what makes a language attractive, JavaScript is doing remarkably well. It certainly is not perfect, but at the moment, it is hard to beat—and things are only getting better.

CHAPTER 3

The Nature of JavaScript

JavaScript's nature can be summarized as follows:

It's dynamic

Many things can be changed. For example, you can freely add and remove *properties* (fields) of objects after they have been created. And you can directly create objects, without creating an object factory (e.g., a class) first.

It's dynamically typed

Variables and object properties can always hold values of any type.

It's functional and object-oriented

JavaScript supports two programming language paradigms: functional programming (first-class functions, closures, partial application via `bind()`, built-in `map()` and `reduce()` for arrays, etc.) and object-oriented programming (mutable state, objects, inheritance, etc.).

It fails silently

JavaScript did not have exception handling until ECMAScript 3. That explains why the language so often fails silently and automatically converts the values of arguments and operands: it initially couldn't throw exceptions.

It's deployed as source code

JavaScript is always deployed as source code and compiled by JavaScript engines. Source code has the benefits of being a flexible delivery format and of abstracting the differences between the engines. Two techniques are used to keep file sizes small: *compression* (mainly gzip) and *minification* (making source code smaller by renaming variables, removing comments, etc.; see Chapter 32 for details).

It's part of the web platform

JavaScript is such an essential part of the web platform (HTML5 APIs, DOM, etc.) that it is easy to forget that the former can also be used without the latter. However, the more JavaScript is used in nonbrowser settings (such as Node.js), the more obvious it becomes.

Quirks and Unorthodox Features

On one hand, JavaScript has several quirks and missing features (for example, it has no block-scoped variables, no built-in modules, and no support for subclassing). Therefore, where you learn language features in other languages, you learn patterns and workarounds in JavaScript. On the other hand, JavaScript includes unorthodox features (such as prototypal inheritance and object properties). These, too, have to be learned, but are more a feature than a bug.

Note that JavaScript engines have become quite smart and fix some of the quirks, under the hood. For example:

- Specification-wise, JavaScript does not have integers, only floating-point numbers. Internally, most engines use integers as much as possible.

- Arguably, arrays in JavaScript are too flexible: they are not indexed sequences of elements, but maps from numbers to elements. Such maps can have holes: indices "inside" the array that have no associated value. Again, engines help by using an optimized representation if an array does not have holes.

Elegant Parts

But JavaScript also has many elegant parts. Brendan Eich's favorites are:[1]

- First-class functions
- Closures
- Prototypes
- Object literals
- Array literals

The last two items, object literals and array literals, let you start with objects and introduce abstractions (such as constructors, JavaScript's analog to classes) later. They also enable JSON (see Chapter 22).

Note that the elegant parts help you work around the quirks. For example, they allow you to implement block scoping, modules, and inheritance APIs—all within the language.

---

1. Brendan Eich, "A Brief History of JavaScript," July 21, 2010, *http://bit.ly/1lKkI0M*.

Influences

JavaScript was influenced by several programming languages (as shown in Figure 3-1):

- Java is the role model for JavaScript's syntax. It also led to JavaScript's partitioning of values into primitives and objects and to the `Date` constructor (which is a port of `java.util.Date`).
- AWK inspired JavaScript's functions. In fact, the keyword `function` comes from AWK.
- Scheme is the reason that JavaScript has first-class functions (they are treated like values and can be passed as arguments to functions) and closures (see Chapter 16).
- Self is responsible for JavaScript's unusual style of object orientation; it supports prototypal inheritance between objects.
- Perl and Python influenced JavaScript's handling of strings, arrays, and regular expressions.
- Beyond the actual language, HyperTalk influenced how JavaScript was integrated into web browsers. It led to HTML tags having event-handling attributes such as `onclick`.

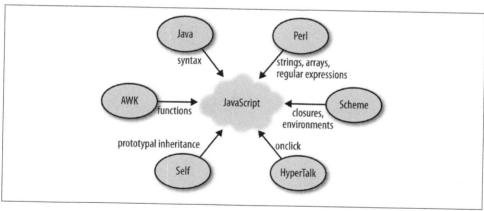

Figure 3-1. Programming languages that influenced JavaScript.

CHAPTER 4

How JavaScript Was Created

Knowing why and how JavaScript was created helps us understand why it is the way it is.

In 1993, NCSA's Mosaic was the first widely popular web browser. In 1994, a company called Netscape was founded to exploit the potential of the nascent World Wide Web. Netscape created the proprietary web browser Netscape Navigator, which was dominant throughout the 1990s. Many of the original Mosaic authors went on to work on Navigator, but the two intentionally shared no code.

Netscape quickly realized that the Web needed to become more dynamic. Even if you simply wanted to check that users entered correct values in a form, you needed to send the data to the server in order to give feedback. In 1995, Netscape hired Brendan Eich with the promise of letting him implement Scheme (a Lisp dialect) in the browser.[1] Before he could get started, Netscape collaborated with hardware and software company Sun (since bought by Oracle) to include its more static programming language, Java, in Navigator. As a consequence, a hotly debated question at Netscape was why the Web needed two programming languages: Java and a scripting language. The proponents of a scripting language offered the following explanation:[2]

> We aimed to provide a "glue language" for the Web designers and part time programmers who were building Web content from components such as images, plugins, and Java applets. We saw Java as the "component language" used by higher-priced programmers, where the glue programmers—the Web page designers—would assemble components and automate their interactions using [a scripting language].

By then, Netscape management had decided that a scripting language had to have a syntax similar to Java's. That ruled out adopting existing languages such as Perl, Python,

---

1. Brendan Eich, "Popularity," April 3, 2008, *http://bit.ly/1lKl6fG*.

2. Naomi Hamilton, "The A–Z of Programming Languages: JavaScript," Computerworld, July 30, 2008, *http://bit.ly/1lKldIe*.

TCL, or Scheme. To defend the idea of JavaScript against competing proposals, Netscape needed a prototype. Eich wrote one in 10 days, in May 1995. JavaScript's first code name was Mocha, coined by Marc Andreesen. Netscape marketing later changed it to Live-Script, for trademark reasons and because the names of several products already had the prefix "Live." In late November 1995, Navigator 2.0B3 came out and included the prototype, which continued its early existence without major changes. In early December 1995, Java's momentum had grown, and Sun licensed the trademark Java to Netscape. The language was renamed again, to its final name, JavaScript.[3]

---

3. Paul Krill, "JavaScript Creator Ponders Past, Future," InfoWorld, June 23, 2008, *http://bit.ly/1lKlpXO*; Brendan Eich, "A Brief History of JavaScript," July 21, 2010, *http://bit.ly/1lKkI0M*.

CHAPTER 5

Standardization: ECMAScript

After JavaScript came out, Microsoft implemented the same language, under the different name JScript, in Internet Explorer 3.0 (August 1996). Partially to keep Microsoft in check, Netscape decided to standardize JavaScript and asked the standards organization Ecma International (*http://en.wikipedia.org/wiki/Ecma*) to host the standard. Work on a specification called ECMA-262 started in November 1996. Because Sun (now Oracle) had a trademark on the word *Java*, the official name of the language to be standardized couldn't be *JavaScript*. Hence, *ECMAScript* was chosen, derived from *JavaScript* and *Ecma*. However, that name is used only to refer to versions of the language (where one refers to the specification). Everyone still calls the language *JavaScript*.

ECMA-262 is managed and evolved by Ecma's Technical Committee 39 (*http://bit.ly/ 1oNTQiP*) (TC39). Its members are companies such as Microsoft, Mozilla, and Google, which appoint employees to participate in committee work; examples include Brendan Eich, Allen Wirfs-Brock (editor of ECMA-262), and David Herman. To advance the design of ECMAScript, TC39 hosts discussions on open channels (such as the mailing list es-discuss (*https://mail.mozilla.org/listinfo/es-discuss*)) and holds regular meetings. The meetings are attended by TC39 members and invited experts. In early 2013, attendee numbers ranged from 15 to 25.

The following is a list of ECMAScript versions (or *editions* of ECMA-262) and their key features:

ECMAScript 1 (June 1997)
 First edition

ECMAScript 2 (August 1998)
 Editorial changes to align ECMA-262 with the standard ISO/IEC 16262

ECMAScript 3 (December 1999)
 `do-while`, regular expressions, new string methods (`concat`, `match`, `replace`, `slice`, `split` with a regular expression, etc.), exception handling, and more

ECMAScript 4 (abandoned July 2008)

ECMAScript 4 was developed as the next version of JavaScript, with a prototype written in ML. However, TC39 could not agree on its feature set. To prevent an impasse, the committee met at the end of July 2008 and came to an accord, summarized in four points (*http://mzl.la/1oNTUiG*):

1. Develop an incremental update of ECMAScript 3 (which became ECMAScript 5).

2. Develop a major new version that does less than ECMAScript 4, but much more than the incremental update of ECMAScript 3. The code name for the new version is Harmony, due to the nature of the meeting in which it was conceived. Harmony will be split into ECMAScript 6 and ECMAScript 7.

3. Features from ECMAScript 4 that would be dropped included packages, namespaces, and early binding.

4. Other ideas were to be developed in consensus with all of TC39.

Thus, the ECMAScript 4 developers agreed to make Harmony less radical than ECMAScript 4, and the rest of TC39 agreed to keep moving things forward.

ECMAScript 5 (December 2009)

Adds a strict mode, getters and setters, new array methods, support for JSON, and more (see Chapter 25)

ECMAScript 5.1 (June 2011)

Editorial changes to align ECMA-262 with the third edition of the international standard ISO/IEC 16262:2011

ECMAScript 6

Currently in development, it is estimated to be ratified by the end of 2014. Most engines will probably support the most important ECMAScript 6 features at ratification. Complete support may take longer.

Reaching consensus and creating a standard is not always easy, but thanks to the collaborative efforts of the aforementioned parties, JavaScript is a truly open language, with implementations by multiple vendors that are remarkably compatible. That compatibility is made possible by a very detailed yet concrete specification. For example, the specification often uses pseudocode, and it is complemented by a test suite, test262 (*http://test262.ecmascript.org/*), that checks an ECMAScript implementation for compliance. It is interesting to note that ECMAScript is not managed by the World Wide Web Consortium (W3C). TC39 and the W3C collaborate wherever there is overlap between JavaScript and HTML5.

CHAPTER 6

Historical JavaScript Milestones

It took JavaScript a long time to make an impact. Many JavaScript-related technologies existed for a while until they were discovered by the mainstream. This section describes what happened from JavaScript's creation until today. Throughout, only the most popular projects are mentioned and many are ignored, even if they were first. For example, the Dojo Toolkit is listed, but there is also the lesser-known qooxdoo (*http://qooxdoo.org/*), which was created around the same time. And Node.js is listed, even though Jaxer (*https://github.com/aptana/Jaxer*) existed before it:

1997—Dynamic HTML (http://bit.ly/1oNVOzH)
Dynamic HTML allows you to dynamically change the content and appearance of a web page. You achieve this by manipulating the Document Object Model (DOM) of the page, a tree-shaped data structure. Things you can do include changing content, changing style, and showing and hiding elements. Dynamic HTML appeared first in Internet Explorer 4 and in Netscape Navigator 4.

1999—XMLHttpRequest (http://www.w3.org/TR/XMLHttpRequest/)
This API lets a client-side script send an HTTP or HTTPS request to a server and get back data, usually in a text format (XML, HTML, JSON). It was introduced in Internet Explorer 5.

2001—JSON (http://json.org/), a JavaScript-based data exchange format
In 2001, Douglas Crockford named and documented JSON (JavaScript Object Notation), whose main idea is to use JavaScript syntax to store data in text format. JSON uses JavaScript literals for objects, arrays, strings, numbers, and booleans to represent structured data. For example:

```
{
    "first": "Jane",
    "last": "Porter",
    "married": true,
    "born": 1890,
```

```
    "friends": [ "Tarzan", "Cheeta" ]
}
```

Over the years, JSON has become a popular lightweight alternative to XML, especially when structured data is to be represented and not markup. Naturally, JSON is easy to consume via JavaScript (see Chapter 22).

2004—Dojo Toolkit (http://dojotoolkit.org/), a framework for programming JavaScript in the large

The Dojo Toolkit facilitates programming in the large by providing the necessary infrastructure: an inheritance library, a module system, an API for desktop-style graphical widgets, and more.

2005—Ajax (http://bit.ly/1oNW3Lf), browser-based desktop-class applications

Ajax is a collection of technologies that brings a level of interactivity to web pages that rivals that of desktop applications. One impressive example of what can be achieved via Ajax was introduced in February 2005: Google Maps. This application allowed you to pan and zoom over a map of the world, but only the content that was currently visible was downloaded to the browser. After Google Maps came out, Jesse James Garrett noticed that it shared certain traits with other interactive websites. He called these traits *Ajax*, a shorthand for *Asynchronous JavaScript and XML*.[1] The two cornerstones of Ajax are loading content asynchronously in the background (via XMLHttpRequest) and dynamically updating the current page with the results (via dynamic HTML). That was a considerable usability improvement from always performing complete page reloads.

Ajax marked the mainstream breakthrough of JavaScript and dynamic web applications. It is interesting to note how long that took—at that point, the Ajax ingredients had been available for years. Since the inception of Ajax, other data formats have become popular (JSON instead of XML), other protocols are used (e.g., Web Sockets in addition to HTTP), and bidirectional communication is possible. But the basic techniques are still the same. However, the term *Ajax* is used much less these days and has mostly been replaced by the more comprehensive terms *HTML5* and *Web Platform* (which both mean JavaScript plus browser APIs).

2005—Apache CouchDB (http://couchdb.apache.org/), a JavaScript-centric database

Roughly, CouchDB is a JSON database: you feed it JSON objects, without the need to specify a schema in advance. Additionally, you can define views and indexes via JavaScript functions that perform map/reduce operations. Hence, CouchDB is a very good fit for JavaScript because you can work directly with native data. Compared to a relational database, there is no mapping-related impedance mismatch. Compared to an object database, you avoid many complications because only data

---

1. Ajax is a shorthand, but not an acronym, which is why it isn't styled as AJAX.

is stored, not behavior. CouchDB is just one of several similar NoSQL databases (*http://bit.ly/1oNYfCp*). Most of them have excellent JavaScript support.

2006—jQuery (http://jquery.com/), helping with DOM manipulation
The browser DOM is one of the most painful parts of client-side web development. jQuery made DOM manipulation fun by abstracting over browser differences and by providing a powerful fluent-style API for querying and modifying the DOM.

2007—WebKit (https://www.webkit.org/), taking the mobile web mainstream
Based on prior work by KDE, WebKit is an HTML engine that was introduced by Apple in 2003. It was open-sourced in 2005. With the introduction of the iPhone in 2007, the mobile Web suddenly became mainstream and had little to no limitations compared to the nonmobile Web.

2008—V8 (http://code.google.com/p/v8/), proving JavaScript can be fast
When Google introduced its Chrome web browser, one of its highlights was a fast JavaScript engine called V8. It changed the perception of JavaScript as being slow and led to a speed race with other browser vendors from which we are still profiting. V8 is open source and can be used as a standalone component whenever you need a fast embedded language that is widely known.

2009—Node.js (http://nodejs.org/), implementing JavaScript on the server
Node.js lets you implement servers that perform well under load. To do so, it uses event-driven, nonblocking I/O and JavaScript (via V8). Node.js creator Ryan Dahl mentions the following reasons for choosing JavaScript:

- "Because it's bare and does not come with I/O APIs." [Node.js can thus introduce its own nonblocking APIs.]

- "Web developers use it already." [JavaScript is a widely known language, especially in a web context.]

- "DOM API is event-based. Everyone is already used to running without threads and on an event loop." [Developers are used to an asynchronous coding style.]

Dahl was able to build on prior work on event-driven servers and server-side Java-Script (mainly the CommonJS (*http://www.commonjs.org/*) project).

The appeal of Node.js for JavaScript programmers goes beyond being able to program in a familiar language; you get to use the same language on both client and server. That means you can share more code (e.g., for validating data) and use techniques such as *isomorphic JavaScript (http://bit.ly/1gWhLIs)*. Isomorphic Java-Script is about assembling web pages on either client or server, with numerous benefits: pages can be rendered on the server for faster initial display, SEO, and running on browsers that either don't support JavaScript or a version that is too old. But they can also be updated on the client, resulting in a more responsive user interface.

2009—PhoneGap (http://phonegap.com/), writing native apps in HTML5
 PhoneGap was created by a company called Nitobi that was later purchased by
 Adobe. The open source foundation of PhoneGap is called *Cordova*. The initial
 mission of PhoneGap was to make it possible to implement native mobile apps via
 HTML5. Since then, support has expanded to nonmobile operating systems. Cur-
 rently supported platforms include Android, Bada, BlackBerry, Firefox OS, iOS,
 Mac OS X, Tizen, Ubuntu, Windows (desktop), and Windows Phone. Apart from
 HTML5 APIs, there are also PhoneGap-specific APIs for accessing native fea-
 tures (*http://bit.ly/1oO22Q9*) such as the accelerometer, camera, and contacts.

2009—Chrome OS (http://bit.ly/1oO27U2), making the browser the operating system
 With Chrome OS, the web platform is the native platform. This approach has several
 advantages:

 - It is much easier to create an operating system, because all of the user interface
   technology is already there.

 - Many developers already (mostly) know how to write apps for the operating
   system.

 - Managing apps is simple. That helps public installations such as Internet cafes
   and schools.

 The introduction of the mobile operating system webOS (*http://bit.ly/1oO2e1N*)
 (which originated at Palm and is now owned by LG Electronics) predates the introduction of Chrome OS, but the "browser as OS" idea is more apparent with the
 latter (which is why it was chosen as a milestone). webOS is both less and more.
 Less, because it is very focused on cell phones and tablets. More, because it has
 Node.js built in, to let you implement services in JavaScript. A more recent entry
 in the web operating system category is Mozilla's Firefox OS (*http://mzl.la/
 1oO2i1J*), which targets cell phones and tablets. Mozilla's wiki (*http://mzl.la/
 1oO2n5m*) mentions a benefit of web operating systems for the Web:

> We also need a hill to take, in order to scope and focus our efforts. Recently we saw
> the pdf.js project [which renders PDFs via HTML5, without plugins] expose small
> gaps that needed filling in order for "HTML5" to be a superset of PDF. We want to
> take a bigger step now, and find the gaps that keep web developers from being able
> to build apps that are—in every way—the equals of native apps built for the iPhone,
> Android, and WP7.

2011—Windows 8 (http://bit.ly/1oO2qhJ), first-class HTML5 apps
 When Microsoft introduced Windows 8, it surprised everyone with the operating
 system's extensive integration of HTML5. HTML5 applications are first-class citi-
 zens in Windows 8, on par with those implemented via incumbent technologies
 such as .NET and C++. To demonstrate that point, Microsoft wrote several important Windows 8 applications in HTML5 (plus calls to native APIs), including the
 app store and the email app.

PART III

JavaScript in Depth

This part is a comprehensive reference of the JavaScript language.

CHAPTER 7

JavaScript's Syntax

JavaScript's syntax is fairly straightforward. This chapter describes things to watch out for.

An Overview of the Syntax

This section gives you a quick impression of what JavaScript's syntax looks like.

The following are five fundamental kinds of values:

- Booleans:

    ```
    true
    false
    ```

- Numbers:

    ```
    1023
    7.851
    ```

- Strings:

    ```
    'hello'
    "hello"
    ```

- Plain objects:

    ```
    {
        firstName: 'Jane',
        lastName: 'Doe'
    }
    ```

- Arrays:

    ```
    [ 'apple', 'banana', 'cherry' ]
    ```

Here are a few examples of basic syntax:

```
// Two slashes start single-linecomments

var x;   // declaring a variable

x = 3 + y;   // assigning a value to the variable `x`

foo(x, y);   // calling function `foo` with parameters `x` and `y`
obj.bar(3);   // calling method `bar` of object `obj`

// A conditional statement
if (x === 0) {   // Is `x` equal to zero?
    x = 123;
}

// Defining function `baz` with parameters `a` and `b`
function baz(a, b) {
    return a + b;
}
```

Note the two different uses of the equals sign:

- A single equals sign (=) is used to assign a value to a variable.
- A triple equals sign (===) is used to compare two values (see "Equality Operators" on page 14).

Comments

There are two kinds of comments:

- Single-line comments via // extend to the rest of the line. Here's an example:

  ```
  var a = 0; // init
  ```

- Multiline comments via /* */ can extend over arbitrary ranges of text. They cannot be nested. Here are two examples:

  ```
  /* temporarily disabled
  processNext(queue);
  */

  function (a /* int */, b /* str */) {
  }
  ```

Expressions Versus Statements

This section looks at an important syntactic distinction in JavaScript: the difference between expressions and statements.

Expressions

An *expression* produces a value and can be written wherever a value is expected—for example, as an argument in a function call or at the right side of an assignment. Each of the following lines contains an expression:

```
myvar
3 + x
myfunc('a', 'b')
```

Statements

Roughly, a *statement* performs an action. Loops and `if` statements are examples of statements. A program is basically a sequence of statements.[1]

Wherever JavaScript expects a statement, you can also write an expression. Such a statement is called an *expression statement*. The reverse does not hold: you cannot write a statement where JavaScript expects an expression. For example, an `if` statement cannot become the argument of a function.

Conditional statement versus conditional expressions

The difference between statements and expressions becomes clearer if we look at members of the two syntactic categories that are similar: the `if` statement and the conditional operator (an expression).

The following is an example of an `if` statement:

```
var salutation;
if (male) {
    salutation = 'Mr.';
} else {
    salutation = 'Mrs.';
}
```

There is a similar kind of expression, the *conditional operator*. The preceding statements are equivalent to the following code:

```
var salutation = (male ? 'Mr.' : 'Mrs.');
```

The code between the equals sign and the semicolon is an expression. The parentheses are not necessary, but I find the conditional operator easier to read if I put it in parens.

Using ambiguous expressions as statements

Two kinds of expressions look like statements—they are ambiguous with regard to their syntactic category:

---

1. To keep things simple, I'm pretending that declarations are statements.

- Object literals (expressions) look like blocks (statements):

```
{
    foo: bar(3, 5)
}
```

The preceding construct is either an object literal (details: "Object Literals" on page 198) or a block followed by the label foo:, followed by the function call bar(3, 5).

- Named function expressions look like function declarations (statements):

```
function foo() { }
```

The preceding construct is either a named function expression or a function declaration. The former produces a function, the latter creates a variable and assigns a function to it (details on both kinds of function definition: "Defining Functions" on page 166).

In order to prevent ambiguity during parsing, JavaScript does not let you use object literals and function expressions as statements. That is, expression statements must not start with:

- A curly brace
- The keyword function

If an expression starts with either of those tokens, it can only appear in an expression context. You can comply with that requirement by, for example, putting parentheses around the expression. Next, we'll look at two examples where that is necessary.

Evaluating an object literal via eval()

eval parses its argument in statement context. You have to put parentheses around an object literal if you want eval to return an object:

```
> eval('{ foo: 123 }')
123
> eval('({ foo: 123 })')
{ foo: 123 }
```

Immediately invoking a function expression

The following code is an *immediately invoked function expression* (IIFE), a function whose body is executed right away (you'll learn what IIFEs are used for in "Introducing a New Scope via an IIFE" on page 183):

```
> (function () { return 'abc' }())
'abc'
```

If you omit the parentheses, you get a syntax error, because JavaScript sees a function declaration, which can't be anonymous:

```
> function () { return 'abc' }()
SyntaxError: function statement requires a name
```

If you add a name, you also get a syntax error, because function declarations can't be immediately invoked:

```
> function foo() { return 'abc' }()
SyntaxError: Unexpected token )
```

Whatever follows a function declaration must be a legal statement and () isn't.

Control Flow Statements and Blocks

For control flow statements, the body is a single statement. Here are two examples:

```
if (obj !== null) obj.foo();

while (x > 0) x--;
```

However, any statement can always be replaced by a *block*, curly braces containing zero or more statements. Thus, you can also write:

```
if (obj !== null) {
    obj.foo();
}

while (x > 0) {
    x--;
}
```

I prefer the latter form of control flow statement. Standardizing on it means that there is no difference between single-statement bodies and multistatement bodies. As a consequence, your code looks more consistent, and alternating between one statement and more than one statement is easier.

Rules for Using Semicolons

In this section, we examine how semicolons are used in JavaScript. The basic rules are:

- Normally, statements are terminated by semicolons.
- The exception is statements ending with blocks.

Semicolons are optional in JavaScript. Missing semicolons are added via so-called *automatic semicolon insertion* (ASI; see "Automatic Semicolon Insertion" on page 59). However, that feature doesn't always work as expected, which is why you should always include semicolons.

No Semicolon After a Statement Ending with a Block

The following statements are not terminated by semicolons if they end with a block:

- Loops: `for`, `while` (but not `do-while`)
- Branching: `if`, `switch`, `try`
- Function declarations (but not function expressions)

Here's an example of `while` versus `do-while`:

```
while (a > 0) {
    a--;
} // no semicolon

do {
    a--;
} while (a > 0);
```

And here's an example of a function declaration versus a function expression. The latter is followed by a semicolon, because it appears inside a `var` declaration (which *is* terminated by a semicolon):

```
function foo() {
    // ...
} // no semicolon

var foo = function () {
    // ...
};
```

 If you do add a semicolon after a block, you do not get a syntax error, because it is considered an empty statement (see the next section).

 That's most of what you need to know about semicolons. If you always add semicolons, you can probably get by without reading the remaining parts of this section.

The Empty Statement

A semicolon on its own is an *empty statement* and does nothing. Empty statements can appear anywhere a statement is expected. They are useful in situations where a statement is demanded, but not needed. In such situations, blocks are usually also allowed. For example, the following two statements are equivalent:

```
while (processNextItem() > 0);
while (processNextItem() > 0) {}
```

The function `processNextItem` is assumed to return the number of remaining items. The following program, consisting of three empty statements, is also syntactically correct:

```
;;;
```

Automatic Semicolon Insertion

The goal of automatic semicolon insertion (ASI) is to make semicolons optional at the end of a line. The image invoked by the term *automatic semicolon insertion* is that the JavaScript parser inserts semicolons for you (internally, things are usually handled differently).

Put another way, ASI helps the parser to determine when a statement ends. Normally, it ends with a semicolon. ASI dictates that a statement also ends if:

- A line terminator (e.g., a newline) is followed by an illegal token.
- A closing brace is encountered.
- The end of the file has been reached.

Example: ASI via illegal token

The following code contains a line terminator followed by an illegal token:

```
if (a < 0) a = 0
console.log(a)
```

The token `console` is illegal after 0 and triggers ASI:

```
if (a < 0) a = 0;
console.log(a);
```

Example: ASI via closing brace

In the following code, the statement inside the braces is not terminated by a semicolon:

```
function add(a,b) { return a+b }
```

ASI creates a syntactically correct version of the preceding code:

```
function add(a,b) { return a+b; }
```

Pitfall: ASI can unexpectedly break up statements

ASI is also triggered if there is a line terminator after the keyword `return`. For example:

```
// Don't do this
return
{
    name: 'John'
};
```

ASI turns the preceding into:

```
return;
{
    name: 'John'
};
```

That's an empty return, followed by a block with the label `name` in front of the expression statement `'John'`. After the block, there is an empty statement.

Pitfall: ASI might unexpectedly not be triggered

Sometimes a statement in a new line starts with a token that is allowed as a continuation of the previous statement. Then ASI is not triggered, even though it seems like it should be. For example:

```
func()
[ 'ul', 'ol' ].foreach(function (t) { handleTag(t) })
```

The square brackets in the second line are interpreted as an index into the result returned by `func()`. The comma inside the brackets is interpreted as the comma operator (which returns `'ol'` in this case; see "The Comma Operator" on page 90). Thus, JavaScript sees the previous code as:

```
func()['ol'].foreach(function (t) { handleTag(t) });
```

Legal Identifiers

Identifiers are used for naming things and appear in various syntactic roles in JavaScript. For example, the names of variables and unquoted property keys must be valid identifiers. Identifiers are case sensitive.

The first character of an identifier is one of:

- Any Unicode letter, including Latin letters such as D, Greek letters such as λ, and Cyrillic letters such as Д
- Dollar sign ($)
- Underscore (_)

Subsequent characters are:

- Any legal first character
- Any Unicode digit in the Unicode category "Decimal number (Nd)"; this includes European numerals such as 7 and Indic numerals such as ٣
- Various other Unicode marks and punctuations

Examples of legal identifiers:

```
var ε = 0.0001;
var строка = '';
var _tmp;
var $foo2;
```

Even though this enables you to use a variety of human languages in JavaScript code, I recommend sticking with English, for both identifiers and comments. That ensures that your code is understandable by the largest possible group of people, which is important, given how much code can spread internationally these days.

The following identifiers are *reserved words*—they are part of the syntax and can't be used as variable names (including function names and parameter names):

arguments	break	case	catch
class	const	continue	debugger
default	delete	do	else
enum	export	extends	false
finally	for	function	if
implements	import	in	instanceof
interface	let	new	null
package	private	protected	public
return	static	super	switch
this	throw	true	try
typeof	var	void	while

The following three identifiers are not reserved words, but you should treat them as if they were:

```
Infinity
NaN
undefined
```

Lastly, you should also stay away from the names of standard global variables (see Chapter 23). You can use them for local variables without breaking anything, but your code still becomes confusing.

Note that you *can* use reserved words as unquoted property keys (as of ECMAScript 5):

```
> var obj = { function: 'abc' };
> obj.function
'abc'
```

You can look up the precise rules for identifiers in Mathias Bynens's blog post "Valid JavaScript variable names" (*http://mathiasbynens.be/notes/javascript-identifiers*).

Invoking Methods on Number Literals

With method invocations, it is important to distinguish between the floating-point dot and the method invocation dot. Thus, you cannot write 1.toString(); you must use one of the following alternatives:

```
1..toString()
1 .toString()  // space before dot
(1).toString()
1.0.toString()
```

Strict Mode

ECMAScript 5 has a *strict mode* that results in cleaner JavaScript, with fewer unsafe features, more warnings, and more logical behavior. The normal (nonstrict) mode is sometimes called "sloppy mode."

Switching on Strict Mode

You switch strict mode on by typing the following line first in your JavaScript file or inside your <script> element:

```
'use strict';
```

Note that JavaScript engines that don't support ECMAScript 5 will simply ignore the preceding statement, as writing strings in this manner (as an expression statement; see "Statements" on page 55) normally does nothing.

You can also switch on strict mode per function. To do so, write your function like this:

```
function foo() {
    'use strict';
    ...
}
```

This is handy when you are working with a legacy code base where switching on strict mode everywhere may break things.

Strict Mode: Recommended, with Caveats

In general, the changes enabled by strict mode are all for the better. Thus, it is highly recommended to use it for new code you write—simply switch it on at the beginning of a file. There are, however, two caveats:

Enabling strict mode for existing code may break it

The code may rely on a feature that is not available anymore, or it may rely on behavior that is different in sloppy mode than in strict mode. Don't forget that you have the option to add single strict mode functions to files that are in sloppy mode.

Package with care

When you concatenate and/or minify files, you have to be careful that strict mode isn't switched off where it should be switched on or vice versa. Both can break code.

The following sections explain the strict mode features in more detail. You normally don't need to know them, as you will mostly get more warnings for things that you shouldn't do anyway.

Variables Must Be Declared in Strict Mode

All variables must be explicitly declared in strict mode. This helps to prevent typos. In sloppy mode, assigning to an undeclared variable creates a global variable:

```
function sloppyFunc() {
    sloppyVar = 123;
}
sloppyFunc();  // creates global variable `sloppyVar`
console.log(sloppyVar);  // 123
```

In strict mode, assigning to an undeclared variable throws an exception:

```
function strictFunc() {
    'use strict';
    strictVar = 123;
}
strictFunc();  // ReferenceError: strictVar is not defined
```

Functions in Strict Mode

Strict mode limits function-related features.

Functions must be declared at the top level of a scope

In strict mode, all functions must be declared at the top level of a scope (global scope or directly inside a function). That means that you can't put a function declaration inside a block. If you do, you get a descriptive SyntaxError. For example, V8 tells you: "In strict mode code, functions can only be declared at top level or immediately within another function":

```
function strictFunc() {
    'use strict';
    {
        // SyntaxError:
        function nested() {
        }
    }
}
```

That is something that isn't useful anyway, because the function is created in the scope of the surrounding function, not "inside" the block.

If you want to work around this limitation, you can create a function inside a block via a variable declaration and a function expression:

```
function strictFunc() {
    'use strict';
    {
        // OK:
        var nested = function () {
        };
    }
}
```

Stricter rules for function parameters

The rules for function parameters are less permissive: using the same parameter name twice is forbidden, as are local variables that have the same name as a parameter.

The arguments objects has fewer properties

The arguments object is simpler in strict mode: the properties arguments.callee and arguments.caller have been eliminated, you can't assign to the variable arguments, and arguments does not track changes to parameters (if a parameter changes, the corresponding array element does not change with it). "Deprecated features of arguments" on page 172 explains the details.

this is undefined in nonmethod functions

In sloppy mode, the value of this in nonmethod functions is the global object (window in browsers; see "The Global Object" on page 188):

```
function sloppyFunc() {
    console.log(this === window);  // true
}
```

In strict mode, it is undefined:

```
function strictFunc() {
    'use strict';
    console.log(this === undefined);  // true
}
```

This is useful for constructors. For example, the following constructor, `Point`, is in strict mode:

```
function Point(x, y) {
    'use strict';
    this.x = x;
    this.y = y;
}
```

Due to strict mode, you get a warning when you accidentally forget new and call it as a function:

```
> var pt = Point(3, 1);
TypeError: Cannot set property 'x' of undefined
```

In sloppy mode, you don't get a warning, and global variables x and y are created. Consult "Tips for Implementing Constructors" on page 239 for details.

Setting and Deleting Immutable Properties Fails with an Exception in Strict Mode

Illegal manipulations of properties throw exceptions in strict mode. For example, attempting to set the value of a read-only property throws an exception, as does attempting to delete a nonconfigurable property. Here is an example of the former:

```
var str = 'abc';
function sloppyFunc() {
    str.length = 7;  // no effect, silent failure
    console.log(str.length);  // 3
}
function strictFunc() {
    'use strict';
    str.length = 7; // TypeError: Cannot assign to
                    // read-only property 'length'
}
```

Unqualified Identifiers Can't Be Deleted in Strict Mode

In sloppy mode, you can delete a global variable foo like this:

```
delete foo
```

In strict mode, you get a syntax error whenever you try to delete unqualified identifiers. You can still delete global variables like this:

```
delete window.foo;  // browsers
delete global.foo;  // Node.js
delete this.foo;    // everywhere (in global scope)
```

eval() Is Cleaner in Strict Mode

In strict mode, the `eval()` function becomes less quirky: variables declared in the evaluated string are not added to the scope surrounding `eval()` anymore. For details, consult "Evaluating Code Using eval()" on page 347.

Features That Are Forbidden in Strict Mode

Two more JavaScript features are forbidden in strict mode:

- The `with` statement is not allowed anymore (see "The with Statement" on page 153). You get a syntax error at compile time (when loading the code).
- No more octal numbers: in sloppy mode, an integer with a leading zero is interpreted as octal (base 8). For example:

```
> 010 === 8
true
```

In strict mode, you get a syntax error if you use this kind of literal:

```
> function f() { 'use strict'; return 010 }
SyntaxError: Octal literals are not allowed in strict mode.
```

Values

JavaScript has most of the values that we have come to expect from programming languages: booleans, numbers, strings, arrays, and so on. All normal values in JavaScript have *properties*.[1] Each property has a *key* (or *name*) and a *value*. You can think of properties like fields of a record. You use the dot (.) operator to access properties:

```
> var obj = {}; // create an empty object
> obj.foo = 123;  // write property
123
> obj.foo  // read property
123
> 'abc'.toUpperCase()  // call method
'ABC'
```

JavaScript's Type System

This chapter gives an overview of JavaScript's type system.

JavaScript's Types

JavaScript has only six types, according to Chapter 8 of the ECMAScript language specification (*http://www.ecma-international.org/ecma-262/5.1/#sec-8*):

> An ECMAScript language type corresponds to values that are directly manipulated by an ECMAScript programmer using the ECMAScript language. The ECMAScript language types are:
>
> - Undefined, Null
> - Boolean, String, Number, and

---

1. Technically, primitive values do not have their own properties, they borrow them from wrapper constructors. But that is something that goes on behind the scenes, so you don't normally see it.

- Object

Therefore, constructors technically don't introduce new types, even though they are said to have instances.

Static Versus Dynamic

In the context of language semantics and type systems, *static* usually means "at compile time" or "without running a program," while *dynamic* means "at runtime."

Static Typing Versus Dynamic Typing

In a statically typed language, variables, parameters, and members of objects (JavaScript calls them properties) have types that the compiler knows at compile time. The compiler can use that information to perform type checks and to optimize the compiled code.

Even in statically typed languages, a variable also has a dynamic type, the type of the variable's value at a given point at runtime. The dynamic type can differ from the static type. For example (Java):

```
Object foo = "abc";
```

The static type of `foo` is `Object`; its dynamic type is `String`.

JavaScript is dynamically typed; types of variables are generally not known at compile time.

Static Type Checking Versus Dynamic Type Checking

If you have type information, you can check whether a value used in an operation (calling a function, applying an operator, etc.) has the correct type. Statically type-checked languages perform this kind of check at compile time, while dynamically type-checked languages do so at runtime. A language can be both statically type-checked and dynamically type-checked. If a check fails, you usually get some kind of error or exception.

JavaScript performs a very limited kind of dynamic type checking:

```
> var foo = null;
> foo.prop
TypeError: Cannot read property 'prop' of null
```

Mostly, however, things silently fail or work. For example, if you access a property that does not exist, you get the value `undefined`:

```
> var bar = {};
> bar.prop
undefined
```

Coercion

In JavaScript, the main way of dealing with a value whose type doesn't fit is to *coerce* it to the correct type. *Coercion* means implicit type conversion. Most operands coerce:

```
> '3' * '4'
12
```

JavaScript's built-in conversion mechanisms support only the types `Boolean`, `Number`, `String`, and `Object`. There is no standard way to convert an instance of one constructor to an instance of another constructor.

 The terms *strongly typed* and *weakly typed* do not have generally meaningful definitions (*http://bit.ly/1oO7t1p*). They are used, but normally incorrectly. It is better to instead use *statically typed*, *statically type-checked*, and so on.

Primitive Values Versus Objects

JavaScript makes a somewhat arbitrary distinction between values:

- The *primitive values* are booleans, numbers, strings, `null`, and `undefined`.
- All other values are *objects*.

A major difference between the two is how they are compared; each object has a unique identity and is only (strictly) equal to itself:

```
> var obj1 = {};  // an empty object
> var obj2 = {};  // another empty object
> obj1 === obj2
false

> var obj3 = obj1;
> obj3 === obj1
true
```

In contrast, all primitive values encoding the same value are considered the same:

```
> var prim1 = 123;
> var prim2 = 123;
> prim1 === prim2
true
```

The following two sections explain primitive values and objects in more detail.

Primitive Values

The following are all of the *primitive values* (*primitives* for short):

- Booleans: `true`, `false` (see Chapter 10)
- Numbers: `1736`, `1.351` (see Chapter 11)
- Strings: `'abc'`, `"abc"` (see Chapter 12)
- Two "nonvalues": `undefined`, `null` (see "undefined and null" on page 71)

Primitives have the following characteristics:

Compared by value
    The "content" is compared:

```
> 3 === 3
true
> 'abc' === 'abc'
true
```

Always immutable
    Properties can't be changed, added, or removed:

```
> var str = 'abc';

> str.length = 1; // try to change property `length`
> str.length      // ⇒ no effect
3

> str.foo = 3; // try to create property `foo`
> str.foo      // ⇒ no effect, unknown property
undefined
```

(Reading an unknown property always returns `undefined`.)

A fixed set of types
    You can't define your own primitive types.

Objects

All nonprimitive values are *objects*. The most common kinds of objects are:

- *Plain objects* (constructor `Object`) can be created by *object literals* (see Chapter 17):

```
{
    firstName: 'Jane',
    lastName: 'Doe'
}
```

The preceding object has two properties: the value of property `firstName` is `'Jane'`, and the value of property `lastName` is `'Doe'`.

- *Arrays* (constructor `Array`) can be created by *array literals* (see Chapter 18):

```
[ 'apple', 'banana', 'cherry' ]
```

The preceding array has three elements that can be accessed via numeric indices. For example, the index of 'apple' is 0.

- *Regular expressions* (constructor RegExp) can be created by *regular expression literals* (see Chapter 19):

```
/^a+b+$/
```

Objects have the following characteristics:

Compared by reference
> Identities are compared; every object has its own identity:

```
> {} === {}   // two different empty objects
false

> var obj1 = {};
> var obj2 = obj1;
> obj1 === obj2
true
```

Mutable by default
> You can normally freely change, add, and remove properties (see "Dot Operator (.): Accessing Properties via Fixed Keys" on page 199):

```
> var obj = {};
> obj.foo = 123; // add property `foo`
> obj.foo
123
```

User-extensible
> Constructors (see "Layer 3: Constructors—Factories for Instances" on page 231) can be seen as implementations of custom types (similar to classes in other languages).

undefined and null

JavaScript has two "nonvalues" that indicate missing information, undefined and null:

- undefined means "no value" (neither primitive nor object). Uninitialized variables, missing parameters, and missing properties have that nonvalue. And functions implicitly return it if nothing has been explicitly returned.

- null means "no object." It is used as a nonvalue where an object is expected (as a parameter, as a member in a chain of objects, etc.).

undefined and null are the only values for which any kind of property access results in an exception:

```
> function returnFoo(x) { return x.foo }
```

```
> returnFoo(true)
undefined
> returnFoo(0)
undefined

> returnFoo(null)
TypeError: Cannot read property 'foo' of null
> returnFoo(undefined)
TypeError: Cannot read property 'foo' of undefined
```

undefined is also sometimes used as more of a metavalue that indicates nonexistence. In contrast, null indicates emptiness. For example, a JSON node visitor (see "Transforming Data via Node Visitors" on page 341) returns:

- undefined to remove an object property or array element
- null to set the property or element to null

Occurrences of undefined and null

Here we review the various scenarios where undefined and null occur.

Occurrences of undefined

Uninitialized variables are undefined:

```
> var foo;
> foo
undefined
```

Missing parameters are undefined:

```
> function f(x) { return x }
> f()
undefined
```

If you read a nonexistent property, you get undefined:

```
> var obj = {}; // empty object
> obj.foo
undefined
```

And functions implicitly return undefined if nothing has been explicitly returned:

```
> function f() {}
> f()
undefined

> function g() { return; }
> g()
undefined
```

Occurrences of null

- null is the last element in the prototype chain (a chain of objects; see "Layer 2: The Prototype Relationship Between Objects" on page 211):

  ```
  > Object.getPrototypeOf(Object.prototype)
  null
  ```

- null is returned by RegExp.prototype.exec() if there was no match for the regular expression in the string:

  ```
  > /x/.exec('aaa')
  null
  ```

Checking for undefined or null

In the following sections we review how to check for undefined and null individually, or to check if either exists.

Checking for null

You check for null via strict equality:

```
if (x === null) ...
```

Checking for undefined

Strict equality (===) is the canonical way of checking for undefined:

```
if (x === undefined) ...
```

You can also check for undefined via the typeof operator ("typeof: Categorizing Primitives" on page 92), but you should normally use the aforementioned approach.

Checking for either undefined or null

Most functions allow you to indicate a missing value via either undefined or null. One way of checking for both of them is via an explicit comparison:

```
// Does x have a value?
if (x !== undefined && x !== null) {
    ...
}
// Is x a non-value?
if (x === undefined || x === null) {
    ...
}
```

Another way is to exploit the fact that both undefined and null are considered false (see "Truthy and Falsy Values" on page 98):

```
// Does x have a value (is it truthy)?
if (x) {
    ...
}
// Is x falsy?
if (!x) {
    ...
}
```

 false, 0, NaN, and '' are also considered `false`.

The History of undefined and null

A single nonvalue could play the roles of both `undefined` and `null`. Why does JavaScript have two such values? The reason is historical.

JavaScript adopted Java's approach of partitioning values into primitives and objects. It also used Java's value for "not an object," `null`. Following the precedent set by C (but not Java), `null` becomes 0 if coerced to a number:

```
> Number(null)
0
> 5 + null
5
```

Remember that the first version of JavaScript did not have exception handling. Therefore, exceptional cases such as uninitialized variables and missing properties had to be indicated via a value. `null` would have been a good choice, but Brendan Eich wanted to avoid two things at the time:

- The value shouldn't have the connotation of a reference, because it was about more than just objects.
- The value shouldn't coerce to 0, because that makes errors harder to spot.

As a result, Eich added `undefined` as an additional nonvalue to the language. It coerces to NaN:

```
> Number(undefined)
NaN
> 5 + undefined
NaN
```

Changing undefined

undefined is a property of the global object (*http://bit.ly/1oO9pXM*) (and thus a global variable; see "The Global Object" on page 188). Under ECMAScript 3, you had to take precautions when reading undefined, because it was easy to accidentally change its value. Under ECMAScript 5, that is not necessary, because undefined is read-only.

To protect against a changed undefined, two techniques were popular (they are still relevant for older JavaScript engines):

Technique 1

Shadow the global undefined (which may have the wrong value):

```
(function (undefined) {
    if (x === undefined) ...  // safe now
}());  // don't hand in a parameter
```

In the preceding code, undefined is guaranteed to have the right value, because it is a parameter whose value has not been provided by the function call.

Technique 2

Compare with void 0, which is always (the correct) undefined (see "The void Operator" on page 90):

```
if (x === void 0)  // always safe
```

Wrapper Objects for Primitives

The three primitive types boolean, number, and string have corresponding constructors: Boolean, Number, String. Their instances (so-called *wrapper objects*) contain (*wrap*) primitive values. The constructors can be used in two ways:

- As constructors, they create objects that are largely incompatible with the primitive values that they wrap:

```
> typeof new String('abc')
'object'
> new String('abc') === 'abc'
false
```

- As functions, they convert values to the corresponding primitive types (see "Functions for Converting to Boolean, Number, String, and Object" on page 78). This is the recommended method of conversion:

```
> String(123)
'123'
```

It's considered a best practice to avoid wrapper objects. You normally don't need them, as there is nothing that objects can do that primitives can't (with the exception of being mutated). (This is different from Java, from which JavaScript inherited the difference between primitives and objects!)

Wrapper Objects Are Different from Primitives

Primitive values such as `'abc'` are fundamentally different from wrapper instances such as `new String('abc')`:

```
> typeof 'abc'  // a primitive value
'string'
> typeof new String('abc')  // an object
'object'
> 'abc' instanceof String  // never true for primitives
false
> 'abc' === new String('abc')
false
```

Wrapper instances are objects, and there is no way of comparing objects in JavaScript, not even via lenient equals == (see "Equality Operators: === Versus ==" on page 83):

```
> var a = new String('abc');
> var b = new String('abc');
> a == b
false
```

Wrapping and Unwrapping Primitives

There is one use case for wrapper objects: you want to add properties to a primitive value. Then you wrap the primitive and add properties to the wrapper object. You need to unwrap the value before you can work with it.

Wrap a primitive by invoking a wrapper constructor:

```
new Boolean(true)
new Number(123)
new String('abc')
```

Unwrap a primitive by invoking the method `valueOf()`. All objects have this method (as discussed in "Conversion to Primitive" on page 258):

```
> new Boolean(true).valueOf()
true
> new Number(123).valueOf()
123
> new String('abc').valueOf()
'abc'
```

Converting wrapper objects to primitives properly extracts numbers and strings, but not booleans:

```
> Boolean(new Boolean(false))  // does not unwrap
true
> Number(new Number(123))  // unwraps
123
> String(new String('abc'))  // unwraps
'abc'
```

The reason for this is explained in "Converting to Boolean" on page 97.

Primitives Borrow Their Methods from Wrappers

Primitives don't have their own methods and borrow them from wrappers:

```
> 'abc'.charAt === String.prototype.charAt
true
```

Sloppy mode and strict mode handle this borrowing differently. In sloppy mode, primitives are converted to wrappers on the fly:

```
String.prototype.sloppyMethod = function () {
    console.log(typeof this); // object
    console.log(this instanceof String); // true
};
''.sloppyMethod(); // call the above method
```

In strict mode, methods from the wrapper prototype are used transparently:

```
String.prototype.strictMethod = function () {
    'use strict';
    console.log(typeof this); // string
    console.log(this instanceof String); // false
};
''.strictMethod(); // call the above method
```

Type Coercion

Type coercion means the implicit conversion of a value of one type to a value of another type. Most of JavaScript's operators, functions, and methods coerce operands and arguments to the types that they need. For example, the operands of the multiplication operator (*) are coerced to numbers:

```
> '3' * '4'
12
```

As another example, if one of the operands is a string, the plus operator (+) converts the other one to a string:

```
> 3 + ' times'
'3 times'
```

Type Coercion Can Hide Bugs

Therefore, JavaScript rarely complains about a value having the wrong type. For example, programs normally receive user input (from online forms or GUI widgets) as strings, even if the user has entered a number. If you treat a number-as-string like a number, you will not get a warning, just unexpected results. For example:

```
var formData = { width: '100' };

// You think formData.width is a number
// and get unexpected results
var w = formData.width;
var outer = w + 20;

// You expect outer to be 120, but it's not
console.log(outer === 120);   // false
console.log(outer === '10020');  // true
```

In cases such as the preceding one, you should convert to the appropriate type early on:

```
var w = Number(formData.width);
```

Functions for Converting to Boolean, Number, String, and Object

The following functions are the preferred way of converting a value to a boolean, number, string, or object:

Boolean() *(see "Converting to Boolean" on page 97)*
> Converts a value to a boolean. The following values are converted to `false`; they are the so-called "falsy" values:
>
> * undefined, null
> * false
> * 0, NaN
> * ' '
>
> All other values are considered "truthy" and converted to `true` (including all objects!).

Number() *(see "Converting to Number" on page 104)*
> Converts a value to a number:
>
> * undefined becomes NaN.
> * null becomes 0.
> * false becomes 0, true becomes 1.
> * Strings are parsed.

- Objects are first converted to primitives (discussed shortly), which are then converted to numbers.

`String()` *(see "Converting to String" on page 135)*

Converts a value to a string. It has the obvious results for all primitives. For example:

```
> String(null)
'null'
> String(123.45)
'123.45'
> String(false)
'false'
```

Objects are first converted to primitives (discussed shortly), which are then converted to strings.

`Object()` *(see "Converting Any Value to an Object" on page 203)*

Converts objects to themselves, `undefined` and `null` to empty objects, and primitives to wrapped primitives. For example:

```
> var obj = { foo: 123 };
> Object(obj) === obj
true

> Object(undefined)
{}
> Object('abc') instanceof String
true
```

Note that `Boolean()`, `Number()`, `String()`, and `Object()` are called as functions. You normally don't use them as constructors. Then they create instances of themselves (see "Wrapper Objects for Primitives" on page 75).

Algorithm: ToPrimitive()—Converting a Value to a Primitive

To convert a value to either a number or a string, it is first converted to an arbitrary primitive value, which is then converted to the final type (as discussed in "Functions for Converting to Boolean, Number, String, and Object" on page 78).

The ECMAScript specification has an internal function, `ToPrimitive()` (which is not accessible from JavaScript), that performs this conversion. Understanding `ToPrimitive()` enables you to configure how objects are converted to numbers and strings. It has the following signature:

```
ToPrimitive(input, PreferredType?)
```

The optional parameter `PreferredType` indicates the final type of the conversion: it is either `Number` or `String`, depending on whether the result of `ToPrimitive()` will be converted to a number or a string.

If `PreferredType` is `Number`, then you perform the following steps:

1. If `input` is primitive, return it (there is nothing more to do).
2. Otherwise, `input` is an object. Call `input.valueOf()`. If the result is primitive, return it.
3. Otherwise, call `input.toString()`. If the result is primitive, return it.
4. Otherwise, throw a `TypeError` (indicating the failure to convert `input` to a primitive).

If `PreferredType` is `String`, steps 2 and 3 are swapped. The `PreferredType` can also be omitted; it is then considered to be `String` for dates and `Number` for all other values. This is how the operators + and == call `ToPrimitive()`.

Examples: ToPrimitive() in action

The default implementation of `valueOf()` returns `this`, while the default implementation of `toString()` returns type information:

```
> var empty = {};
> empty.valueOf() === empty
true
> empty.toString()
'[object Object]'
```

Therefore, `Number()` skips `valueOf()` and converts the result of `toString()` to a number; that is, it converts `'[object Object]'` to NaN:

```
> Number({})
NaN
```

The following object customizes `valueOf()`, which influences `Number()`, but doesn't change anything for `String()`:

```
> var n = { valueOf: function () { return 123 } };
> Number(n)
123
> String(n)
'[object Object]'
```

The following object customizes `toString()`. Because the result can be converted to a number, `Number()` can return a number:

```
> var s = { toString: function () { return '7'; } };
> String(s)
'7'
> Number(s)
7
```

CHAPTER 9

Operators

This chapter gives an overview of operators.

Operators and Objects

All operators coerce (as discussed in "Type Coercion" on page 77) their operands to appropriate types. Most operators only work with primitive values (e.g., arithmetic operators and comparison operators). That means that objects are converted to primitives before anything is done with them. One example where that is unfortunate is the plus operator, which many languages use for array concatenation. That's not so with JavaScript, however, where this operator converts arrays to strings and appends them:

```
> [1, 2] + [3]
'1,23'
> String([1, 2])
'1,2'
> String([3])
'3'
```

 There is no way to overload or customize operators in JavaScript, not even equality.

Assignment Operators

There are several ways to use the plain assignment operator:

```
x = value
```
Assigns to a variable x that has previously been declared

```
var x = value
```
   Combines a variable declaration with an assignment

```
obj.propKey = value
```
   Sets a property

```
obj['propKey'] = value
```
   Sets a property

```
arr[index] = value
```
   Sets an array element[1]

An assignment is an expression that evaluates to the assigned value. That allows you to chain assignments. For example, the following statement assigns 0 to both y and x:

```
x = y = 0;
```

Compound Assignment Operators

A *compound assignment operator* is written as op=, where op is one of several binary operators and = is the assignment operator. The following two expressions are equivalent:

```
myvar op= value
myvar = myvar op value
```

In other words, a compound assignment operator op= applies op to both operands and assigns the result to the first operand. Let's look at an example of using the plus operator (+) via compound assignment:

```
> var x = 2;
> x += 3
5
> x
5
```

The following are all compound assignment operators:

- Arithmetic operations (see "Arithmetic Operators" on page 122): *=, /=, %=, +=, -=
- Bitwise operations (see "Binary Bitwise Operators" on page 126): <<=, >>=, >>>=, &=, ^=, |=
- String concatenation (see "Concatenation: The Plus (+) Operator" on page 137): +=

---

1. Strictly speaking, setting an array element is a special case of setting a property.

Equality Operators: === Versus ==

JavaScript has two ways of determining whether two values are equal:

- Strict equality (===) and strict inequality (!==) consider only values that have the same type to be equal.
- Normal (or "lenient") equality (==) and inequality (!=) try to convert values of different types before comparing them as with strict (in)equality.

Lenient equality is problematic in two regards. First, how it performs conversion is confusing. Second, due to the operators being so forgiving, type errors can remain hidden longer.

Always use strict equality and avoid lenient equality. You only need to learn about the latter if you want to know why it should be avoided.

Equality is not customizable. Operators can't be overloaded in JavaScript, and you can't customize how equality works. There are some operations where you often need to influence comparison—for example, `Array.prototype.sort()` (see "Sorting and Reversing Elements (Destructive)" on page 287). That method optionally accepts a callback that performs all comparisons between array elements.

Strict Equality (===, !==)

Values with different types are never strictly equal. If both values have the same type, then the following assertions hold:

- `undefined === undefined`
- `null === null`
- Two numbers:

```
x === x  // unless x is NaN
+0 === -0
NaN !== NaN  // read explanation that follows
```

- Two booleans, two strings: obvious results
- Two objects (including arrays and functions): x === y if and only if x and y are the same object; that is, if you want to compare different objects, you have to implement your own comparison algorithm:

```
> var b = {}, c = {};
> b === c
false
> b === b
true
```

- Everything else: not strictly equal.

Pitfall: NaN

The special number value NaN (see "NaN" on page 106) is not equal to itself:

```
> NaN === NaN
false
```

Thus, you need to use other means to check for it, which are described in "Pitfall: checking whether a value is NaN" on page 107.

Strict inequality (!==)

A strict inequality comparison:

```
x !== y
```

is equivalent to the negation of a strict equality comparison:

```
!(x === y)
```

Normal (Lenient) Equality (==, !=)

The algorithm for comparing via normal equality works as follows. If both operands have the same type (one of the six specification types—Undefined, Null, Boolean, Number, String, and Object), then compare them via strict equality.

Otherwise, if the operands are:

1. undefined and null, then they are considered leniently equal:

    ```
    > undefined == null
    true
    ```

2. A string and a number, then convert the string to a number and compare both operands via strict equality.

3. A boolean and a nonboolean, then convert the boolean to a number and compare leniently (again).

4. An object and a number or a string, then try to convert the object to a primitive (via the algorithm described in "Algorithm: ToPrimitive()—Converting a Value to a Primitive" on page 79) and compare leniently (again).

Otherwise—if none of the aforementioned cases apply—the result of the lenient comparison is false.

Lenient inequality (!=)

An inequality comparison:

```
  x != y
```

is equivalent to the negation of an equality comparison:

```
  !(x == y)
```

Pitfall: lenient equality is different from conversion to boolean

Step 3 means that equality and conversion to boolean (see "Converting to Boolean" on page 97) work differently. If converted to boolean, numbers greater than 1 become `true` (e.g., in `if` statements). But those numbers are not leniently equal to `true`. The comments explain how the results were computed:

```
> 2 == true   // 2 === 1
false
> 2 == false  // 2 === 0
false

> 1 == true   // 1 === 1
true
> 0 == false  // 0 === 0
true
```

Similarly, while the empty string is equal to `false`, not all nonempty strings are equal to `true`:

```
> '' == false    // 0 === 0
true
> '1' == true    // 1 === 1
true
> '2' == true    // 2 === 1
false
> 'abc' == true  // NaN === 1
false
```

Pitfall: lenient equality and strings

Some of the leniency can be useful, depending on what you want:

```
> 'abc' == new String('abc')  // 'abc' == 'abc'
true
> '123' == 123   // 123 === 123
true
```

Other cases are problematic, due to how JavaScript converts strings to numbers (see "Converting to Number" on page 104):

```
> '\n\t123\r ' == 123  // usually not OK
true
> '' == 0  // 0 === 0
true
```

Pitfall: lenient equality and objects

If you compare an object to a nonobject, it is converted to a primitive, which leads to strange results:

```
> {} == '[object Object]'
true
> ['123'] == 123
true
> [] == 0
true
```

However, two objects are only equal if they are they same object. That means that you can't really compare two wrapper objects:

```
> new Boolean(true) === new Boolean(true)
false
> new Number(123) === new Number(123)
false
> new String('abc') == new String('abc')
false
```

There Are No Valid Use Cases for ==

You sometimes read about valid use cases for lenient equality (==). This section lists them and points out better alternatives.

Use case: checking for undefined or null

The following comparison ensures that x is neither undefined nor null:

```
if (x != null) ...
```

While this is a compact way of writing this check, it confuses beginners, and experts can't be sure whether it is a typo or not. Thus, if you want to check whether x has a value, use the standard check for truthiness (covered in "Truthy and Falsy Values" on page 98):

```
if (x) ...
```

If you want to be more precise, you should perform an explicit check for both values:

```
if (x !== undefined && x !== null) ...
```

Use case: working with numbers in strings

If you are not sure whether a value x is a number or a number-as-a-string, you can use checks such as the following:

```
if (x == 123) ...
```

The preceding checks whether x is either 123 or '123'. Again, this is very compact, and again, it is better to be explicit:

```
if (Number(x) === 123) ...
```

Use case: comparing wrapper instances with primitives

Lenient equals lets you compare primitives with wrapped primitives:

```
> 'abc' == new String('abc')
true
```

There are three reasons against this approach. First, lenient equality does not work between wrapped primitives:

```
> new String('abc') == new String('abc')
false
```

Second, you should avoid wrappers anyway. Third, if you do use them, it is better to be explicit:

```
if (wrapped.valueOf() === 'abc') ...
```

Ordering Operators

JavaScript knows the following ordering operators:

- Less than (<)
- Less than or equal (<=)
- Greater than (>)
- Greater than or equal (>=)

These operators work for numbers and for strings:

```
> 7 >= 5
true
> 'apple' < 'orange'
true
```

For strings, they are not very useful, because they are case-sensitive and don't handle features such as accents well (for details, see "Comparing Strings" on page 136).

The Algorithm

You evaluate a comparison:

```
x < y
```

by taking the following steps:

1. Ensure that both operands are primitives. Objects `obj` are converted to primitives via the internal operation `ToPrimitive(obj, Number)` (refer to "Algorithm: ToPrimitive()—Converting a Value to a Primitive" on page 79), which calls `obj.valueOf()` and, possibly, `obj.toString()` to do so.

2. If both operands are strings, then compare them by lexicographically comparing the 16-bit code units (see Chapter 24) that represent the JavaScript characters of the string.

3. Otherwise, convert both operands to numbers and compare them numerically.

The other ordering operators are handled similarly.

The Plus Operator (+)

Roughly, the plus operator examines its operands. If one of them is a string, the other is also converted to a string and both are concatenated:

```
> 'foo' + 3
'foo3'
> 3 + 'foo'
'3foo'

> 'Colors: ' + [ 'red', 'green', 'blue' ]
'Colors: red,green,blue'
```

Otherwise, both operands are converted to numbers (see "Converting to Number" on page 104) and added:

```
> 3 + 1
4
> 3 + true
4
```

That means that the order in which you evaluate matters:

```
> 'foo' + (1 + 2)
'foo3'
> ('foo' + 1) + 2
'foo12'
```

The Algorithm

You evaluate an addition:

```
value1 + value2
```

by taking the following steps:

1. Ensure that both operands are primitives. Objects `obj` are converted to primitives via the internal operation `ToPrimitive(obj)` (refer to "Algorithm: ToPrimitive()—Converting a Value to a Primitive" on page 79), which calls `obj.valueOf()` and, possibly, `obj.toString()` to do so. For dates, `obj.toString()` is called first.

2. If either operand is a string, then convert both to strings and return the concatenation of the results.

3. Otherwise, convert both operands to numbers and return the sum of the results.

Operators for Booleans and Numbers

The following operators only have operands of a single type and also produce results of that type. They are covered elsewhere.

Boolean operators:

- Binary logical operators (see "Binary Logical Operators: And (&&) and Or (||)" on page 99):

  ```
  x && y, x || y
  ```

- Logical Not (see "Logical Not (!)" on page 101):

  ```
  !x
  ```

Number operators:

- Arithmetic operators (see "Arithmetic Operators" on page 122):

  ```
  x + y, x - y, x * y, x / y, x % y
  ++x, --x, x++, x--
  -x, +x
  ```

- Bitwise operators (see "Bitwise Operators" on page 124):

  ```
  ~x
  x & y, x | y, x ^ y
  x << y, x >> y, x >>> y
  ```

Special Operators

Here we will review special operators, namely the conditional, comma, and `void` operators.

The Conditional Operator (? :)

The conditional operator is an expression:

```
    «condition» ? «if_true» : «if_false»
```

If the condition is true, the result is if_true; otherwise, the result is if_false. For example:

```
    var x = (obj ? obj.prop : null);
```

The parentheses around the operator are not needed, but they make it easier to read.

The Comma Operator

```
    «left» , «right»
```

The comma operator evaluates both operands and returns the result of right. Roughly, it does for expressions what the semicolon does for statements.

This example demonstrates that the second operand becomes the result of the operator:

```
    > 123, 'abc'
    'abc'
```

This example demonstrates that both operands are evaluated:

```
    > var x = 0;
    > var y = (x++, 10);

    > x
    1
    > y
    10
```

The comma operator is confusing. It's better to not be clever and to write two separate statements whenever you can.

The void Operator

The syntax for the void operator is:

```
    void «expr»
```

which evaluates expr and returns undefined. Here are some examples:

```
    > void 0
    undefined
    > void (0)
    undefined

    > void 4+7   // same as (void 4)+7
    NaN
    > void (4+7)
    undefined

    > var x;
    > x = 3
```

```
3
> void (x = 5)
undefined
> x
5
```

Thus, if you implement void as a function, it looks as follows:

```
function myVoid(expr) {
    return undefined;
}
```

The void operator is associated closely with its operand, so use parentheses as necessary. For example, void 4+7 binds as (void 4)+7.

What is void used for?

Under ECMAScript 5, void is rarely useful. Its main use cases are:

void 0 *as a synonym for* undefined
>   The latter can be changed, while the former will always have the correct value. However, undefined is reasonably safe from being changed under ECMAScript 5, which makes this use case less important (for details, see "Changing undefined" on page 75).

Discarding the result of an expression
>   In some situations, it is important to return undefined as opposed to the result of an expression. Then void can be used to discard that result. One such situation involves javascript: URLs, which should be avoided for links, but are useful for bookmarklets. When you visit one of those URLs, many browsers replace the current document with the result of evaluating the URL's "content," but only if the result isn't undefined. Hence, if you want to open a new window without changing the currently displayed content, you can do the following:

```
javascript:void window.open("http://example.com/")
```

Prefixing an IIFE
>   An IIFE must be parsed as an expression. One of several ways to ensure that is by prefixing it with void (see "IIFE Variation: Prefix Operators" on page 185).[2]

Why does JavaScript have a void operator?

According to JavaScript creator Brendan Eich, he added it to the language to help with javascript: links (one of the aforementioned use cases):

---

2. Thanks to Brandon Benvie (@benvie), who told me about using void for IIFEs.

I added the void operator to JS before Netscape 2 shipped to make it easy to discard any non-undefined value in a javascript: URL.[3]

Categorizing Values via typeof and instanceof

If you want to categorize a value, you unfortunately have to distinguish between primitives and objects (refer back to Chapter 8) in JavaScript:

- The typeof operator distinguishes primitives from objects and determines the types of primitives.
- The instanceof operator determines whether an object is an instance of a given constructor. Consult Chapter 17 for more information on object-oriented programming in JavaScript.

typeof: Categorizing Primitives

The typeof operator:

    typeof «value»

returns a string describing what kind of value value is. Here are some examples:

```
> typeof undefined
'undefined'
> typeof 'abc'
'string'
> typeof {}
'object'
> typeof []
'object'
```

typeof is used to distinguish primitives and objects and to categorize primitives (which cannot be handled by instanceof). Unfortunately, the results of this operator are not completely logical and only loosely correspond to the types of the ECMAScript specification (which are explained in "JavaScript's Types" on page 67):

Operand	Result
undefined, undeclared variable	'undefined'
null	'object'
Boolean value	'boolean'
Number value	'number'
String value	'string'

---

3. Source: *http://en.wikipedia.org/wiki/Bookmarklet*

Operand	Result
Function	`'function'`
All other normal values	`'object'`
(Engine-created value)	JavaScript engines are allowed to create values for whom `typeof` returns arbitrary strings (different from all results listed in this table).

Pitfall: typeof null

Unfortunately, `typeof null` is `'object'`. This is considered a bug (`null` is not a member of the internal type Object), but it can't be fixed, because doing so would break existing code. You thus have to be wary of `null`. For example, the following function checks whether `value` is an object:

```
function isObject(value) {
    return (value !== null
        && (typeof value === 'object'
            || typeof value === 'function'));
}
```

Trying it out:

```
> isObject(123)
false
> isObject(null)
false
> isObject({})
true
```

The history of typeof null

The first JavaScript engine (*http://mzl.la/1oO9VF7*) represented JavaScript values as 32-bit words. The lowest 3 bits of such a word were used as a type tag, to indicate whether the value was an object, an integer, a double, a string, or a boolean (as you can see, even this early engine already stored numbers as integers if possible).

The type tag for objects was 000. In order to represent the value `null`, the engine used the machine language NULL pointer, a word where all bits are zero. `typeof` checked the type tag to determine the type of value, which is why it reported `null` to be an object.[4]

Checking whether a variable exists

The check:

```
typeof x === 'undefined'
```

has two use cases:

---

4. Thanks to Tom Schuster (@evilpies) for pointing me to the source code of the first JavaScript engine.

1. It determines whether x is undefined.

2. It determines whether the variable x exists.

Here are examples of both use cases:

```
> var foo;
> typeof foo === 'undefined'
true

> typeof undeclaredVariable === 'undefined'
true
```

For the first use case, comparing directly with undefined is usually a better choice. However, it doesn't work for the second use case:

```
> var foo;
> foo === undefined
true

> undeclaredVariable === undefined
ReferenceError: undeclaredVariable is not defined
```

instanceof: Checking Whether an Object Is an Instance of a Given Constructor

The instanceof operator:

«value» **instanceof** «Constr»

determines whether value has been created by the constructor Constr or a subconstructor. Here are some examples:

```
> {} instanceof Object
true
> [] instanceof Array  // constructor of []
true
> [] instanceof Object  // super-constructor of []
true
```

As expected, instanceof is false for the nonvalues undefined and null:

```
> undefined instanceof Object
false
> null instanceof Object
false
```

But it is also false for all other primitive values:

```
> 'abc' instanceof Object
false
> 123 instanceof Object
false
```

For details on `instanceof`, consult "The instanceof Operator" on page 237.

Object Operators

The following three operators work on objects. They are explained elsewhere:

`new` *(see "Layer 3: Constructors—Factories for Instances" on page 231)*
> Invoke a constructor—for example, `new Point(3, 5)`

`delete` *(see "Deleting properties" on page 200)*
> Delete a property—for example, `delete obj.prop`

`in` *(see "Iteration and Detection of Properties" on page 217)*
> Check whether an object has a given property—for example, `'prop' in obj`

CHAPTER 10

Booleans

The primitive boolean type comprises the values `true` and `false`:

```
> typeof false
'boolean'
> typeof true
'boolean'
```

Converting to Boolean

Values are converted to booleans as follows:

Value	Converted to boolean
undefined	false
null	false
A boolean	Same as input (nothing to convert)
A number	0, NaN → false
	other numbers → true
A string	'' → false
	other strings → true
An object	true (always!)

Manually Converting to Boolean

There are three ways any value can be converted to a boolean:

`Boolean(value)`	(Invoked as a function, not as a constructor)
`value ? true : false`	
`!!value`	A single "not" converts to negated boolean; use twice for the nonnegated conversion.

I prefer `Boolean()`, because it is more descriptive. Here are some examples:

```
> Boolean(undefined)
false
> Boolean(null)
false

> Boolean(0)
false
> Boolean(1)
true
> Boolean(2)
true

> Boolean('')
false
> Boolean('abc')
true
> Boolean('false')
true
```

Truthy and Falsy Values

Wherever JavaScript expects a boolean, you can provide any kind of value and it is automatically converted to boolean. Thus, there are two sets of values in JavaScript: one set is converted to `false`, while the other set is converted to `true`. These sets are called *falsy values* and *truthy values*. Given the preceding table, the following are all falsy values:

- undefined, null
- Boolean: false
- Number: 0, NaN
- String: ''

All other values—including *all* objects, even empty objects, empty arrays, and `new Boolean(false)`—are truthy. Because `undefined` and `null` are falsy, you can use the `if` statement to check whether a variable x has a value:

```
if (x) {
    // x has a value
}
```

The caveat is that the preceding check interprets all falsy values as "does not have a value," not just `undefined` and `null`. But if you can live with that limitation, you get to use a compact and established pattern.

Pitfall: all objects are truthy

All objects are truthy:

```
> Boolean(new Boolean(false))
true
> Boolean([])
true
> Boolean({})
true
```

That is different from how objects are converted to a number or string, where you can control the result by implementing the methods valueOf() and toString():

```
> Number({ valueOf: function () { return 123 } })
123
> String({ toString: function () { return 'abc' } })
'abc'
```

History: Why are objects always truthy?

The conversion to boolean is different for historic reasons. For ECMAScript 1, it was decided to not enable objects to configure that conversion (e.g., via a toBoolean() method). The rationale was that the boolean operators || and && preserve the values of their operands. Therefore, if you chain those operators, the same value may be checked multiple times for truthiness or falsiness. Such checks are cheap for primitives, but would be costly for objects if they were able to configure their conversion to boolean. ECMAScript 1 avoided that cost by making objects always truthy.

Logical Operators

In this section, we cover the basics of the And (&&), Or (||), and Not (!) logical operators.

Binary Logical Operators: And (&&) and Or (||)

Binary logical operators are:

Value-preserving
> They always return either one of the operands, unchanged:

```
> 'abc' || 123
'abc'
> false || 123
123
```

Short-circuiting
> The second operand is not evaluated if the first operand already determines the result. For example (the result of console.log is undefined):

```
> true || console.log('Hello')
true
> false || console.log('Hello')
Hello
undefined
```

That is uncommon behavior for operators. Normally, all operands are evaluated before an operator is invoked (just like for functions).

Logical And (&&)

If the first operand can be converted to `false`, return it. Otherwise, return the second operand:

```
> true && false
false
> false && 'def'
false
> '' && 'def'
''
> 'abc' && 'def'
'def'
```

Logical Or (||)

If the first operand can be converted to `true`, return it. Otherwise, return the second operand:

```
> true || false
true
> true || 'def'
true
> 'abc' || 'def'
'abc'
> '' || 'def'
'def'
```

Pattern: providing a default value

Sometimes there are situations where a value (a parameter, the result of a function, etc.) can be either a nonvalue (`undefined`, `null`) or an actual value. If you want to provide a default value for the former case, you can use the Or operator:

```
theValue || defaultValue
```

The preceding expression evaluates to `theValue` if it is truthy and to `defaultValue` otherwise. The usual caveat applies: `defaultValue` will also be returned if `theValue` has a falsy value other than `undefined` and `null`. Let's look at three examples of using that pattern.

Example 1: a default for a parameter

The parameter `text` of the function `saveText()` is optional and should be the empty string if it has been omitted:

```
function saveText(text) {
    text = text || '';
    ...
}
```

This is the most common use of `||` as a default operator. Consult "Optional Parameters" on page 173 for more on optional parameters.

Example 2: a default for a property

The object `options` may or may not have the property `title`. If it is missing, the value `'Untitled'` should be used when setting the title:

```
setTitle(options.title || 'Untitled');
```

Example 3: a default for the result of a function

The function `countOccurrences` counts how often `regex` matches inside `str`:

```
function countOccurrences(regex, str) {
    // Omitted: check that /g is set for `regex`
    return (str.match(regex) || []).length;
}
```

The problem is that `match()` (see "String.prototype.match: Capture Groups or Return All Matching Substrings" on page 307) either returns an array or `null`. Thanks to `||`, a default value is used in the latter case. Therefore, you can safely access the property `length` in both cases.

Logical Not (!)

The logical not operator `!` converts its operand to boolean and then negates it:

```
> !true
false
> !43
false
> !''
true
> !{}
false
```

Equality Operators, Ordering Operators

The following operators are covered elsewhere:

- Equality operators: ===, !==, ==, != (see "Equality Operators: === Versus ==" on page 83)
- Ordering operators: >, >=, <, <= (see "Ordering Operators" on page 87)

The Function Boolean

The function `Boolean` can be invoked in two ways:

`Boolean(value)`

As a normal function, it converts `value` to a primitive boolean (see "Converting to Boolean" on page 97):

```
> Boolean(0)
false
> typeof Boolean(false)  // no change
'boolean'
```

`new Boolean(bool)`

As a constructor, it creates a new instance of `Boolean` (see "Wrapper Objects for Primitives" on page 75), an object that wraps `bool` (after converting it to a boolean). For example:

```
> typeof new Boolean(false)
'object'
```

The former invocation is the common one.

CHAPTER 11

Numbers

JavaScript has a single type for all numbers: it treats all of them as floating-point numbers. However, the dot is not displayed if there are no digits after the decimal point:

```
> 5.000
5
```

Internally, most JavaScript engines optimize and do distinguish between floating-point numbers and integers (details: "Integers in JavaScript" on page 114). But that is something that programmers don't see.

JavaScript numbers are double (64-bit) values, based on the IEEE Standard for Floating-Point Arithmetic (IEEE 754). That standard is used by many programming languages.

Number Literals

A number literal can be an integer, floating point, or (integer) hexadecimal:

```
> 35  // integer
35
> 3.141  // floating point
3.141
> 0xFF  // hexadecimal
255
```

Exponent

An exponent, eX, is an abbreviation for "multiply with 10^X":

```
> 5e2
500
> 5e-2
0.05
> 0.5e2
50
```

Invoking Methods on Literals

With number literals, the dot for accessing a property must be distinguished from the decimal dot. This leaves you with the following options if you want to invoke to String() on the number literal 123:

```
123..toString()
123 .toString()  // space before the dot
123.0.toString()
(123).toString()
```

Converting to Number

Values are converted to numbers as follows:

Value	Result
undefined	NaN
null	0
A boolean	false → 0
	true → 1
A number	Same as input (nothing to convert)
A string	Parse the number in the string (ignoring leading and trailing whitespace); the empty string is converted to 0. Example: '3.141' → 3.141
An object	Call ToPrimitive(value, Number) (see "Algorithm: ToPrimitive()—Converting a Value to a Primitive" on page 79) and convert the resulting primitive.

When converting the empty string to a number, NaN would arguably be a better result. The result 0 was chosen to help with empty numeric input fields, in line with what other programming languages did in the mid-1990s.[1]

Manually Converting to Number

The two most common ways to convert any value to a number are:

```
Number(value)
```
(Invoked as a function, not as a constructor)
```
+value
```

I prefer Number(), because it is more descriptive. Here are some examples:

```
> Number('')
0
> Number('123')
123
```

---

1. Source: Brendan Eich, *http://bit.ly/1lKzQeC*.

```
> Number('\t\v\r12.34\n ')  // ignores leading and trailing whitespace
12.34

> Number(false)
0
> Number(true)
1
```

parseFloat()

The global function `parseFloat()` provides another way to convert values to numbers. However, `Number()` is usually a better choice, as we shall see in a moment. This code:

```
parseFloat(str)
```

converts `str` to string, trims leading whitespace, and then parses the longest prefix that is a floating-point number. If no such prefix exists (e.g., in an empty string), NaN is returned.

Comparing `parseFloat()` and `Number()`:

- Applying `parseFloat()` to a nonstring is less efficient, because it coerces its argument to a string before parsing it. As a consequence, many values that `Number()` converts to actual numbers are converted to NaN by `parseFloat()`:

    ```
    > parseFloat(true)  // same as parseFloat('true')
    NaN
    > Number(true)
    1

    > parseFloat(null)  // same as parseFloat('null')
    NaN
    > Number(null)
    0
    ```

- `parseFloat()` parses the empty string as NaN:

    ```
    > parseFloat('')
    NaN
    > Number('')
    0
    ```

- `parseFloat()` parses until the last legal character, meaning you get a result where you may not want one:

    ```
    > parseFloat('123.45#')
    123.45
    > Number('123.45#')
    NaN
    ```

- `parseFloat()` ignores leading whitespace and stops before illegal characters (which include whitespace):

```
> parseFloat('\t\v\r12.34\n ')
12.34
```

Number() ignores both leading and trailing whitespace (but other illegal characters lead to NaN).

Special Number Values

JavaScript has several special number values:

- Two error values, NaN and Infinity.
- Two values for zero, +0 and -0. JavaScript has two zeros, a positive zero and a negative zero, because the sign and the magnitude of a number are stored separately. In most of this book, I pretend that there is only a single zero, and you almost never see in JavaScript that there are two of them.

NaN

The error value NaN (an abbreviation for "not a number") is, ironically, a number value:

```
> typeof NaN
'number'
```

It is produced by errors such as the following:

- A number could not be parsed:

    ```
    > Number('xyz')
    NaN
    > Number(undefined)
    NaN
    ```

- An operation failed:

    ```
    > Math.acos(2)
    NaN
    > Math.log(-1)
    NaN
    > Math.sqrt(-1)
    NaN
    ```

- One of the operands is NaN (this ensures that, if an error occurs during a longer computation, you can see it in the final result):

    ```
    > NaN + 3
    NaN
    > 25 / NaN
    NaN
    ```

Pitfall: checking whether a value is NaN

NaN is the only value that is not equal to itself:

```
> NaN === NaN
false
```

Strict equality (===) is also used by Array.prototype.indexOf. You therefore can't search for NaN in an array via that method:

```
> [ NaN ].indexOf(NaN)
-1
```

If you want to check whether a value is NaN, you have to use the global function isNaN():

```
> isNaN(NaN)
true
> isNaN(33)
false
```

However, isNaN does not work properly with nonnumbers, because it first converts those to numbers. That conversion can produce NaN and then the function incorrectly returns true:

```
> isNaN('xyz')
true
```

Thus, it is best to combine isNaN with a type check:

```
function myIsNaN(value) {
    return typeof value === 'number' && isNaN(value);
}
```

Alternatively, you can check whether the value is unequal to itself (as NaN is the only value with this trait). But that is less self-explanatory:

```
function myIsNaN(value) {
    return value !== value;
}
```

Note that this behavior is dictated by IEEE 754. As noted in Section 7.11, "Details of comparison predicates":[2]

> Every NaN shall compare unordered with everything, including itself.

Infinity

Infinity is an error value indicating one of two problems: a number can't be represented because its magnitude is too large, or a division by zero has happened.

---

2. Béla Varga (@netzzwerg) pointed out that IEEE 754 specifies NaN as not equal to itself.

`Infinity` is larger than any other number (except `NaN`). Similarly, `-Infinity` is smaller than any other number (except `NaN`). That makes them useful as default values—for example, when you are looking for a minimum or maximum.

Error: a number's magnitude is too large

How large a number's magnitude can become is determined by its internal representation (as discussed in "The Internal Representation of Numbers" on page 111), which is the arithmetic product of:

- A mantissa (a binary number $1.f_1f_2...$)
- 2 to the power of an exponent

The exponent must be between (and excluding) -1023 and 1024. If the exponent is too small, the number becomes 0. If the exponent is too large, it becomes `Infinity`. 2^{1023} can still be represented, but 2^{1024} can't:

```
> Math.pow(2, 1023)
8.98846567431158e+307
> Math.pow(2, 1024)
Infinity
```

Error: division by zero

Dividing by zero produces `Infinity` as an error value:

```
> 3 / 0
Infinity
> 3 / -0
-Infinity
```

Computing with Infinity

You get the error result `NaN` if you try to "neutralize" one `Infinity` with another one:

```
> Infinity - Infinity
NaN
> Infinity / Infinity
NaN
```

If you try to go beyond `Infinity`, you still get `Infinity`:

```
> Infinity + Infinity
Infinity
> Infinity * Infinity
Infinity
```

Checking for Infinity

Strict and lenient equality work fine for `Infinity`:

```
> var x = Infinity;
> x === Infinity
true
```

Additionally, the global function `isFinite()` allows you to check whether a value is an actual number (neither infinite nor `NaN`):

```
> isFinite(5)
true
> isFinite(Infinity)
false
> isFinite(NaN)
false
```

Two Zeros

Because JavaScript's numbers keep magnitude and sign separate, each nonnegative number has a negative, including `0`.

The rationale for this is that whenever you represent a number digitally, it can become so small that it is indistinguishable from 0, because the encoding is not precise enough to represent the difference. Then a signed zero allows you to record "from which direction" you approached zero; that is, what sign the number had before it was considered zero. Wikipedia nicely sums up the pros and cons of signed zeros (*http://en.wikipe dia.org/wiki/Signed_zero*):

> It is claimed that the inclusion of signed zero in IEEE 754 makes it much easier to achieve numerical accuracy in some critical problems, in particular when computing with complex elementary functions. On the other hand, the concept of signed zero runs contrary to the general assumption made in most mathematical fields (and in most mathematics courses) that negative zero is the same thing as zero. Representations that allow negative zero can be a source of errors in programs, as software developers do not realize (or may forget) that, while the two zero representations behave as equal under numeric comparisons, they are different bit patterns and yield different results in some operations.

Best practice: pretend there's only one zero

JavaScript goes to great lengths to hide the fact that there are two zeros. Given that it normally doesn't matter that they are different, it is recommended that you play along with the illusion of the single zero. Let's examine how that illusion is maintained.

In JavaScript, you normally write `0`, which means `+0`. But `-0` is also displayed as simply `0`. This is what you see when you use a browser command line or the Node.js REPL:

```
> -0
0
```

That is because the standard `toString()` method converts both zeros to the same `'0'`:

```
> (-0).toString()
'0'
```

```
> (+0).toString()
'0'
```

Equality doesn't distinguish zeros, either. Not even ===:

```
> +0 === -0
true
```

Array.prototype.indexOf uses === to search for elements, maintaining the illusion:

```
> [ -0, +0 ].indexOf(+0)
0
> [ +0, -0 ].indexOf(-0)
0
```

The ordering operators also consider the zeros to be equal:

```
> -0 < +0
false
> +0 < -0
false
```

Distinguishing the two zeros

How *can* you actually observe that the two zeros are different? You can divide by zero (-Infinity and +Infinity *can* be distinguished by ===):

```
> 3 / -0
-Infinity
> 3 / +0
Infinity
```

Another way to perform the division by zero is via Math.pow() (see "Numerical Functions" on page 328):

```
> Math.pow(-0, -1)
-Infinity
> Math.pow(+0, -1)
Infinity
```

Math.atan2() (see "Trigonometric Functions" on page 329) also reveals that the zeros are different:

```
> Math.atan2(-0, -1)
-3.141592653589793
> Math.atan2(+0, -1)
3.141592653589793
```

The canonical way of telling the two zeros apart is the division by zero. Therefore, a function for detecting negative zeros would look like this:

```
function isNegativeZero(x) {
    return x === 0 && (1/x < 0);
}
```

Here is the function in use:

```
> isNegativeZero(0)
false
> isNegativeZero(-0)
true
> isNegativeZero(33)
false
```

The Internal Representation of Numbers

JavaScript numbers have 64-bit precision, which is also called *double precision* (type `double` in some programming languages). The internal representation is based on the IEEE 754 standard. The 64 bits are distributed between a number's sign, exponent, and fraction as follows:

Sign	Exponent $\in [-1023, 1024]$	Fraction
1 bit	11 bits	52 bits
Bit 63	Bits 62–52	Bits 51–0

The value of a number is computed by the following formula:

$$(-1)^{\text{sign}} \times \%1.\text{fraction} \times 2^{\text{exponent}}$$

The prefixed percentage sign (%) means that the number in the middle is written in binary notation: a 1, followed by a binary point, followed by a binary fraction—namely the binary digits of the fraction (a natural number). Here are some examples of this representation:

+0		(sign = 0, fraction = 0, exponent = −1023)
−0		(sign = 1, fraction = 0, exponent = −1023)
1	$= (-1)^0 \times \%1.0 \times 2^0$	(sign = 0, fraction = 0, exponent = 0)
2	$= (-1)^0 \times \%1.0 \times 2^1$	
3	$= (-1)^0 \times \%1.1 \times 2^1$	(sign = 0, fraction = 2^{51}, exponent = 0)
0.5	$= (-1)^0 \times \%1.0 \times 2^{-1}$	
−1	$= (-1)^1 \times \%1.0 \times 2^0$	

The encodings of +0, −0, and 3 can be explained as follows:

- ±0: Given that the fraction is always prefixed by a 1, it's impossible to represent 0 with it. Hence, JavaScript encodes a zero via the fraction 0 and the special exponent −1023. The sign can be either positive or negative, meaning that JavaScript has two zeros (see "Two Zeros" on page 109).
- 3: Bit 51 is the most significant (highest) bit of the fraction. That bit is 1.

Special Exponents

The previously mentioned representation of numbers is called *normalized*. In that case, the exponent e is in the range $-1023 < e < 1024$ (excluding lower and upper bounds). −1023 and 1024 are special exponents:

- 1024 is used for error values such as NaN and Infinity.
- −1023 is used for:
  - Zero (if the fraction is 0, as just explained)
  - Small numbers close to zero (if the fraction is not 0).

To enable both applications, a different, so-called *denormalized*, representation is used:

$$(-1)^{\text{sign}} \times \%0.\text{fraction} \times 2^{-1022}$$

To compare, the smallest (as in "closest to zero") numbers in normalized representation are:

$$(-1)^{\text{sign}} \times \%1.\text{fraction} \times 2^{-1022}$$

Denormalized numbers are smaller, because there is no leading digit 1.

Handling Rounding Errors

JavaScript's numbers are usually entered as decimal floating-point numbers, but they are internally represented as binary floating-point numbers. That leads to imprecision. To understand why, let's forget JavaScript's internal storage format and take a general look at what fractions can be well represented by decimal floating-point numbers and by binary floating-point numbers. In the decimal system, all fractions are a mantissa m divided by a power of 10:

$$\frac{m}{10^e}$$

So, in the denominator, there are only tens. That's why $\frac{1}{3}$ cannot be expressed precisely as a decimal floating-point number—there is no way to get a 3 into the denominator. Binary floating-point numbers only have twos in the denominator. Let's examine which decimal floating-point numbers can be represented well as binary and which can't. If there are only twos in the denominator, the decimal number can be represented:

- $0.5_{dec} = \frac{5}{10} = \frac{1}{2} = 0.1_{bin}$
- $0.75_{dec} = \frac{75}{100} = \frac{3}{4} = 0.11_{bin}$
- $0.125_{dec} = \frac{125}{1000} = \frac{1}{8} = 0.001_{bin}$

Other fractions cannot be represented precisely, because they have numbers other than 2 in the denominator (after prime factorization):

- $0.1_{dec} = \frac{1}{10} = \frac{1}{2 \times 5}$
- $0.2_{dec} = \frac{2}{10} = \frac{1}{5}$

You can't normally see that JavaScript doesn't store exactly 0.1 internally. But you can make it visible by multiplying it with a high enough power of 10:

```
> 0.1 * Math.pow(10, 24)
1.0000000000000001e+23
```

And if you add two imprecisely represented numbers, the result is sometimes imprecise enough that the imprecision becomes visible:

```
> 0.1 + 0.2
0.30000000000000004
```

Another example:

```
> 0.1 + 1 - 1
0.10000000000000009
```

Due to rounding errors, as a best practice you should not compare nonintegers directly. Instead, take an upper bound for rounding errors into consideration. Such an upper bound is called a *machine epsilon* (*http://en.wikipedia.org/wiki/Machine_epsilon*). The standard epsilon value for double precision is 2^{-53}:

```
var EPSILON = Math.pow(2, -53);
function epsEqu(x, y) {
    return Math.abs(x - y) < EPSILON;
}
```

epsEqu() ensures correct results where a normal comparison would be inadequate:

```
> 0.1 + 0.2 === 0.3
false
```

```
> epsEqu(0.1+0.2, 0.3)
true
```

Integers in JavaScript

As mentioned before, JavaScript has only floating-point numbers. Integers appear internally in two ways. First, most JavaScript engines store a small enough number without a decimal fraction as an integer (with, for example, 31 bits) and maintain that representation as long as possible. They have to switch back to a floating-point representation if a number's magnitude grows too large or if a decimal fraction appears.

Second, the ECMAScript specification has integer operators: namely, all of the bitwise operators. Those operators convert their operands to 32-bit integers and return 32-bit integers. For the specification, *integer* only means that the numbers don't have a decimal fraction, and *32-bit* means that they are within a certain range. For engines, *32-bit integer* means that an actual integer (non-floating-point) representation can usually be introduced or maintained.

Ranges of Integers

Internally, the following ranges of integers are important in JavaScript:

- Safe integers (see "Safe Integers" on page 116), the largest practically usable range of integers that JavaScript supports:
    - 53 bits plus a sign, range $(-2^{53}, 2^{53})$
- Array indices (see "Array Indices" on page 276):
    - 32 bits, unsigned
    - Maximum length: $2^{32}-1$
    - Range of indices: $[0, 2^{32}-1)$ (excluding the maximum length!)
- Bitwise operands (see "Bitwise Operators" on page 124):
    - Unsigned right shift operator (>>>): 32 bits, unsigned, range $[0, 2^{32})$
    - All other bitwise operators: 32 bits, including a sign, range $[-2^{31}, 2^{31})$
- "Char codes," UTF-16 code units as numbers:
    - Accepted by `String.fromCharCode()` (see "String Constructor Method" on page 138)
    - Returned by `String.prototype.charCodeAt()` (see "Extract Substrings" on page 139)
    - 16 bits, unsigned

Representing Integers as Floating-Point Numbers

JavaScript can only handle integer values up to a magnitude of 53 bits (the 52 bits of the fraction plus 1 indirect bit, via the exponent; see "The Internal Representation of Numbers" on page 111 for details).

The following table explains how JavaScript represents 53-bit integers as floating-point numbers:

Bits	Range	Encoding
1 bit	0	(See "The Internal Representation of Numbers" on page 111.)
1 bit	1	$\%1 \times 2^0$
2 bits	2–3	$\%1.f_{51} \times 2^1$
3 bits	$4–7 = 2^2–(2^3–1)$	$\%1.f_{51}f_{50} \times 2^2$
4 bits	$2^3–(2^4–1)$	$\%1.f_{51}f_{50}f_{49} \times 2^3$
...	...	...
53 bits	$2^{52}–(2^{53}–1)$	$\%1.f_{51}\cdots f_0 \times 2^{52}$

There is no fixed sequence of bits that represents the integer. Instead, the mantissa %1.f is shifted by the exponent, so that the leading digit 1 is in the right place. In a way, the exponent counts the number of digits of the fraction that are in active use (the remaining digits are 0). That means that for 2 bits, we use one digit of the fraction and for 53 bits, we use all digits of the fraction. Additionally, we can represent 2^{53} as $\%1.0 \times 2^{53}$, but we get problems with higher numbers:

Bits	Range	Encoding
54 bits	$2^{53}–(2^{54}–1)$	$\%1.f_{51}\cdots f_0 0 \times 2^{53}$
55 bits	$2^{54}–(2^{55}–1)$	$\%1.f_{51}\cdots f_0 00 \times 2^{54}$
...		

For 54 bits, the least significant digit is always 0, for 55 bits the two least significant digits are always 0, and so on. That means that for 54 bits, we can only represent every second number, for 55 bits only every fourth number, and so on. For example:

```
> Math.pow(2, 53) - 1  // OK
9007199254740991
> Math.pow(2, 53)  // OK
9007199254740992
> Math.pow(2, 53) + 1  // can't be represented
9007199254740992
> Math.pow(2, 53) + 2  // OK
9007199254740994
```

Best practice

If you work with integers of up to 53 bits magnitude, you are fine. Unfortunately, you'll often encounter 64-bit unsigned integers in programming (Twitter IDs, databases, etc.). These must be stored in strings in JavaScript. If you want to perform arithmetic with such integers, you need special libraries. There are plans to bring larger integers to JavaScript, but that will take a while.

Safe Integers

JavaScript can only safely represent integers i in the range $-2^{53} < i < 2^{53}$. This section examines what that means and what the consequences are. It is based on an email by Mark S. Miller to the es-discuss mailing list (*http://mzl.la/1oOaCOO*).

The idea of a safe integer centers on how mathematical integers are represented in JavaScript. In the range $(-2^{53}, 2^{53})$ (excluding the lower and upper bounds), JavaScript integers are *safe*: there is a one-to-one mapping between mathematical integers and their representations in JavaScript.

Beyond this range, JavaScript integers are *unsafe*: two or more mathematical integers are represented as the same JavaScript integer. For example, starting at 2^{53}, JavaScript can represent only every second mathematical integer (the previous section explains why). Therefore, a safe JavaScript integer is one that unambiguously represents a single mathematical integer.

Definitions in ECMAScript 6

ECMAScript 6 will provide the following constants:

```
Number.MAX_SAFE_INTEGER = Math.pow(2, 53)-1;
Number.MIN_SAFE_INTEGER = -Number.MAX_SAFE_INTEGER;
```

It will also provide a function for determining whether an integer is safe:

```
Number.isSafeInteger = function (n) {
    return (typeof n === 'number' &&
        Math.round(n) === n &&
        Number.MIN_SAFE_INTEGER <= n &&
        n <= Number.MAX_SAFE_INTEGER);
}
```

For a given value n, this function first checks whether n is a number and an integer. If both checks succeed, n is safe if it is greater than or equal to MIN_SAFE_INTEGER and less than or equal to MAX_SAFE_INTEGER.

Safe results of arithmetic computations

How can we make sure that results of arithmetic computations are correct? For example, the following result is clearly not correct:

```
> 9007199254740990 + 3
9007199254740992
```

We have two safe operands, but an unsafe result:

```
> Number.isSafeInteger(9007199254740990)
true
> Number.isSafeInteger(3)
true
> Number.isSafeInteger(9007199254740992)
false
```

The following result is also incorrect:

```
> 9007199254740995 - 10
9007199254740986
```

This time, the result is safe, but one of the operands isn't:

```
> Number.isSafeInteger(9007199254740995)
false
> Number.isSafeInteger(10)
true
> Number.isSafeInteger(9007199254740986)
true
```

Therefore, the result of applying an integer operator `op` is guaranteed to be correct only if all operands and the result are safe. More formally:

```
isSafeInteger(a) && isSafeInteger(b) && isSafeInteger(a op b)
```

implies that `a op b` is a correct result.

Converting to Integer

In JavaScript, all numbers are floating point. Integers are floating-point numbers without a fraction. Converting a number `n` to an integer means finding the integer that is "closest" to `n` (where the meaning of "closest" depends on how you convert). You have several options for performing this conversion:

1. The `Math` functions `Math.floor()`, `Math.ceil()`, and `Math.round()` (see "Integers via Math.floor(), Math.ceil(), and Math.round()" on page 118)

2. The custom function `ToInteger()` (see "Integers via the Custom Function ToInteger()" on page 118)

3. Binary bitwise operators (see "32-bit Integers via Bitwise Operators" on page 119)

4. The global function `parseInt()` (see "Integers via parseInt()" on page 120)

Spoiler: #1 is usually the best choice, #2 and #3 have niche applications, and #4 is OK for parsing strings, but not for converting numbers to integers.

Integers via Math.floor(), Math.ceil(), and Math.round()

The following three functions are usually the best way of converting a number to an integer:

- `Math.floor()` converts its argument to the closest lower integer:

    ```
    > Math.floor(3.8)
    3
    > Math.floor(-3.8)
    -4
    ```

- `Math.ceil()` converts its argument to the closest higher integer:

    ```
    > Math.ceil(3.2)
    4
    > Math.ceil(-3.2)
    -3
    ```

- `Math.round()` converts its argument to the closest integer:

    ```
    > Math.round(3.2)
    3
    > Math.round(3.5)
    4
    > Math.round(3.8)
    4
    ```

    The result of rounding -3.5 may be surprising:

    ```
    > Math.round(-3.2)
    -3
    > Math.round(-3.5)
    -3
    > Math.round(-3.8)
    -4
    ```

    Therefore, `Math.round(x)` is the same as:

    ```
    Math.ceil(x + 0.5)
    ```

Integers via the Custom Function ToInteger()

Another good option for converting any value to an integer is the internal ECMAScript operation `ToInteger()`, which removes the fraction of a floating-point number. If it was accessible in JavaScript, it would work like this:

```
> ToInteger(3.2)
3
> ToInteger(3.5)
3
> ToInteger(3.8)
3
```

```
> ToInteger(-3.2)
-3
> ToInteger(-3.5)
-3
> ToInteger(-3.8)
-3
```

The ECMAScript specification defines the result of `ToInteger(number)` as:

$$\text{sign(number)} \times \text{floor(abs(number))}$$

For what it does, this formula is relatively complicated because `floor` seeks the closest *larger* integer; if you want to remove the fraction of a negative integer, you have to seek the closest smaller integer. The following code implements the operation in JavaScript. We avoid the `sign` operation by using `ceil` if the number is negative:

```
function ToInteger(x) {
    x = Number(x);
    return x < 0 ? Math.ceil(x) : Math.floor(x);
}
```

32-bit Integers via Bitwise Operators

Binary bitwise operators (see "Binary Bitwise Operators" on page 126) convert (at least) one of their operands to a 32-bit integer that is then manipulated to produce a result that is also a 32-bit integer. Therefore, if you choose the other operand appropriately, you get a fast way to convert an arbitrary number to a 32-bit integer (that is either signed or unsigned).

Bitwise Or (|)

If the mask, the second operand, is 0, you don't change any bits and the result is the first operand, coerced to a signed 32-bit integer. This is the canonical way to execute this kind of coercion and is used, for example, by asm.js (refer back to "Is JavaScript Fast Enough?" on page 37):

```
// Convert x to a signed 32-bit integer
function ToInt32(x) {
    return x | 0;
}
```

`ToInt32()` removes the fraction and applies modulo 2^{32}:

```
> ToInt32(1.001)
1
> ToInt32(1.999)
1
> ToInt32(1)
1
```

```
> ToInt32(-1)
-1
> ToInt32(Math.pow(2, 32)+1)
1
> ToInt32(Math.pow(2, 32)-1)
-1
```

Shift operators

The same trick that worked for bitwise Or also works for shift operators: if you shift by zero bits, the result of a shift operation is the first operand, coerced to a 32-bit integer. Here are some examples of implementing operations of the ECMAScript specification via shift operators:

```
// Convert x to a signed 32-bit integer
function ToInt32(x) {
    return x << 0;
}

// Convert x to a signed 32-bit integer
function ToInt32(x) {
    return x >> 0;
}

// Convert x to an unsigned 32-bit integer
function ToUint32(x) {
    return x >>> 0;
}
```

Here is ToUint32() in action:

```
> ToUint32(-1)
4294967295
> ToUint32(Math.pow(2, 32)-1)
4294967295
> ToUint32(Math.pow(2, 32))
0
```

Should I use bitwise operators to coerce to integer?

You have to decide for yourself if the slight increase in efficiency is worth your code being harder to understand. Also note that bitwise operators artificially limit themselves to 32 bits, which is often neither necessary nor useful. Using one of the Math functions, possibly in addition to Math.abs(), is a more self-explanatory and arguably better choice.

Integers via parseInt()

The parseInt() function:

```
parseInt(str, radix?)
```

parses the string str (nonstrings are coerced) as an integer. The function ignores leading whitespace and considers as many consecutive legal digits as it can find.

The radix

The range of the radix is $2 \leq radix \leq 36$. It determines the base of the number to be parsed. If the radix is greater than 10, letters are used as digits (case-insensitively), in addition to 0–9.

If radix is missing, then it is assumed to be 10, except if str begins with "0x" or "0X," in which case radix is set to 16 (hexadecimal):

```
> parseInt('0xA')
10
```

If radix is already 16, then the hexadecimal prefix is optional:

```
> parseInt('0xA', 16)
10
> parseInt('A', 16)
10
```

So far I have described the behavior of parseInt() according to the ECMAScript specification. Additionally, some engines set the radix to 8 if str starts with a zero:

```
> parseInt('010')
8
> parseInt('0109')  // ignores digits ≥ 8
8
```

Thus, it is best to always explicitly state the radix, to always call parseInt() with two arguments.

Here are a few examples:

```
> parseInt('')
NaN
> parseInt('zz', 36)
1295
> parseInt('  81', 10)
81

> parseInt('12**', 10)
12
> parseInt('12.34', 10)
12
> parseInt(12.34, 10)
12
```

Don't use parseInt() to convert a number to an integer. The last example gives us hope that we might be able to use parseInt() for converting numbers to integers. Alas, here is an example where the conversion is incorrect:

```
> parseInt(1000000000000000000000.5, 10)
1
```

Explanation

The argument is first converted to a string:

```
> String(1000000000000000000000.5)
'1e+21'
```

parseInt doesn't consider "e" to be an integer digit and thus stops parsing after the 1. Here's another example:

```
> parseInt(0.0000008, 10)
8
> String(0.0000008)
'8e-7'
```

Summary

parseInt() shouldn't be used to convert numbers to integers: coercion to string is an unnecessary detour and even then, the result is not always correct.

parseInt() *is* useful for parsing strings, but you have to be aware that it stops at the first illegal digit. Parsing strings via Number() (see "The Function Number" on page 127) is less forgiving, but may produce nonintegers.

Arithmetic Operators

The following operators are available for numbers:

number1 + number2
    Numerical addition, unless either of the operands is a string. Then both operands are converted to strings and concatenated (see "The Plus Operator (+)" on page 88):

```
> 3.1 + 4.3
7.4
> 4 + ' messages'
'4 messages'
```

number1 - number2
    Subtraction.

number1 * number2
    Multiplication.

number1 / number2
    Division.

number1 % number2
    Remainder:

```
> 9 % 7
2
> -9 % 7
-2
```

This operation is not modulo. It returns a value whose sign is the same as the first operand (more details in a moment).

`-number`

Negates its argument.

`+number`

Leaves its argument as is; nonnumbers are converted to a number.

`++variable, --variable`

Returns the current value of the variable after incrementing (or decrementing) it by 1:

```
> var x = 3;
> ++x
4
> x
4
```

`variable++, variable--`

Increments (or decrements) the value of the variable by 1 and returns it:

```
> var x = 3;
> x++
3
> x
4
```

Mnemonic: increment (++) and decrement (--) operators
The position of the operand can help you remember whether it is returned before or after incrementing (or decrementing) it. If the operand comes before the increment operator, it is returned before incrementing it. If the operand comes after the operator, it is incremented and then returned. (The decrement operator works similarly.)

Bitwise Operators

JavaScript has several bitwise operators that work with 32-bit integers. That is, they convert their operands to 32-bit integers and produce a result that is a 32-bit integer. Use cases for these operators include processing binary protocols, special algorithms, etc.

Background Knowledge

This section explains a few concepts that will help you understand bitwise operators.

Binary complements

Two common ways of computing a binary complement (or inverse) of a binary number are:

Ones' complement

You compute the ones' complement ~x of a number x by inverting each of the 32 digits. Let's illustrate the ones' complement via four-digit numbers. The ones' complement of `1100` is `0011`. Adding a number to its ones' complement results in a number whose digits are all 1:

```
1 + ~1 = 0001 + 1110 = 1111
```

Twos' complement

The twos' complement `-x` of a number `x` is the ones' complement plus one. Adding a number to its twos' complement results in 0 (ignoring overflow beyond the most significant digit). Here's an example using four-digit numbers:

```
1 + -1 = 0001 + 1111 = 0000
```

Signed 32-bit integers

32-bit integers don't have an explicit sign, but you can still encode negative numbers. For example, -1 can be encoded as the twos' complement of 1: adding 1 to the result yields 0 (within 32 bits). The boundary between positive and negative numbers is fluid; 4294967295 ($2^{32}-1$) and -1 are the same integer here. But you have to decide on a sign when you convert such an integer from or to a JavaScript number, which has an explicit sign as opposed to an implicit one. Therefore, *signed 32-bit integers* are partitioned into two groups:

- Highest bit is 0: number is zero or positive.
- Highest bit is 1: number is negative.

The highest bit is often called the *sign bit*. Accordingly, 4294967295, interpreted as a signed 32-bit integer, becomes -1 when converted to a JavaScript number:

```
> ToInt32(4294967295)
-1
```

`ToInt32()` is explained in "32-bit Integers via Bitwise Operators" on page 119.

 Only the unsigned right shift operator (`>>>`) works with unsigned 32-bit integers; all other bitwise operators work with signed 32-bit integers.

Inputting and outputting binary numbers

In the following examples, we work with binary numbers via the following two operations:

- `parseInt(str, 2)` (see "Integers via parseInt()" on page 120) parses a string `str` in binary notation (base 2). For example:

```
> parseInt('110', 2)
6
```

- num.toString(2) (see "Number.prototype.toString(radix?)" on page 129) converts the number num to a string in binary notation. For example:

```
> 6..toString(2)
'110'
```

Bitwise Not Operator

~number computes the ones' complement of number:

```
> (~parseInt('11111111111111111111111111111111', 2)).toString(2)
'0'
```

Binary Bitwise Operators

JavaScript has three binary bitwise operators:

- number1 & number2 (bitwise And):

```
> (parseInt('11001010', 2) & parseInt('1111', 2)).toString(2)
'1010'
```

- number1 | number2 (bitwise Or):

```
> (parseInt('11001010', 2) | parseInt('1111', 2)).toString(2)
'11001111'
```

- number1 ^ number2 (bitwise Xor; eXclusive Or):

```
> (parseInt('11001010', 2) ^ parseInt('1111', 2)).toString(2)
'11000101'
```

There are two ways to intuitively understand binary bitwise operators:

One boolean operation per bit

In the following formulas, n_i means bit i of number n interpreted as a boolean (0 is false, 1 is true). For example, 2_0 is false; 2_1 is true:

- And: $result_i$ = $number1_i$ && $number2_i$
- Or: $result_i$ = $number1_i$ || $number2_i$
- Xor: $result_i$ = $number1_i$ ^^ $number2_i$

  The operator ^^ does not exist. If it did, it would work like this (the result is true if exactly one of the operands is true):

```
x ^^ y === (x && !y) || (!x && y)
```

Changing bits of `number1` *via* `number2`

- And: Keeps only those bits of `number1` that are set in `number2`. This operation is also called *masking*, with `number2` being the *mask*.

- Or: Sets all bits of `number1` that are set in `number2` and keeps all other bits unchanged.

- Xor: Inverts all bits of `number1` that are set in `number2` and keeps all other bits unchanged.

Bitwise Shift Operators

JavaScript has three bitwise shift operators:

- `number << digitCount` (left shift):

    ```
    > (parseInt('1', 2) << 1).toString(2)
    '10'
    ```

- `number >> digitCount` (signed right shift):

    The 32-bit binary number is interpreted as signed (see the preceding section). When shifting right, the sign is preserved:

    ```
    > (parseInt('11111111111111111111111111111110', 2) >> 1).toString(2)
    '-1'
    ```

    We have right-shifted –2. The result, –1, is equivalent to a 32-bit integer whose digits are all 1 (the twos' complement of 1). In other words, a signed right shift by one digit divides both negative and positive integers by two.

- `number >>> digitCount`` (unsigned right shift):

    ```
    > (parseInt('11100', 2) >>> 1).toString(2)
    '1110'
    ```

As you can see, this operator shifts in zeros from the left.

The Function Number

The function `Number` can be invoked in two ways:

`Number(value)`

  As a normal function, it converts `value` to a primitive number (see "Converting to Number" on page 104):

```
> Number('123')
123
> typeof Number(3)  // no change
'number'
```

```
new Number(num)
```
As a constructor, it creates a new instance of Number (see "Wrapper Objects for Primitives" on page 75), an object that wraps num (after converting it to a number). For example:

```
> typeof new Number(3)
'object'
```

The former invocation is the common one.

Number Constructor Properties

The object Number has the following properties:

Number.MAX_VALUE

The largest positive number that can be represented. Internally, all digits of its fraction are ones and the exponent is maximal, at 1023. If you try to increment the exponent by multiplying it by two, the result is the error value Infinity (see "Infinity" on page 107):

```
> Number.MAX_VALUE
1.7976931348623157e+308
> Number.MAX_VALUE * 2
Infinity
```

Number.MIN_VALUE

The smallest representable positive number (greater than zero, a tiny fraction):

```
> Number.MIN_VALUE
5e-324
```

Number.NaN

The same value as the global NaN.

Number.NEGATIVE_INFINITY

The same value as -Infinity:

```
> Number.NEGATIVE_INFINITY === -Infinity
true
```

Number.POSITIVE_INFINITY

The same value as Infinity:

```
> Number.POSITIVE_INFINITY === Infinity
true
```

Number Prototype Methods

All methods of primitive numbers are stored in Number.prototype (see "Primitives Borrow Their Methods from Wrappers" on page 77).

Number.prototype.toFixed(fractionDigits?)

`Number.prototype.toFixed(fractionDigits?)` returns an exponent-free representation of the number, rounded to `fractionDigits` digits. If the parameter is omitted, the value 0 is used:

```
> 0.0000003.toFixed(10)
'0.0000003000'
> 0.0000003.toString()
'3e-7'
```

If the number is greater than or equal to 10^{21}, then this method works the same as `toString()`. You get a number in exponential notation:

```
> 1234567890123456789012..toFixed()
'1.2345678901234568e+21'
> 1234567890123456789012..toString()
'1.2345678901234568e+21'
```

Number.prototype.toPrecision(precision?)

`Number.prototype.toPrecision(precision?)` prunes the mantissa to `precision` digits before using a conversion algorithm similar to `toString()`. If no precision is given, `toString()` is used directly:

```
> 1234..toPrecision(3)
'1.23e+3'

> 1234..toPrecision(4)
'1234'

> 1234..toPrecision(5)
'1234.0'

> 1.234.toPrecision(3)
'1.23'
```

You need the exponential notation to display 1234 with a precision of three digits.

Number.prototype.toString(radix?)

For `Number.prototype.toString(radix?)`, the parameter `radix` indicates the base of the system in which the number is to be displayed. The most common radices are 10 (decimal), 2 (binary), and 16 (hexadecimal):

```
> 15..toString(2)
'1111'
> 65535..toString(16)
'ffff'
```

The radix must be at least 2 and at most 36. Any radix greater than 10 leads to alphabetical characters being used as digits, which explains the maximum 36, as the Latin alphabet has 26 characters:

```
> 1234567890..toString(36)
'kf12oi'
```

The global function `parseInt` (see "Integers via parseInt()" on page 120) allows you to convert such notations back to a number:

```
> parseInt('kf12oi', 36)
1234567890
```

Decimal exponential notation

For the radix 10, `toString()` uses exponential notation (with a single digit before the decimal point) in two cases. First, if there are more than 21 digits before the decimal point of a number:

```
> 1234567890123456789012
1.2345678901234568e+21
> 123456789012345678901
123456789012345680000
```

Second, if a number starts with `0.` followed by more than five zeros and a non-zero digit:

```
> 0.0000003
3e-7
> 0.000003
0.000003
```

In all other cases, a fixed notation is used.

Number.prototype.toExponential(fractionDigits?)

`Number.prototype.toExponential(fractionDigits?)` forces a number to be expressed in exponential notation. `fractionDigits` is a number between 0 and 20 that determines how many digits should be shown after the decimal point. If it is omitted, then as many significant digits are included as necessary to uniquely specify the number.

In this example, we force more precision when `toString()` would also use exponential notation. Results are mixed, because we reach the limits of the precision that can be achieved when converting binary numbers to a decimal notation:

```
> 1234567890123456789012..toString()
'1.2345678901234568e+21'

> 1234567890123456789012..toExponential(20)
'1.23456789012345677414e+21'
```

In this example, the magnitude of the number is not large enough for an exponent being displayed by toString(). However, toExponential() does display an exponent:

```
> 1234..toString()
'1234'

> 1234..toExponential(5)
'1.23400e+3'

> 1234..toExponential()
'1.234e+3'
```

In this example, we get exponential notation when the fraction is not small enough:

```
> 0.003.toString()
'0.003'

> 0.003.toExponential(4)
'3.0000e-3'

> 0.003.toExponential()
'3e-3'
```

Functions for Numbers

The following functions operate on numbers:

isFinite(number)

Checks whether number is an actual number (neither Infinity nor NaN). For details, see "Checking for Infinity" on page 108.

isNaN(number)

Returns true if number is NaN. For details, see "Pitfall: checking whether a value is NaN" on page 107.

parseFloat(str)

Turns str into a floating-point number. For details, see "parseFloat()" on page 105.

parseInt(str, radix?)

Parses str as an integer whose base is radix (2–36). For details, see "Integers via parseInt()" on page 120.

Sources for This Chapter

I referred to the following sources while writing this chapter:

- "IEEE Standard 754 Floating Point Numbers" (*http://bit.ly/1oOc43P*) by Steve Hollasch
- "Data Types and Scaling (Fixed-Point Blockset)" (*http://bit.ly/1oOc83t*) in the MATLAB documentation
- "IEEE floating point" (*http://en.wikipedia.org/wiki/IEEE_754*) on Wikipedia

CHAPTER 12

Strings

Strings are immutable sequences of JavaScript characters. Each such character is a 16-bit UTF-16 code unit. That means that a single Unicode character is represented by either one or two JavaScript characters. You mainly need to worry about the two-character case whenever you are counting characters or splitting strings (see Chapter 24).

String Literals

Both single and double quotes can be used to delimit string literals:

```
'He said: "Hello"'
"He said: \"Hello\""

'Everyone\'s a winner'
"Everyone's a winner"
```

Thus, you are free to use either kind of quote. There are several considerations, though:

- The most common style in the community is to use double quotes for HTML and single quotes for JavaScript.
- On the other hand, double quotes are used exclusively for strings in some languages (e.g., C and Java). Therefore, it may make sense to use them in a multilanguage code base.
- For JSON (discussed in Chapter 22), you must use double quotes.

Your code will look cleaner if you quote consistently. But sometimes, a different quote means that you don't have to escape, which can justify your being less consistent (e.g., you may normally use single quotes, but temporarily switch to double quotes to write the last one of the preceding examples).

Escaping in String Literals

Most characters in string literals simply represent themselves. The backslash is used for *escaping* and enables several special features:

Line continuations

You can spread a string over multiple lines by escaping the end of the line (the line-terminating character, the *line terminator*) with a backslash:

```
var str = 'written \
over \
multiple \
lines';
console.log(str === 'written over multiple lines'); // true
```

An alternative is to use the plus operator to concatenate:

```
var str = 'written ' +
          'over ' +
          'multiple ' +
          'lines';
```

Character escape sequences

These sequences start with a backslash:

- Control characters: \b is a backspace, \f is a form feed, \n is a line feed (newline), \r is a carriage return, \t is a horizontal tab, and \v is a vertical tab.

- Escaped characters that represent themselves: \' is a single quote, \" is a double quote, and \\ is a backslash. All characters except b f n r t v x u and decimal digits represent themselves, too. Here are two examples:

    ```
    > '\"'
    '"'
    > '\q'
    'q'
    ```

NUL character (Unicode code point 0)

This character is represented by \0.

Hexadecimal escape sequences

\xHH (HH are two hexadecimal digits) specifies a character via an ASCII code. For example:

```
> '\x4D'
'M'
```

Unicode escape sequences

\uHHHH (HHHH are four hexadecimal digits) specifies a UTF-16 code unit (see Chapter 24). Here are two examples:

```
> '\u004D'
'M'
> '\u03C0'
'π'
```

Character Access

There are two operations that return the *n*th character of a string.[1] Note that JavaScript does not have a special data type for characters; these operations return strings:

```
> 'abc'.charAt(1)
'b'
> 'abc'[1]
'b'
```

Some older browsers don't support the array-like access to characters via square brackets.

Converting to String

Values are converted to a string as follows:

Value	Result
undefined	'undefined'
null	'null'
A boolean	false → 'false'
	true → 'true'
A number	The number as a string (e.g., 3.141 → '3.141')
A string	Same as input (nothing to convert)
An object	Call ToPrimitive(value, String) (see "Algorithm: ToPrimitive()—Converting a Value to a Primitive" on page 79) and convert the resulting primitive.

Manually Converting to String

The three most common ways to convert any value to a string are:

String(value)	(Invoked as a function, not as a constructor)
''+value	
value.toString()	(Does not work for undefined and null!)

I prefer String(), because it is more descriptive. Here are some examples:

---

1. Strictly speaking, a JavaScript string consists of a sequence of UTF-16 code units. That is, JavaScript characters are Unicode code units (see Chapter 24).

```
> String(false)
'false'
> String(7.35)
'7.35'
> String({ first: 'John', last: 'Doe' })
'[object Object]'
> String([ 'a', 'b', 'c' ])
'a,b,c'
```

Note that for displaying data, `JSON.stringify()` ("JSON.stringify(value, replacer?, space?)" on page 337) often works better than the canonical conversion to string:

```
> console.log(JSON.stringify({ first: 'John', last: 'Doe' }))
{"first":"John","last":"Doe"}
> console.log(JSON.stringify([ 'a', 'b', 'c' ]))
["a","b","c"]
```

Naturally, you have to be aware of the limitations of `JSON.stringify()`—it doesn't always show everything. For example, it hides properties whose values it can't handle (functions and more!). On the plus side, its output can be parsed by `eval()` and it can display deeply nested data as nicely formatted trees.

Pitfall: conversion is not invertible

Given how often JavaScript automatically converts, it is a shame that the conversion isn't always invertible, especially with regard to booleans:

```
> String(false)
'false'
> Boolean('false')
true
```

For `undefined` and `null`, we face similar problems.

Comparing Strings

There are two ways of comparing strings. First, you can use the comparison operators: `<`, `>`, `===`, `<=`, `>=`. They have the following drawbacks:

- They're case-sensitive:

  ```
  > 'B' > 'A'  // ok
  true
  > 'B' > 'a'  // should be true
  false
  ```

- They don't handle umlauts and accents well:

  ```
  > 'ä' < 'b'  // should be true
  false
  ```

```
> 'é' < 'f'   // should be true
false
```

Second, you can use `String.prototype.localeCompare(other)`, which tends to fare better, but isn't always supported (consult "Search and Compare" on page 141 for details). The following is an interaction in Firefox's console:

```
> 'B'.localeCompare('A')
2
> 'B'.localeCompare('a')
2

> 'ä'.localeCompare('b')
-2
> 'é'.localeCompare('f')
-2
```

A result less than zero means that the receiver is "smaller" than the argument. A result greater than zero means that the receiver is "larger" than the argument.

Concatenating Strings

There are two main approaches for concatenating strings.

Concatenation: The Plus (+) Operator

The operator + does string concatenation as soon as one of its operands is a string. If you want to collect string pieces in a variable, the compound assignment operator += is useful:

```
> var str = '';
> str += 'Say hello ';
> str += 7;
> str += ' times fast!';
> str
'Say hello 7 times fast!'
```

Concatenation: Joining an Array of String Fragments

It may seem that the previous approach creates a new string whenever a piece is added to `str`. Older JavaScript engines do it that way, which means that you can improve the performance of string concatenation by collecting all the pieces in an array first and joining them as a last step:

```
> var arr = [];

> arr.push('Say hello ');
> arr.push(7);
> arr.push(' times fast');
```

```
> arr.join('')
'Say hello 7 times fast'
```

However, newer engines optimize string concatenation via + and use a similar method internally. Therefore, the plus operator is faster on those engines.

The Function String

The function `String` can be invoked in two ways:

`String(value)`

As a normal function, it converts `value` to a primitive string (see "Converting to String" on page 135):

```
> String(123)
'123'
> typeof String('abc')  // no change
'string'
```

`new String(str)`

As a constructor, it creates a new instance of `String` (see "Wrapper Objects for Primitives" on page 75), an object that wraps `str` (nonstrings are coerced to string). For example:

```
> typeof new String('abc')
'object'
```

The former invocation is the common one.

String Constructor Method

`String.fromCharCode(codeUnit1, codeUnit2, ...)` produces a string whose characters are the UTF-16 code units specified by the 16-bit unsigned integers `codeUnit1`, `codeUnit2`, and so on. For example:

```
> String.fromCharCode(97, 98, 99)
'abc'
```

If you want to turn an array of numbers into a string, you can do so via `apply()` (see "func.apply(thisValue, argArray)" on page 170):

```
> String.fromCharCode.apply(null, [97, 98, 99])
'abc'
```

The inverse of `String.fromCharCode()` is `String.prototype.charCodeAt()`.

String Instance Property length

The length property indicates the number of JavaScript characters in the string and is immutable:

```
> 'abc'.length
3
```

String Prototype Methods

All methods of primitive strings are stored in String.prototype (refer back to "Primitives Borrow Their Methods from Wrappers" on page 77). Next, I describe how they work for primitive strings, not for instances of String.

Extract Substrings

The following methods extract substrings from the receiver:

String.prototype.charAt(pos)
> Returns a string with the character at position pos. For example:
>
> ```
> > 'abc'.charAt(1)
> 'b'
> ```
>
> The following two expressions return the same result, but some older JavaScript engines support only charAt() for accessing characters:
>
> ```
> str.charAt(n)
> str[n]
> ```

String.prototype.charCodeAt(pos)
> Returns the code (a 16-bit unsigned integer) of the JavaScript character (a UTF-16 code unit; see Chapter 24) at position pos.
>
> This is how you create an array of character codes:
>
> ```
> > 'abc'.split('').map(function (x) { return x.charCodeAt(0) })
> [ 97, 98, 99 ]
> ```
>
> The inverse of charCodeAt() is String.fromCharCode().

String.prototype.slice(start, end?)
> Returns the substring starting at position start up to and excluding position end. Both of the two parameters can be negative, and then the length of the string is added to them:
>
> ```
> > 'abc'.slice(2)
> 'c'
> > 'abc'.slice(1, 2)
> 'b'
> ```

```
> 'abc'.slice(-2)
'bc'
```

String.prototype.substring(start, end?)

Should be avoided in favor of `slice()`, which is similar, but can handle negative positions and is implemented more consistently across browsers.

String.prototype.split(separator?, limit?)

Extracts the substrings of the receiver that are delimited by `separator` and returns them in an array. The method has two parameters:

- `separator`: Either a string or a regular expression. If missing, the complete string is returned, wrapped in an array.

- `limit`: If given, the returned array contains at most `limit` elements.

Here are some examples:

```
> 'a,  b,c, d'.split(',')  // string
[ 'a', '  b', 'c', ' d' ]
> 'a,  b,c, d'.split(/,/)  // simple regular expression
[ 'a', '  b', 'c', ' d' ]
> 'a,  b,c, d'.split(/, */)   // more complex regular expression
[ 'a', 'b', 'c', 'd' ]
> 'a,  b,c, d'.split(/, */, 2)  // setting a limit
[ 'a', 'b' ]
> 'test'.split()  // no separator provided
[ 'test' ]
```

If there is a group, then the matches are also returned as array elements:

```
> 'a, b  ,  '.split(/(,)/)
[ 'a', ',', '  b  ', ',', '  ' ]
> 'a, b  ,  '.split(/ *(,) */)
[ 'a', ',', 'b', ',', '' ]
```

Use `''` (empty string) as a separator to produce an array with the characters of a string:

```
> 'abc'.split('')
[ 'a', 'b', 'c' ]
```

Transform

While the previous section was about extracting substrings, this section is about transforming a given string into a new one. These methods are typically used as follows:

```
var str = str.trim();
```

In other words, the original string is discarded after it has been (nondestructively) transformed:

```
String.prototype.trim()
```
Removes all whitespace from the beginning and the end of the string:

```
> '\r\nabc \t'.trim()
'abc'
```

```
String.prototype.concat(str1?, str2?, ...)
```
Returns the concatenation of the receiver and `str1`, `str2`, etc.:

```
> 'hello'.concat(' ', 'world', '!')
'hello world!'
```

```
String.prototype.toLowerCase()
```
Creates a new string with all of the original string's characters converted to lowercase:

```
> 'MJÖLNIR'.toLowerCase()
'mjölnir'
```

```
String.prototype.toLocaleLowerCase()
```
Works the same as `toLowerCase()`, but respects the rules of the current locale. According to the ECMAScript spec: "There will only be a difference in the few cases (such as Turkish) where the rules for that language conflict with the regular Unicode case mappings."

```
String.prototype.toUpperCase()
```
Creates a new string with all of the original string's characters converted to uppercase:

```
> 'mjölnir'.toUpperCase()
'MJÖLNIR'
```

```
String.prototype.toLocaleUpperCase()
```
Works the same as `toUpperCase()`, but respects the rules of the current locale.

Search and Compare

The following methods are used for searching and comparing strings:

```
String.prototype.indexOf(searchString, position?)
```
Searches for `searchString` starting at `position` (the default is 0). It returns the position where `searchString` has been found or –1 if it can't be found:

```
> 'aXaX'.indexOf('X')
1
> 'aXaX'.indexOf('X', 2)
3
```

Note that when it comes to finding text inside a string, a regular expression works just as well. For example, the following two expressions are equivalent:

```
str.indexOf('abc') >= 0
/abc/.test(str)
```

`String.prototype.lastIndexOf(searchString, position?)`

Searches for `searchString`, starting at `position` (the default is the end), backward. It returns the position where `searchString` has been found or −1 if it can't be found:

```
> 'aXaX'.lastIndexOf('X')
3
> 'aXaX'.lastIndexOf('X', 2)
1
```

`String.prototype.localeCompare(other)`

Performs a locale-sensitive comparison of the string with `other`. It returns a number:

- < 0 if the string comes before `other`
- = 0 if the string is equivalent to `other`
- > 0 if the string comes after `other`

For example:

```
> 'apple'.localeCompare('banana')
-2
> 'apple'.localeCompare('apple')
0
```

 Not all JavaScript engines implement this method properly. Some just base it on the comparison operators. However, the ECMAScript Internationalization API (see "The ECMAScript Internationalization API" on page 406) does provide a Unicode-aware implementation. That is, if that API is available in an engine, `localeCompare()` will work.

If it is supported, `localeCompare()` is a better choice for comparing strings than the comparison operators. Consult "Comparing Strings" on page 136 for more information.

Test, Match, and Replace with Regular Expressions

The following methods work with regular expressions:

`String.prototype.search(regexp)` *(more thoroughly explained in "String.prototype.search: At What Index Is There a Match?" on page 305)*

Returns the first index at which `regexp` matches in the receiver (or −1 if it doesn't):

```
> '-yy-xxx-y-'.search(/x+/)
4
```

`String.prototype.match(regexp)` *(more thoroughly explained in "String.proto-type.match: Capture Groups or Return All Matching Substrings" on page 307)*

Matches the given regular expression against the receiver. It returns a match object for the first match if the flag `/g` of `regexp` is not set:

```
> '-abb--aaab-'.match(/(a+)b/)
[ 'ab',
  'a',
  index: 1,
  input: '-abb--aaab-' ]
```

If the flag `/g` is set, then all complete matches (group 0) are returned in an array:

```
> '-abb--aaab-'.match(/(a+)b/g)
[ 'ab', 'aaab' ]
```

`String.prototype.replace(search, replacement)` *(more thoroughly explained in "String.prototype.replace: Search and Replace" on page 307)*

Searches for `search` and replaces it with `replacement`. `search` can be a string or a regular expression, and `replacement` can be a string or a function. Unless you use a regular expression as `search` whose flag `/g` is set, only the first occurrence will be replaced:

```
> 'iixxxixx'.replace('i', 'o')
'oixxxixx'
> 'iixxxixx'.replace(/i/, 'o')
'oixxxixx'
> 'iixxxixx'.replace(/i/g, 'o')
'ooxxxoxx'
```

A dollar sign ($) in a replacement string allows you to refer to the complete match or a captured group:

```
> 'iixxxixx'.replace(/i+/g, '($&)') // complete match
'(ii)xxx(i)xx'
> 'iixxxixx'.replace(/(i+)/g, '($1)') // group 1
'(ii)xxx(i)xx'
```

You can also compute a replacement via a function:

```
> function repl(all) { return '('+all.toUpperCase()+')' }
> 'axbbyyxaa'.repl(/a+|b+/g, replacement)
'(A)x(BB)yyx(AA)'
```

CHAPTER 13

Statements

This chapter covers JavaScript's statements: variable declarations, loops, conditionals, and others.

Declaring and Assigning Variables

var is used to *declare* a variable, which creates the variable and enables you to work with it. The equals operator (=) is used to assign a value to it:

```
var foo;
foo = 'abc';
```

var also lets you combine the preceding two statements into a single one:

```
var foo = 'abc';
```

Finally, you can also combine multiple var statements into one:

```
var x, y=123, z;
```

Read more about how variables work in Chapter 16.

The Bodies of Loops and Conditionals

Compound statements such as loops and conditionals have one or more "bodies" embedded—for example, the while loop:

```
while («condition»)
    «statement»
```

For the body «statement», you have a choice. You can either use a single statement:

```
while (x >= 0) x--;
```

or you can use a block (which counts as a single statement):

```
while (x > 0) {
    x--;
}
```

You need to use a block if you want the body to comprise multiple statements. Unless the complete compound statement can be written in a single line, I recommend using a block.

Loops

This section explores JavaScript's loop statements.

Mechanisms to Be Used with Loops

The following mechanisms can be used with all loops:

break [«label»]
:   Exit from a loop.

continue [«label»]
:   Stop the current loop iteration, and immediately continue with the next one.

Labels
:   A label is an identifier followed by a colon. In front of a loop, a label allows you to break or continue that loop even from a loop nested inside of it. In front of a block, you can break out of that block. In both cases, the name of the label becomes an argument of break or continue. Here's an example of breaking out of a block:

```
function findEvenNumber(arr) {
    loop: { // label
        for (var i=0; i<arr.length; i++) {
            var elem = arr[i];
            if ((elem % 2) === 0) {
                console.log('Found: ' + elem);
                break loop;
            }
        }
        console.log('No even number found.');
    }
    console.log('DONE');
}
```

while

A while loop:

```
while («condition»)
    «statement»
```

---

executes `statement` as long as `condition` holds. If `condition` is always `true`, you get an infinite loop:

```
while (true) { ... }
```

In the following example, we remove all elements of an array and log them to the console:

```
var arr = [ 'a', 'b', 'c' ];
while (arr.length > 0) {
    console.log(arr.shift());
}
```

Here is the output:

```
a
b
c
```

do-while

A do-while loop:

```
do «statement»
while («condition»);
```

executes `statement` at least once and then as long as `condition` holds. For example:

```
var line;
do {
    line = prompt('Enter a number:');
} while (!/^[0-9]+$/.test(line));
```

for

In a `for` loop:

```
for ([«init»]; [«condition»]; [«post_iteration»])
    «statement»
```

`init` is executed once before the loop, which continues as long as `condition` is `true`. You can use `var` in `init` to declare variables, but the scope of those variables is always the complete surrounding function. `post_iteration` is executed after each iteration of the loop. Taking all of this into consideration, the preceding loop is equivalent to the following `while` loop:

```
«init»;
while («condition») {
    «statement»
    «post_iteration»;
}
```

The following example is the traditional way of iterating over arrays (other possibilities are described in "Best Practices: Iterating over Arrays" on page 295):

```
var arr = [ 'a', 'b', 'c' ];
for (var i=0; i<arr.length; i++) {
    console.log(arr[i]);
}
```

A for loop becomes infinite if you omit all parts of the head:

```
for (;;) {
    ...
}
```

for-in

A for-in loop:

```
for («variable» in «object»)
    «statement»
```

iterates over all property keys of object, including inherited ones. However, properties
that are marked as not enumerable are ignored (see "Property Attributes and Property
Descriptors" on page 222). The following rules apply to for-in loops:

- You can use var to declare variables, but the scope of those variables is always the
  complete surrounding function.
- Properties can be deleted during iteration.

Best practice: don't use for-in for arrays

Don't use for-in to iterate over arrays. First, it iterates over indices, not over values:

```
> var arr = [ 'a', 'b', 'c' ];
> for (var key in arr) { console.log(key); }
0
1
2
```

Second, it also iterates over all (nonindex) property keys. The following example illustrates what happens when you add a property foo to an array:

```
> var arr = [ 'a', 'b', 'c' ];
> arr.foo = true;
> for (var key in arr) { console.log(key); }
0
1
2
foo
```

Thus, you are better off with a normal for loop or the array method forEach() (see
"Best Practices: Iterating over Arrays" on page 295).

Best practice: be careful with for-in for objects

The `for-in` loop iterates over *all* (enumerable) properties, including inherited ones. That may not be what you want. Let's use the following constructor to illustrate the problem:

```
function Person(name) {
    this.name = name;
}
Person.prototype.describe = function () {
    return 'Name: '+this.name;
};
```

Instances of `Person` inherit the property `describe` from `Person.prototype`, which is seen by `for-in`:

```
var person = new Person('Jane');
for (var key in person) {
    console.log(key);
}
```

Here is the output:

```
name
describe
```

Normally, the best way to use `for-in` is to skip inherited properties via `hasOwnProperty()`:

```
for (var key in person) {
    if (person.hasOwnProperty(key)) {
        console.log(key);
    }
}
```

And here is the output:

```
name
```

There is one last caveat: `person` may have a property `hasOwnProperty`, which would prevent the check from working. To be safe, you have to refer to the generic method (see "Generic Methods: Borrowing Methods from Prototypes" on page 260) `Object.prototype.hasOwnProperty` directly:

```
for (var key in person) {
    if (Object.prototype.hasOwnProperty.call(person, key)) {
        console.log(key);
    }
}
```

There are other, more comfortable, means for iterating over property keys, which are described in "Best Practices: Iterating over Own Properties" on page 220.

for each-in

This loop exists only on Firefox. Don't use it.

Conditionals

This section covers JavaScript's conditional statements.

if-then-else

In an `if-then-else` statement:

```
if («condition»)
    «then_branch»
[else
    «else_branch»]
```

then_branch and else_branch can be either single statements or blocks of statements (see "The Bodies of Loops and Conditionals" on page 145).

Chaining if statements

You can chain several `if` statements:

```
if (s1 > s2) {
    return 1;
} else if (s1 < s2) {
    return -1;
} else {
    return 0;
}
```

Note that in the preceding example, all the `else` branches are single statements (`if` statements). Programming languages that only allow blocks for `else` branches need some kind of `else-if` branch for chaining.

Pitfall: dangling else

The `else` branch of the following example is called *dangling*, because it is not clear to which of the two `if` statements it belongs:

```
if («cond1») if («cond2») «stmt1» else «stmt2»
```

Here's a simple rule: use braces. The preceding snippet is equivalent to the following code (where it is obvious who the `else` belongs to):

```
if («cond1») {
    if («cond2») {
        «stmt1»
    } else {
        «stmt2»
```

```
    }
}
```

switch

A `switch` statement:

```
switch («expression») {
    case «label1_1»:
    case «label1_2»:
        ...
        «statements1»
        ⟦break;⟧
    case «label2_1»:
    case «label2_2»:
        ...
        «statements2»
        ⟦break;⟧
    ...
    ⟦default:
        «statements_default»
        ⟦break;⟧⟧
}
```

evaluates `expression` and then jumps to the `case` clause whose label matches the result. If no label matches, `switch` jumps to the `default` clause if it exists or does nothing otherwise.

The "operand" after `case` can be any expression; it is compared via `===` with the parameter of `switch`.

If you don't finish a clause with a terminating statement, execution continues into the next clause. The most frequently used terminating statement is `break`. But `return` and `throw` also work, even though they normally leave more than just the `switch` statement.

The following example illustrates that you don't need to `break` if you use `throw` or `return`:

```
function divide(dividend, divisor) {
    switch (divisor) {
        case 0:
            throw 'Division by zero';
        default:
            return dividend / divisor;
    }
}
```

In this example, there is no `default` clause. Therefore, nothing happens if `fruit` matches none of the `case` labels:

```
function useFruit(fruit) {
    switch (fruit) {
```

```
        case 'apple':
            makeCider();
            break;
        case 'grape':
            makeWine();
            break;
        // neither apple nor grape: do nothing
    }
}
```

Here, there are multiple case labels in a row:

```
function categorizeColor(color) {
    var result;
    switch (color) {
        case 'red':
        case 'yellow':
        case 'blue':
            result = 'Primary color: '+color;
            break;
        case 'or':
        case 'green':
        case 'violet':
            result = 'Secondary color: '+color;
            break;
        case 'black':
        case 'white':
            result = 'Not a color';
            break;
        default:
            throw 'Illegal argument: '+color;
    }
    console.log(result);
}
```

This example demonstrates that the value after case can be an arbitrary expression:

```
function compare(x, y) {
    switch (true) {
        case x < y:
            return -1;
        case x === y:
            return 0;
        default:
            return 1;
    }
}
```

The preceding switch statement looks for a match for its parameter true by going through the case clauses. If one of the case expressions evaluates to true, the corresponding case body is executed. Therefore, the preceding code is equivalent to the following if statement:

```
function compare(x, y) {
    if (x < y) {
        return -1;
    } else if (x === y) {
        return 0;
    } else {
        return 1;
    }
}
```

You normally should prefer the latter solution; it is more self-explanatory.

The with Statement

This section explains how the with statement works in JavaScript and why its use is discouraged.

Syntax and Semantics

The syntax of the with statement is as follows:

```
with («object»)
    «statement»
```

It turns the properties of object into local variables for statement. For example:

```
var obj = { first: 'John' };
with (obj) {
    console.log('Hello '+first); // Hello John
}
```

Its intended use is to avoid redundancy when accessing an object several times. The following is an example of code with redundancies:

```
foo.bar.baz.bla   = 123;
foo.bar.baz.yadda = 'abc';
```

with makes this shorter:

```
with (foo.bar.baz) {
    bla   = 123;
    yadda = 'abc';
}
```

The with Statement Is Deprecated

The use of the with statement is generally discouraged (the next section explains why). For example, it is forbidden in strict mode:

```
> function foo() { 'use strict'; with ({}); }
SyntaxError: strict mode code may not contain 'with' statements
```

Techniques for avoiding the with statement

Avoid code like this:

```
// Don't do this:
with (foo.bar.baz) {
    console.log('Hello '+first+' '+last);
}
```

Instead, use a temporary variable with a short name:

```
var b = foo.bar.baz;
console.log('Hello '+b.first+' '+b.last);
```

If you don't want to expose the temporary variable b to the current scope, you can use an IIFE (see "Introducing a New Scope via an IIFE" on page 183):

```
(function () {
    var b = foo.bar.baz;
    console.log('Hello '+b.first+' '+b.last);
}());
```

You also have the option of making the object that you want to access a parameter of the IIFE:

```
(function (b) {
    console.log('Hello '+b.first+' '+b.last);
}(foo.bar.baz));
```

The Rationale for the Deprecation

To understand why with is deprecated, look at the following example and notice how the function's argument completely changes how it works:

```
function logit(msg, opts) {
    with (opts) {
        console.log('msg: '+msg); // (1)
    }
}
```

If opts has a property msg, then the statement in line (1) doesn't access the parameter msg anymore. It accesses the property:

```
> logit('hello', {})  // parameter msg
msg: hello
> logit('hello', { msg: 'world' })  // property opts.msg
msg: world
```

There are three problems that the with statement causes:

Performance suffers
> Variable lookup becomes slower, because an object is temporarily inserted into the scope chain.

Code becomes less predictable
> You cannot determine what an identifier refers to by looking at its syntactic surroundings (its lexical context). According to Brendan Eich (*http://bit.ly/1jCrTKj*), that was the actual reason why `with` was deprecated, not performance considerations:
>
>> `with` violates lexical scope, making program analysis (e.g. for security) hard to infeasible.

Minifiers (described in Chapter 32) can't shorten variable names
> Inside a `with` statement, you can't statically determine whether a name refers to a variable or a property. Only variables can be renamed by minifiers.

Here is an example of `with` making code brittle:

```
function foo(someArray) {
    var values = ...;  // (1)
    with (someArray) {
        values.someMethod(...);  // (2)
        ...
    }
}
foo(myData);  // (3)
```

You can prevent the function call in line (3) from working, even if you don't have access to the array `myData`.

How? By adding a property `values` to `Array.prototype`. For example:

```
Array.prototype.values = function () {
    ...
};
```

Now the code in line (2) calls `someArray.values.someMethod()` instead of `values.some Method()`. The reason is that, inside the `with` statement, `values` now refers to `someAr ray.values` and not the local variable from line (1) anymore.

This is not just a thought experiment: the array method `values()` was added to Firefox and broke the TYPO3 content management system. Brandon Benvie figured out what went wrong (*http://mzl.la/1jCrXti*).

The debugger Statement

The syntax for the `debugger` statement is as follows:

```
debugger;
```

If a debugger is active, this statement functions as a breakpoint; if not, it has no observable effect.

CHAPTER 14

Exception Handling

This chapter describes how JavaScript's exception handling works. It begins with a general explanation of what exception handling is.

What Is Exception Handling?

In exception handling, you often group statements that are tightly coupled. If, while you are executing those statements, one of them causes an error, then it makes no sense to continue with the remaining statements. Instead, you try to recover from the error as gracefully as you can. This is loosely reminiscent of transactions (but without the atomicity).

Let's look at code without exception handling:

```
function processFiles() {
    var fileNames = collectFileNames();
    var entries = extractAllEntries(fileNames);
    processEntries(entries);
}
function extractAllEntries(fileNames) {
    var allEntries = new Entries();
    fileNames.forEach(function (fileName) {
        var entry = extractOneEntry(fileName);
        allEntries.add(entry);  // (1)
    });
}
function extractOneEntry(fileName) {
    var file = openFile(fileName);  // (2)
    ...
}
...
```

What is the best way to react to an error in `openFile()` at (2)? Clearly, the statement (1) should not be executed anymore. But we wouldn't want to abort `extractAllEn` tries(), either. Instead, it is enough to skip the current file and continue with the next one. To do that, we add exception handling to the previous code:

```
function extractAllEntries(fileNames) {
    var allEntries = new Entries();
    fileNames.forEach(function (fileName) {
        try {
            var entry = extractOneEntry(fileName);
            allEntries.add(entry);
        } catch (exception) {  // (2)
            errorLog.log('Error in '+fileName, exception);
        }
    });
}
function extractOneEntry(fileName) {
    var file = openFile(fileName);
    ...
}
function openFile(fileName) {
    if (!exists(fileName)) {
        throw new Error('Could not find file '+fileName); // (1)
    }
    ...
}
```

There are two aspects to exception handling:

1. If there is a problem that can't be handled meaningfully where it occurs, throw an exception.

2. Find a place where errors can be handled: catch exceptions.

At (1), the following constructs are active:

```
processFile()
    extractAllEntries(...)
        fileNames.forEach(...)
            function (fileName) { ... }
                try { ... } catch (exception) { ... }
                    extractOneEntry(...)
                        openFile(...)
```

The throw statement at (1) walks up that tree and leaves all constructs until it encounters an active try statement. It then invokes that statement's catch block and passes it the exception value.

Exception Handling in JavaScript

Exception handling in JavaScript works like in most programming languages: a try statement groups statements and lets you intercept exceptions in those statements.

throw

The syntax of `throw` is as follows:

```
throw «value»;
```

Any JavaScript value can be thrown. For simplicity's sake, many JavaScript programs just throw strings:

```
// Don't do this
if (somethingBadHappened) {
    throw 'Something bad happened';
}
```

Don't do this. JavaScript has special constructors for exception objects (see "Error Constructors" on page 161). Use those or subclass them (see Chapter 28). Their advantage is that JavaScript automatically adds a stack trace (on most engines) and that they have room for additional context-specific properties. The simplest solution is to use the built-in constructor `Error()`:

```
if (somethingBadHappened) {
    throw new Error('Something bad happened');
}
```

try-catch-finally

The syntax of `try-catch-finally` looks as follows. `try` is mandatory, and at least one of `catch` and `finally` must be there, too:

```
try {
    «try_statements»
}
[catch («exceptionVar») {
    «catch_statements»
}]
[finally {
    «finally_statements»
}]
```

Here's how it works:

- `catch` catches any exception that is thrown in `try_statements`, whether directly or in functions they invoke. Tip: If you want to distinguish between different kinds of exceptions, you can use the `constructor` property to switch over the exceptions' constructors (see "Use cases for the constructor property" on page 235).

- `finally` is always executed, no matter what happens in `try_statements` (or in functions they invoke). Use it for clean-up operations that should always be performed, no matter what happens in `try_statements`:

```
var resource = allocateResource();
try {
    ...
} finally {
    resource.deallocate();
}
```

If one of the try_statements is a return, then the try block is executed afterward (immediately before leaving the function or method; see the examples that follow).

Examples

Any value can be thrown:

```
function throwIt(exception) {
    try {
        throw exception;
    } catch (e) {
        console.log('Caught: '+e);
    }
}
```

Here is the interaction:

```
> throwIt(3);
Caught: 3
> throwIt('hello');
Caught: hello
> throwIt(new Error('An error happened'));
Caught: Error: An error happened
```

finally is always executed:

```
function throwsError() {
    throw new Error('Sorry...');
}
function cleansUp() {
    try {
        throwsError();
    } finally {
        console.log('Performing clean-up');
    }
}
```

Here is the interaction:

```
> cleansUp();
Performing clean-up
Error: Sorry...
```

finally is executed *after* a return statement:

```
function idLog(x) {
    try {
        console.log(x);
        return 'result';
    } finally {
        console.log("FINALLY");
    }
}
```

Here is the interaction:

```
> idLog('arg')
arg
FINALLY
'result'
```

The return value is queued before executing `finally`:

```
var count = 0;
function countUp() {
    try {
        return count;
    } finally {
        count++;   // (1)
    }
}
```

By the time statement (1) is executed, the value of count has already been queued for returning:

```
> countUp()
0
> count
1
```

Error Constructors

ECMAScript standardizes the following error constructors. The descriptions are quoted from the ECMAScript 5 specification:

- `Error` is a generic constructor for errors. All other error constructors mentioned here are subconstructors.

- `EvalError` "is not currently used within this specification. This object remains for compatibility with previous editions of this specification."

- `RangeError` "indicates a numeric value has exceeded the allowable range." For example:

    ```
    > new Array(-1)
    RangeError: Invalid array length
    ```

- `ReferenceError` "indicates that an invalid reference value has been detected." Usually, this is an unknown variable. For example:

    ```
    > unknownVariable
    ReferenceError: unknownVariable is not defined
    ```

- `SyntaxError` "indicates that a parsing error has occurred"—for example, while parsing code via `eval()`:

    ```
    > eval('3 +')
    SyntaxError: Unexpected end of file
    ```

- `TypeError` "indicates the actual type of an operand is different than the expected type." For example:

    ```
    > undefined.foo
    TypeError: Cannot read property 'foo' of undefined
    ```

- `URIError` "indicates that one of the global URI handling functions was used in a way that is incompatible with its definition." For example:

    ```
    > decodeURI('%2')
    URIError: URI malformed
    ```

Here are the properties of errors:

`message`
: The error message.

`name`
: The name of the error.

`stack`
: A stack trace. This is nonstandard, but is available on many platforms—for example, Chrome, Node.js, and Firefox.

Stack Traces

The usual sources of errors are either external (wrong input, missing file, etc.) or internal (a bug in the program). Especially in the latter case, you will get unexpected exceptions and need to debug. Often you don't have a debugger running. For "manual" debugging, two pieces of information are helpful:

1. Data: What values do variables have?

2. Execution: In what line did the exception happen, and what function calls were active?

You can put some of the first item (data) into either the message or the properties of an exception object. The second item (execution) is supported on many JavaScript engines

---

via *stack traces*, snapshots of the call stack when the exception objects were created. The following example prints a stack trace:

```
function catchit() {
    try {
        throwit();
    } catch(e) {
        console.log(e.stack); // print stack trace
    }
}
function throwit() {
    throw new Error('');
}
```

Here's the interaction:

```
> catchit()
Error
    at throwit (~/examples/throwcatch.js:9:11)
    at catchit (~/examples/throwcatch.js:3:9)
    at repl:1:5
```

Implementing Your Own Error Constructor

If you want stack traces, you need the services of the built-in error constructors. You can use an existing constructor and attach your own data to it. Or you can create a subconstructor, whose instances can be distinguished from those of other error constructors via `instanceof`. Alas, doing so (for built-in constructors) is complicated; see Chapter 28 to learn how to do it.

CHAPTER 15

Functions

Functions are values that can be called. One way of defining a function is called a *function declaration*. For example, the following code defines the function id that has a single parameter, x:

```
function id(x) {
    return x;
}
```

The return statement returns a value from id. You can call a function by mentioning its name, followed by arguments in parentheses:

```
> id('hello')
'hello'
```

If you don't return anything from a function, undefined is returned (implicitly):

```
> function f() { }
> f()
undefined
```

This section showed just one way of defining and one way of calling a function. Others are described later.

The Three Roles of Functions in JavaScript

Once you have defined a function as just shown, it can play several roles:

Nonmethod function ("normal function")
    You can call a function directly. Then it works as a normal function. Here's an example invocation:

    ```
    id('hello')
    ```

    By convention, the names of normal functions start with lowercase letters.

Constructor

You can invoke a function via the new operator. Then it becomes a constructor, a factory for objects. Here's an example invocation:

```
new Date()
```

By convention, the names of constructors start with uppercase letters.

Method

You can store a function in a property of an object, which turns it into a *method* that you can invoke via that object. Here's an example invocation:

```
obj.method()
```

By convention, the names of methods start with lowercase letters.

Nonmethod functions are explained in this chapter; constructors and methods are explained in Chapter 17.

Terminology: "Parameter" Versus "Argument"

The terms *parameter* and *argument* are often used interchangeably, because the context usually makes it clear what the intended meaning is. The following is a rule of thumb for distinguishing them.

- *Parameters* are used to define a function. They are also called formal parameters and formal arguments. In the following example, param1 and param2 are parameters:

  ```
  function foo(param1, param2) {
      ...
  }
  ```

- *Arguments* are used to invoke a function. They are also called actual parameters and actual arguments. In the following example, 3 and 7 are arguments:

  ```
  foo(3, 7);
  ```

Defining Functions

This section describes three ways to create a function:

- Via a function expression
- Via a function declaration
- Via the constructor Function()

All functions are objects, instances of Function:

```
function id(x) {
    return x;
}
console.log(id instanceof Function); // true
```

Therefore, functions get their methods from `Function.prototype`.

Function Expressions

A function expression produces a value—a function object. For example:

```
var add = function (x, y) { return x + y };
console.log(add(2, 3)); // 5
```

The preceding code assigned the result of a function expression to the variable `add` and called it via that variable. The value produced by a function expression can be assigned to a variable (as shown in the last example), passed as an argument to another function, and more. Because normal function expressions don't have a name, they are also called *anonymous function expressions*.

Named function expressions

You can give a function expression a name. *Named function expressions* allow a function expression to refer to itself, which is useful for self-recursion:

```
var fac = function me(n) {
    if (n > 0) {
        return n * me(n-1);
    } else {
        return 1;
    }
};
console.log(fac(3)); // 6
```

> The name of a named function expression is only accessible inside the function expression:
>
> ```
> var repeat = function me(n, str) {
>     return n > 0 ? str + me(n-1, str) : '';
> };
> console.log(repeat(3, 'Yeah')); // YeahYeahYeah
> console.log(me); // ReferenceError: me is not defined
> ```

Function Declarations

The following is a function declaration:

```
function add(x, y) {
    return x + y;
}
```

The preceding looks like a function expression, but it is a statement (see "Expressions Versus Statements" on page 54). It is roughly equivalent to the following code:

```
var add = function (x, y) {
    return x + y;
};
```

In other words, a function declaration declares a new variable, creates a function object, and assigns it to the variable.

The Function Constructor

The constructor `Function()` evaluates JavaScript code stored in strings. For example, the following code is equivalent to the previous example:

```
var add = new Function('x', 'y', 'return x + y');
```

However, this way of defining a function is slow and keeps code in strings (inaccessible to tools). Therefore, it is much better to use a function expression or a function declaration if possible. "Evaluating Code Using new Function()" on page 350 explains `Function()` in more detail; it works similarly to `eval()`.

Hoisting

Hoisting means "moving to the beginning of a scope." Function declarations are hoisted completely, variable declarations only partially.

Function declarations are completely hoisted. That allows you to call a function before it has been declared:

```
foo();
function foo() {  // this function is hoisted
    ...
}
```

The reason the preceding code works is that JavaScript engines move the declaration of `foo` to the beginning of the scope. They execute the code as if it looked like this:

```
function foo() {
    ...
}
foo();
```

`var` declarations are hoisted, too, but only the declarations, not assignments made with them. Therefore, using a `var` declaration and a function expression similarly to the previous example results in an error:

```
foo();  // TypeError: undefined is not a function
var foo = function foo() {
    ...
};
```

Only the variable declaration is hoisted. The engine executes the preceding code as:

```
var foo;
foo();  // TypeError: undefined is not a function
foo = function foo() {
    ...
};
```

The Name of a Function

Most JavaScript engines support the nonstandard property `name` for function objects. Function declarations have it:

```
> function f1() {}
> f1.name
'f1'
```

The name of anonymous function expressions is the empty string:

```
> var f2 = function () {};
> f2.name
' '
```

Named function expressions, however, do have a name:

```
> var f3 = function myName() {};
> f3.name
'myName'
```

The name of a function is useful for debugging. Some people always give their function expressions names for that reason.

Which Is Better: A Function Declaration or a Function Expression?

Should you prefer a function declaration like the following?

```
function id(x) {
    return x;
}
```

Or the equivalent combination of a `var` declaration plus a function expression?

```
var id = function (x) {
    return x;
};
```

They are basically the same, but function declarations have two advantages over function expressions:

- They are hoisted (see "Hoisting" on page 168), so you can call them before they appear in the source code.

- They have a name (see "The Name of a Function" on page 169). However, JavaScript engines are getting better at inferring the names of anonymous function expressions.

More Control over Function Calls: call(), apply(), and bind()

call(), apply(), and bind() are methods that all functions have (remember that functions are objects and therefore have methods). They can supply a value for this when invoking a method and thus are mainly interesting in an object-oriented context (see "Calling Functions While Setting this: call(), apply(), and bind()" on page 204). This section explains two use cases for nonmethods.

func.apply(thisValue, argArray)

This method uses the elements of argArray as arguments while calling the function func; that is, the following two expressions are equivalent:

```
func(arg1, arg2, arg3)
func.apply(null, [arg1, arg2, arg3])
```

thisValue is the value that this has while executing func. It is not needed in a non-object-oriented setting and is thus null here.

apply() is useful whenever a function accepts multiple arguments in an array-like manner, but not an array.

Thanks to apply(), we can use Math.max() (see "Other Functions" on page 330) to determine the maximum element of an array:

```
> Math.max(17, 33, 2)
33
> Math.max.apply(null, [17, 33, 2])
33
```

func.bind(thisValue, arg1, ..., argN)

This performs *partial function application*—a new function is created that calls func with this set to thisValue and the following arguments: first arg1 until argN, and then the actual arguments of the new function. thisValue is not needed in the following non-object-oriented setting, which is why it is null.

Here, we use `bind()` to create a new function `plus1()` that is like `add()`, but only requires the parameter y, because x is always 1:

```
function add(x, y) {
    return x + y;
}
var plus1 = add.bind(null, 1);
console.log(plus1(5));  // 6
```

In other words, we have created a new function that is equivalent to the following code:

```
function plus1(y) {
    return add(1, y);
}
```

Handling Missing or Extra Parameters

JavaScript does not enforce a function's arity: you can call it with any number of actual parameters, independent of what formal parameters have been defined. Hence, the number of actual parameters and formal parameters can differ in two ways:

More actual parameters than formal parameters
    The extra parameters are ignored but can be retrieved via the special array-like variable `arguments` (discussed momentarily).

Fewer actual parameters than formal parameters
    The missing formal parameters all have the value `undefined`.

All Parameters by Index: The Special Variable arguments

The special variable `arguments` exists only inside functions (including methods). It is an array-like object that holds all of the actual parameters of the current function call. The following code uses it:

```
function logArgs() {
    for (var i=0; i<arguments.length; i++) {
        console.log(i+'. '+arguments[i]);
    }
}
```

And here is the interaction:

```
> logArgs('hello', 'world')
0. hello
1. world
```

`arguments` has the following characteristics:

- It is array-like, but not an array. On one hand, it has a property `length`, and individual parameters can be read and written by index.

On the other hand, arguments is not an array, it is only similar to one. It has none of the array methods (slice(), forEach(), etc.). Thankfully, you can borrow array methods or convert arguments to an array, as explained in "Array-Like Objects and Generic Methods" on page 262.

- It is an object, so all object methods and operators are available. For example, you can use the in operator ("Iteration and Detection of Properties" on page 217) to check whether arguments "has" a given index:

```
> function f() { return 1 in arguments }
> f('a')
false
> f('a', 'b')
true
```

You can use hasOwnProperty() ("Iteration and Detection of Properties" on page 217) in a similar manner:

```
> function g() { return arguments.hasOwnProperty(1) }
> g('a', 'b')
true
```

Deprecated features of arguments

Strict mode drops several of the more unusual features of arguments:

- arguments.callee refers to the current function. It is mainly used to do self-recursion in anonymous functions, and is not allowed in strict mode. As a work-around, use a named function expression (see "Named function expressions" on page 167), which can refer to itself via its name.

- In nonstrict mode, arguments stays up-to-date if you change a parameter:

```
function sloppyFunc(param) {
    param = 'changed';
    return arguments[0];
}
console.log(sloppyFunc('value'));  // changed
```

But this kind of updating is not done in strict mode:

```
function strictFunc(param) {
    'use strict';
    param = 'changed';
    return arguments[0];
}
console.log(strictFunc('value'));  // value
```

- Strict mode forbids assigning to the variable arguments (e.g., via arguments++). Assigning to elements and properties is still allowed.

Mandatory Parameters, Enforcing a Minimum Arity

There are three ways to find out whether a parameter is missing. First, you can check if it is undefined:

```
function foo(mandatory, optional) {
    if (mandatory === undefined) {
        throw new Error('Missing parameter: mandatory');
    }
}
```

Second, you can interpret the parameter as a boolean. Then undefined is considered false. However, there is a caveat: several other values are also considered false (see "Truthy and Falsy Values" on page 98), so the check cannot distinguish between, say, 0 and a missing parameter:

```
if (!mandatory) {
    throw new Error('Missing parameter: mandatory');
}
```

Third, you can also check the length of arguments to enforce a minimum arity:

```
if (arguments.length < 1) {
    throw new Error('You need to provide at least 1 argument');
}
```

The last approach differs from the other ones:

- The first two approaches don't distinguish between foo() and foo(undefined). In both cases, an exception is thrown.

- The third approach throws an exception for foo() and sets optional to unde fined for foo(undefined).

Optional Parameters

If a parameter is optional, it means that you give it a default value if it is missing. Similarly to mandatory parameters, there are four alternatives.

First, check for undefined:

```
function bar(arg1, arg2, optional) {
    if (optional === undefined) {
        optional = 'default value';
    }
}
```

Second, interpret optional as a boolean:

```
if (!optional) {
    optional = 'default value';
}
```

Third, you can use the Or operator || (see "Logical Or (||)" on page 100), which returns the left operand, if it isn't falsy. Otherwise, it returns the right operand:

```
// Or operator: use left operand if it isn't falsy
optional = optional || 'default value';
```

Fourth, you can check a function's arity via `arguments.length`:

```
if (arguments.length < 3) {
    optional = 'default value';
}
```

Again, the last approach differs from the other ones:

- The first three approaches don't distinguish between `bar(1, 2)` and `bar(1, 2, undefined)`. In both cases, `optional` is `'default value'`.
- The fourth approach sets `optional` to `'default value'` for `bar(1, 2)` and leaves it `undefined` (i.e., unchanged) for `bar(1, 2, undefined)`.

Another possibility is to hand in optional parameters as *named parameters*, as properties of an object literal (see "Named Parameters" on page 176).

Simulating Pass-by-Reference Parameters

In JavaScript, you cannot pass parameters by reference; that is, if you pass a variable to a function, its value is copied and handed to the function (pass by value). Therefore, the function can't change the variable. If you need to do so, you must wrap the value of the variable in an array.

This example demonstates a function that increments a variable:

```
function incRef(numberRef) {
    numberRef[0]++;
}
var n = [7];
incRef(n);
console.log(n[0]);  // 8
```

Pitfall: Unexpected Optional Parameters

If you hand a function c as a parameter to another function f, then you have to be aware of two signatures:

- The signature that f expects its parameter to have. f might provide several parameters, and c can decide how many (if any) of them to use.

- The actual signature of c. For example, it might support optional parameters.

If the two diverge, then you can get unexpected results: c could have optional parameters that you don't know about and that would interpret additional arguments provided by f incorrectly.

As an example, consider the array method map() (see "Transformation Methods" on page 293) whose parameter is normally a function with a single parameter:

```
> [ 1, 2, 3 ].map(function (x) { return x * x })
[ 1, 4, 9 ]
```

One function that you could pass as an argument is parseInt() (see "Integers via parseInt()" on page 120):

```
> parseInt('1024')
1024
```

You may (incorrectly) think that map() provides only a single argument and that parseInt() accepts only a single argument. Then you would be surprised by the following result:

```
> [ '1', '2', '3' ].map(parseInt)
[ 1, NaN, NaN ]
```

map() expects a function with the following signature:

```
function (element, index, array)
```

But parseInt() has the following signature:

```
parseInt(string, radix?)
```

Thus, map() not only fills in string (via element), but also radix (via index). That means that the values of the preceding array are produced as follows:

```
> parseInt('1', 0)
1
> parseInt('2', 1)
NaN
> parseInt('3', 2)
NaN
```

To sum up, be careful with functions and methods whose signature you are not sure about. If you use them, it often makes sense to be explicit about what parameters are received and what parameters are passed on. That is achieved via a callback:

```
> ['1', '2', '3'].map(function (x) { return parseInt(x, 10) })
[ 1, 2, 3 ]
```

Named Parameters

When calling a function (or method) in a programming language, you must map the actual parameters (specified by the caller) to the formal parameters (of a function definition). There are two common ways to do so:

- *Positional parameters* are mapped by position. The first actual parameter is mapped to the first formal parameter, the second actual to the second formal, and so on.
- *Named parameters* use *names* (labels) to perform the mapping. Names are associated with formal parameters in a function definition and label actual parameters in a function call. It does not matter in which order named parameters appear, as long as they are correctly labeled.

Named parameters have two main benefits: they provide descriptions for arguments in function calls and they work well for optional parameters. I'll first explain the benefits and then show you how to simulate named parameters in JavaScript via object literals.

Named Parameters as Descriptions

As soon as a function has more than one parameter, you might get confused about what each parameter is used for. For example, let's say you have a function, `selectEntries()`, that returns entries from a database. Given the following function call:

```
selectEntries(3, 20, 2);
```

what do these two numbers mean? Python supports named parameters, and they make it easy to figure out what is going on:

```
selectEntries(start=3, end=20, step=2)  # Python syntax
```

Optional Named Parameters

Optional positional parameters work well only if they are omitted at the end. Anywhere else, you have to insert placeholders such as `null` so that the remaining parameters have correct positions. With optional named parameters, that is not an issue. You can easily omit any of them. Here are some examples:

```
# Python syntax
selectEntries(step=2)
selectEntries(end=20, start=3)
selectEntries()
```

Simulating Named Parameters in JavaScript

JavaScript does not have native support for named parameters like Python and many other languages. But there is a reasonably elegant simulation: name parameters via an object literal, passed as a single actual parameter. When you use this technique, an invocation of `selectEntries()` looks like:

```
selectEntries({ start: 3, end: 20, step: 2 });
```

The function receives an object with the properties `start`, `end`, and `step`. You can omit any of them:

```
selectEntries({ step: 2 });
selectEntries({ end: 20, start: 3 });
selectEntries();
```

You could implement `selectEntries()` as follows:

```
function selectEntries(options) {
    options = options || {};
    var start = options.start || 0;
    var end = options.end || getDbLength();
    var step = options.step || 1;
    ...
}
```

You can also combine positional parameters with named parameters. It is customary for the latter to come last:

```
selectEntries(posArg1, posArg2, { namedArg1: 7, namedArg2: true });
```

 In JavaScript, the pattern for named parameters shown here is sometimes called *options* or *option object* (e.g., by the jQuery documentation).

CHAPTER 16

Variables: Scopes, Environments, and Closures

This chapter first explains how to use variables and then goes into detail on how they work (environments, closures, etc.).

Declaring a Variable

In JavaScript, you declare a variable via a `var` statement before you use it:

```
var foo;
foo = 3; // OK, has been declared
bar = 5; // not OK, an undeclared variable
```

You can also combine a declaration with an assignment, to immediately initialize a variable:

```
var foo = 3;
```

The value of an uninitialized variable is `undefined`:

```
> var x;
> x
undefined
```

Background: Static Versus Dynamic

There are two angles from which you can examine the workings of a program:

Statically (or lexically)
    You examine the program as it exists in source code, without running it. Given the following code, we can make the static assertion that function g is nested inside function f:

```
function f() {
    function g() {
    }
}
```

The adjective *lexical* is used synonymously with *static*, because both pertain to the *lexicon* (the words, the source) of the program.

Dynamically

You examine what happens while executing the program ("at runtime"). Given the following code:

```
function g() {
}
function f() {
    g();
}
```

when we call f(), it calls g(). During runtime, g being called by f represents a dynamic relationship.

Background: The Scope of a Variable

For the rest of this chapter, you should understand the following concepts:

The scope of a variable

The scope of a variable are the locations where it is accessible. For example:

```
function foo() {
    var x;
}
```

Here, the *direct scope* of x is the function foo().

Lexical scoping

Variables in JavaScript are *lexically scoped*, so the static structure of a program determines the scope of a variable (it is not influenced by, say, where a function is called from).

Nested scopes

If scopes are nested within the direct scope of a variable, then the variable is accessible in all of those scopes:

```
function foo(arg) {
    function bar() {
        console.log('arg: '+arg);
    }
    bar();
}
console.log(foo('hello')); // arg: hello
```

The direct scope of arg is foo(), but it is also accessible in the nested scope bar(). With regard to nesting, foo() is the *outer scope* and bar() is the *inner scope*.

Shadowing

If a scope declares a variable that has the same name as one in a surrounding scope, access to the outer variable is blocked in the inner scope and all scopes nested inside it. Changes to the inner variable do not affect the outer variable, which is accessible again after the inner scope is left:

```
var x = "global";
function f() {
    var x = "local";
    console.log(x); // local
}
f();
console.log(x); // global
```

Inside the function f(), the global x is shadowed by a local x.

Variables Are Function-Scoped

Most mainstream languages are *block-scoped*: variables "live inside" the innermost surrounding code block. Here is an example from Java:

```
public static void main(String[] args) {
    { // block starts
        int foo = 4;
    } // block ends
    System.out.println(foo); // Error: cannot find symbol
}
```

In the preceding code, the variable foo is accessible only inside the block that directly surrounds it. If we try to access it after the end of the block, we get a compilation error.

In contrast, JavaScript's variables are *function-scoped*: only functions introduce new scopes; blocks are ignored when it comes to scoping. For example:

```
function main() {
    { // block starts
        var foo = 4;
    } // block ends
    console.log(foo); // 4
}
```

Put another way, foo is accessible within all of main(), not just inside the block.

Variable Declarations Are Hoisted

JavaScript *hoists* all variable declarations, it moves them to the beginning of their direct scopes. This makes it clear what happens if a variable is accessed before it has been declared:

```
function f() {
    console.log(bar);  // undefined
    var bar = 'abc';
    console.log(bar);  // abc
}
```

We can see that the variable bar already exists in the first line of f(), but it does not have a value yet; that is, the declaration has been hoisted, but not the assignment. Java-Script executes f() as if its code were:

```
function f() {
    var bar;
    console.log(bar);  // undefined
    bar = 'abc';
    console.log(bar);  // abc
}
```

If you declare a variable that has already been declared, nothing happens (the variable's value is unchanged):

```
> var x = 123;
> var x;
> x
123
```

Each function declaration is also hoisted, but in a slightly different manner. The complete function is hoisted, not just the creation of the variable in which it is stored (see "Hoisting" on page 168).

Best practice: be aware of hoisting, but don't be scared of it

Some JavaScript style guides recommend that you only put variable declarations at the beginning of a function, in order to avoid being tricked by hoisting. If your function is relatively small (which it should be anyway), then you can afford to relax that rule a bit and declare variables close to where they are used (e.g., inside a for loop). That better encapsulates pieces of code. Obviously, you should be aware that that encapsulation is only conceptual, because function-wide hoisting still happens.

Pitfall: Assigning to an Undeclared Variable Makes It Global

In sloppy mode, assigning to a variable that hasn't been declared via var creates a global variable:

```
> function sloppyFunc() { x = 123 }
> sloppyFunc()
> x
123
```

Thankfully, strict mode throws an exception when that happens:

```
> function strictFunc() { 'use strict'; x = 123 }
> strictFunc()
ReferenceError: x is not defined
```

Introducing a New Scope via an IIFE

You typically introduce a new scope to restrict the lifetime of a variable. One example where you may want to do so is the "then" part of an if statement: it is executed only if the condition holds; and if it exclusively uses helper variables, we don't want them to "leak out" into the surrounding scope:

```
function f() {
    if (condition) {
        var tmp = ...;
        ...
    }
    // tmp still exists here
    // => not what we want
}
```

If you want to introduce a new scope for the then block, you can define a function and immediately invoke it. This is a workaround, a simulation of block scoping:

```
function f() {
    if (condition) {
```

```
    (function () {  // open block
        var tmp = ...;
        ...
    }());  // close block
  }
}
```

This is a common pattern in JavaScript. Ben Alman suggested it be called *immediately invoked function expression* (*http://bit.ly/i-ife*) (IIFE, pronounced "iffy"). In general, an IIFE looks like this:

```
(function () { // open IIFE
    // inside IIFE
}()); // close IIFE
```

Here are some things to note about an IIFE:

It is immediately invoked

> The parentheses following the closing brace of the function immediately invoke it. That means its body is executed right away.

It must be an expression

> If a statement starts with the keyword function, the parser expects it to be a function declaration (see "Expressions Versus Statements" on page 54). But a function declaration cannot be immediately invoked. Thus, we tell the parser that the keyword function is the beginning of a function expression by starting the statement with an open parenthesis. Inside parentheses, there can only be expressions.

The trailing semicolon is required

> If you forget it between two IIFEs, then your code won't work anymore:

> ```
> (function () {
>     ...
> }()) // no semicolon
> (function () {
>     ...
> }());
> ```

The preceding code is interpreted as a function call—the first IIFE (including the parentheses) is the function to be called, and the second IIFE is the parameter.

> An IIFE incurs costs (both cognitively and performance-wise), so it rarely makes sense to use it inside an if statement. The preceding example was chosen for didactic reasons.

IIFE Variation: Prefix Operators

You can also enforce the expression context via prefix operators. For example, you can do so via the logical Not operator:

```
!function () { // open IIFE
    // inside IIFE
}(); // close IIFE
```

or via the void operator (see "The void Operator" on page 90):

```
void function () { // open IIFE
    // inside IIFE
}(); // close IIFE
```

The advantage of using prefix operators is that forgetting the terminating semicolon does not cause trouble.

IIFE Variation: Already Inside Expression Context

Note that enforcing the expression context for an IIFE is not necessary, if you are already in the expression context. Then you need no parentheses or prefix operators. For example:

```
var File = function () { // open IIFE
    var UNTITLED = 'Untitled';
    function File(name) {
        this.name = name || UNTITLED;
    }
    return File;
}(); // close IIFE
```

In the preceding example, there are two different variables that have the name File. On one hand, there is the function that is only directly accessible inside the IIFE. On the other hand, there is the variable that is declared in the first line. It is assigned the value that is returned in the IIFE.

IIFE Variation: An IIFE with Parameters

You can use parameters to define variables for the inside of the IIFE:

```
var x = 23;
(function (twice) {
    console.log(twice);
}(x * 2));
```

This is similar to:

```
var x = 23;
(function () {
    var twice = x * 2;
```

```
    console.log(twice);
}());
```

IIFE Applications

An IIFE enables you to attach private data to a function. Then you don't have to declare a global variable and can tightly package the function with its state. You avoid polluting the global namespace:

```
var setValue = function () {
    var prevValue;
    return function (value) { // define setValue
        if (value !== prevValue) {
            console.log('Changed: ' + value);
            prevValue = value;
        }
    };
}();
```

Other applications of IIFEs are mentioned elsewhere in this book:

- Avoiding global variables; hiding variables from global scope (see "Best Practice: Avoid Creating Global Variables" on page 187)
- Creating fresh environments; avoiding sharing (see "Pitfall: Inadvertently Sharing an Environment" on page 195)
- Keeping global data private to all of a constructor (see "Keeping global data private to all of a constructor" on page 250)
- Attaching global data to a singleton object (see "Attaching private global data to a singleton object" on page 249)
- Attaching global data to a method (see "Attaching global data to a method" on page 250)

Global Variables

The scope containing all of a program is called *global scope* or *program scope*. This is the scope you are in when entering a script (be it a `<script>` tag in a web page or be it a *.js* file). Inside the global scope, you can create a nested scope by defining a function. Inside such a function, you can again nest scopes. Each scope has access to its own variables and to the variables in the scopes that surround it. As the global scope surrounds all other scopes, its variables can be accessed everywhere:

```
// here we are in global scope
var globalVariable = 'xyz';
function f() {
    var localVariable = true;
```

```
function g() {
    var anotherLocalVariable = 123;

    // All variables of surround scopes are accessible
    localVariable = false;
    globalVariable = 'abc';
}
}
// here we are again in global scope
```

Best Practice: Avoid Creating Global Variables

Global variables have two disadvantages. First, pieces of software that rely on global variables are subject to side effects; they are less robust, behave less predictably, and are less reusable.

Second, all of the JavaScript on a web page shares the same global variables: your code, built-ins, analytics code, social media buttons, and so on. That means that name clashes can become a problem. That is why it is best to hide as many variables from the global scope as possible. For example, don't do this:

```
<!-- Don't do this -->
<script>
    // Global scope
    var tmp = generateData();
    processData(tmp);
    persistData(tmp);
</script>
```

The variable tmp becomes global, because its declaration is executed in global scope. But it is only used locally. Hence, we can use an IIFE (see "Introducing a New Scope via an IIFE" on page 183) to hide it inside a nested scope:

```
<script>
    (function () {  // open IIFE
        // Local scope
        var tmp = generateData();
        processData(tmp);
        persistData(tmp);
    }());  // close IIFE
</script>
```

Module Systems Lead to Fewer Globals

Thankfully, module systems (see "Module Systems" on page 411) mostly eliminate the problem of global variables, because modules don't interface via the global scope and because each module has its own scope for module-global variables.

The Global Object

The ECMAScript specification uses the internal data structure *environment* to store variables (see "Environments: Managing Variables" on page 190). The language has the somewhat unusual feature of making the environment for global variables accessible via an object, the so-called *global object*. The global object can be used to create, read, and change global variables. In global scope, this points to it:

```
> var foo = 'hello';
> this.foo  // read global variable
'hello'

> this.bar = 'world';  // create global variable
> bar
'world'
```

Note that the global object has prototypes. If you want to list all of its (own and inherited) properties, you need a function such as getAllPropertyNames() from "Listing All Property Keys" on page 218:

```
> getAllPropertyNames(window).sort().slice(0, 5)
[ 'AnalyserNode', 'Array', 'ArrayBuffer', 'Attr', 'Audio' ]
```

JavaScript creator Brendan Eich considers the global object one of his "biggest regrets" (*http://mzl.la/1oOeCif*). It affects performance negatively, makes the implementation of variable scoping more complicated, and leads to less modular code.

Cross-Platform Considerations

Browsers and Node.js have global variables for referring to the global object. Unfortunately, they are different:

- Browsers include window, which is standardized as part of the Document Object Model (DOM), not as part of ECMAScript 5. There is one global object per frame or window.

- Node.js contains global, which is a Node.js-specific variable. Each module has its own scope in which this points to an object with that scopes variables. Accordingly, this and global are different inside modules.

On both platforms, this refers to the global object, but only when you are in global scope. That is almost never the case on Node.js. If you want to access the global object in a cross-platform manner, you can use a pattern such as the following:

```
(function (glob) {
    // glob points to global object
}(typeof window !== 'undefined' ? window : global));
```

From now on, I use `window` to refer to the global object, but in cross-platform code, you should use the preceding pattern and `glob` instead.

Use Cases for window

This section describes use cases for accessing global variables via `window`. But the general rule is: avoid doing that as much as you can.

Use case: marking global variables

The prefix `window` is a visual clue that code is referring to a global variable and not to a local one:

```
var foo = 123;
(function () {
    console.log(window.foo);  // 123
}());
```

However, this makes your code brittle. It ceases to work as soon as you move `foo` from global scope to another surrounding scope:

```
(function () {
    var foo = 123;
    console.log(window.foo);  // undefined
}());
```

Thus, it is better to refer to `foo` as a variable, not as a property of `window`. If you want to make it obvious that `foo` is a global or global-like variable, you can add a name prefix such as `g_`:

```
var g_foo = 123;
(function () {
    console.log(g_foo);
}());
```

Use case: built-ins

I prefer not to refer to built-in global variables via `window`. They are well-known names, so you gain little from an indicator that they are global. And the prefixed `window` adds clutter:

```
window.isNaN(...)  // no
isNaN(...)  // yes
```

Use case: style checkers

When you are working with a style checking tool such as JSLint and JSHint, using `window` means that you don't get an error when referring to a global variable that is not declared in the current file. However, both tools provide ways to tell them about such variables and prevent such errors (search for "global variable" in their documentation).

Use case: checking whether a global variable exists

It's not a frequent use case, but shims and polyfills especially (see "Shims Versus Polyfills" on page 405) need to check whether a global variable `someVariable` exists. In that case, `window` helps:

```
if (window.someVariable) { ... }
```

This is a safe way of performing this check. The following statement throws an exception if `someVariable` has not been declared:

```
// Don't do this
if (someVariable) { ... }
```

There are two additional ways in which you can check via `window`; they are roughly equivalent, but a little more explicit:

```
if (window.someVariable !== undefined) { ... }
if ('someVariable' in window) { ... }
```

The general way of checking whether a variable exists (and has a value) is via `typeof` (see "typeof: Categorizing Primitives" on page 92):

```
if (typeof someVariable !== 'undefined') { ... }
```

Use case: creating things in global scope

`window` lets you add things to the global scope (even if you are in a nested scope), and it lets you do so conditionally:

```
if (!window.someApiFunction) {
    window.someApiFunction = ...;
}
```

It is normally best to add things to the global scope via `var`, while you are in the global scope. However, `window` provides a clean way of making additions conditionally.

Environments: Managing Variables

 Environments are an advanced topic. They are a detail of JavaScript's internals. Read this section if you want to get a deeper understanding of how variables work.

Variables come into existence when program execution enters their scope. Then they need storage space. The data structure that provides that storage space is called an *environment* in JavaScript. It maps variable names to values. Its structure is very similar

---

to that of JavaScript objects. Environments sometimes live on after you leave their scope. Therefore, they are stored on a heap, not on a stack.

Variables are passed on in two ways. There are two dimensions to them, if you will:

Dynamic dimension: invoking functions

Every time a function is invoked, it needs new storage for its parameters and variables. After it is finished, that storage can usually be reclaimed. As an example, take the following implementation of the faculty function. It calls itself recursively several times and each time, it needs fresh storage for n:

```
function fac(n) {
    if (n <= 1) {
        return 1;
    }
    return n * fac(n - 1);
}
```

Lexical (static) dimension: staying connected to your surrounding scopes

No matter how often a function is called, it always needs access to both its own (fresh) local variables and the variables of the surrounding scopes. For example, the following function, doNTimes, has a helper function, doNTimesRec, inside it. When doNTimesRec calls itself several times, a new environment is created each time. However, doNTimesRec also stays connected to the single environment of doN Times during those calls (similar to all functions sharing a single global environment). doNTimesRec needs that connection to access action in line (1):

```
function doNTimes(n, action) {
    function doNTimesRec(x) {
        if (x >= 1) {
            action();  // (1)
            doNTimesRec(x-1);
        }
    }
    doNTimesRec(n);
}
```

These two dimensions are handled as follows:

Dynamic dimension: stack of execution contexts

Each time a function is invoked, a new *environment* is created to map identifiers (of parameters and variables) to values. To handle recursion, *execution contexts*—references to environments—are managed in a stack. That stack mirrors the call stack.

Lexical dimension: chain of environments

To support this dimension, a function records the scope it was created in via the internal property [[Scope]]. When a function is called, an environment is created for the new scope that is entered. That environment has a field called outer that points to the outer scope's environment and is set up via [[Scope]]. Therefore, there is always a chain of environments, starting with the currently active environment, continuing with its outer environment, and so on. Every chain ends with the global environment (the scope of all initially invoked functions). The field outer of the global environment is null.

To resolve an identifier, the complete environment chain is traversed, starting with the active environment.

Let's look at an example:

```
function myFunction(myParam) {
    var myVar = 123;
    return myFloat;
}
var myFloat = 1.3;
// Step 1
myFunction('abc');  // Step 2
```

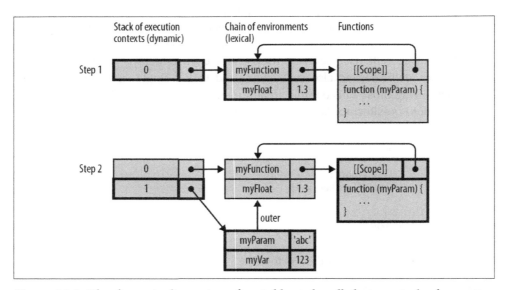

Figure 16-1. The dynamic dimension of variables is handled via a stack of execution contexts, and the static dimension is handled by chaining environments. The active execution contexts, environments, and functions are highlighted. Step 1 shows those data structures before the function call myFunction(abc). Step 2 shows them during the function call.

Figure 16-1 illustrates what happens when the preceding code is executed:

1. `myFunction` and `myFloat` have been stored in the global environment (#0). Note that the `function` object referred to by `myFunction` points to its scope (the global scope) via the internal property `[[Scope]]`.
2. For the execution of `myFunction('abc')`, a new environment (#1) is created that holds the parameter and the local variable. It refers to its outer environment via `outer` (which is initialized from `myFunction.[[Scope]]`). Thanks to the outer environment, `myFunction` can access `myFloat`.

Closures: Functions Stay Connected to Their Birth Scopes

If a function leaves the scope in which it was created, it stays connected to the variables of that scope (and of the surrounding scopes). For example:

```
function createInc(startValue) {
    return function (step) {
        startValue += step;
        return startValue;
    };
}
```

The function returned by `createInc()` does not lose its connection to `startValue`—the variable provides the function with state that persists across function calls:

```
> var inc = createInc(5);
> inc(1)
6
> inc(2)
8
```

A *closure* is a function plus the connection to the scope in which the function was created. The name stems from the fact that a closure "closes over" the free variables of a function. A variable is free if it is not declared within the function—that is, if it comes "from outside."

Handling Closures via Environments

 This is an advanced section that goes deeper into how closures work. You should be familiar with environments (review "Environments: Managing Variables" on page 190).

A closure is an example of an environment surviving after execution has left its scope. To illustrate how closures work, let's examine the previous interaction with `createInc()` and split it up into four steps (during each step, the active execution context and its environment are highlighted; if a function is active, it is highlighted, too):

1. This step takes place before the interaction, and after the evaluation of the function declaration of `createInc`. An entry for `createInc` has been added to the global environment (#0) and points to a function object.

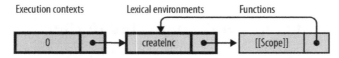

2. This step occurs during the execution of the function call `createInc(5)`. A fresh environment (#1) for `createInc` is created and pushed onto the stack. Its outer environment is the global environment (the same as `createInc.[[Scope]]`). The environment holds the parameter `startValue`.

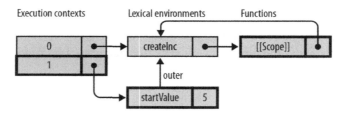

3. This step happens after the assignment to `inc`. After we returned from `createInc`, the execution context pointing to its environment was removed from the stack, but the environment still exists on the heap, because `inc.[[Scope]]` refers to it. `inc` is a closure (function plus birth environment).

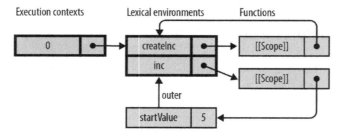

4. This step takes place during the execution of `inc(1)`. A new environment (#1) has been created and an execution context pointing to it has been pushed onto the stack.

Its outer environment is the `[[Scope]]` of inc. The outer environment gives inc access to startValue.

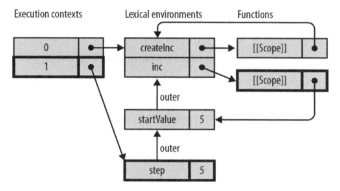

5. This step happens after the execution of `inc(1)`. No reference (execution context, outer field, or `[[Scope]]`) points to inc's environment, anymore. It is therefore not needed and can be removed from the heap.

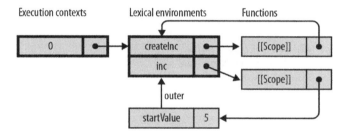

Pitfall: Inadvertently Sharing an Environment

Sometimes the behavior of functions you create is influenced by a variable in the current scope. In JavaScript, that can be problematic, because each function should work with the value that the variable had when the function was created. However, due to functions being closures, the function will always work with the *current* value of the variable. In for loops, that can prevent things from working properly. An example will make things clearer:

```
function f() {
    var result = [];
    for (var i=0; i<3; i++) {
        var func = function () {
            return i;
        };
        result.push(func);
```

```
    }
    return result;
}
console.log(f()[1]());  // 3
```

f returns an array with three functions in it. All of these functions can still access the environment of f and thus i. In fact, they share the same environment. Alas, after the loop is finished, i has the value 3 in that environment. Therefore, all functions return 3.

This is not what we want. To fix things, we need to make a snapshot of the index i before creating a function that uses it. In other words, we want to package each function with the value that i had at the time of the function's creation. We therefore take the following steps:

1. Create a new environment for each function in the returned array.

2. Store (a copy of) the current value of *i* in that environment.

Only functions create environments, so we use an IIFE (see "Introducing a New Scope via an IIFE" on page 183) to accomplish step 1:

```
function f() {
    var result = [];
    for (var i=0; i<3; i++) {
        (function () { // step 1: IIFE
            var pos = i; // step 2: copy
            var func = function () {
                return pos;
            };
            result.push(func);
        }());
    }
    return result;
}
console.log(f()[1]());  // 1
```

Note that the example has real-world relevance, because similar scenarios arise when you add event handlers to DOM elements via loops.

CHAPTER 17

Objects and Inheritance

There are several layers to object-oriented programming (OOP) in JavaScript:

- Layer 1: Object-orientation with single objects (covered in "Layer 1: Single Objects" on page 197)
- Layer 2: Prototype chains of objects (described in "Layer 2: The Prototype Relationship Between Objects" on page 211)
- Layer 3: Constructors as factories for instances, similar to classes in other languages (discussed in "Layer 3: Constructors—Factories for Instances" on page 231)
- Layer 4: Subclassing, creating new constructors by inheriting from existing ones (covered in "Layer 4: Inheritance Between Constructors" on page 251)

Each new layer only depends on prior ones, enabling you to learn JavaScript OOP incrementally. Layers 1 and 2 form a simple core that you can refer back to whenever you are getting confused by the more complicated layers 3 and 4.

Layer 1: Single Objects

Roughly, all objects in JavaScript are maps (dictionaries) from strings to values. A (key, value) entry in an object is called a *property*. The key of a property is always a text string. The value of a property can be any JavaScript value, including a function. *Methods* are properties whose values are functions.

Kinds of Properties

There are three kinds of properties:

Properties (or named data properties)
> Normal properties in an object—that is, mappings from string keys to values. Named data properties include methods. This is by far the most common kind of property.

Accessors (or named accessor properties)
> Special methods whose invocations look like reading or writing properties. Normal properties are storage locations for property values; accessors allow you to compute the values of properties. They are virtual properties, if you will. See "Accessors (Getters and Setters)" on page 221 for details.

Internal properties
> Exist only in the ECMAScript language specification. They are not directly accessible from JavaScript, but there might be indirect ways of accessing them. The specification writes the keys of internal properties in brackets. For example, [[Prototype]] holds the prototype of an object and is readable via Object.getPrototypeOf().

Object Literals

JavaScript's *object literals* allow you to directly create *plain objects* (direct instances of Object). The following code uses an object literal to assign an object to the variable jane. The object has the two properties: name and describe. describe is a method:

```
var jane = {
    name: 'Jane',

    describe: function () {
        return 'Person named '+this.name;  // (1)
    },  // (2)
};
```

1. Use this in methods to refer to the current object (also called the *receiver* of a method invocation).

2. ECMAScript 5 allows a trailing comma (after the last property) in an object literal. Alas, not all older browsers support it. A trailing comma is useful, because you can rearrange properties without having to worry which property is last.

You may get the impression that objects are *only* maps from strings to values. But they are more than that: they are real general-purpose objects. For example, you can use inheritance between objects (see "Layer 2: The Prototype Relationship Between Objects" on page 211), and you can protect objects from being changed. The ability to directly create objects is one of JavaScript's standout features: you can start with concrete objects (no classes needed!) and introduce abstractions later. For example, *constructors*, which are factories for objects (as discussed in "Layer 3: Constructors—Factories for Instances" on page 231), are roughly similar to classes in other languages.

Dot Operator (.): Accessing Properties via Fixed Keys

The dot operator provides a compact syntax for accessing properties. The property keys must be identifiers (consult "Legal Identifiers" on page 60). If you want to read or write properties with arbitrary names, you need to use the bracket operator (see "Bracket Operator ([]): Accessing Properties via Computed Keys" on page 202).

The examples in this section work with the following object:

```
var jane = {
    name: 'Jane',

    describe: function () {
        return 'Person named '+this.name;
    }
};
```

Getting properties

The dot operator lets you "get" a property (read its value). Here are some examples:

```
> jane.name  // get property `name`
'Jane'
> jane.describe  // get property `describe`
[Function]
```

Getting a property that doesn't exist returns undefined:

```
> jane.unknownProperty
undefined
```

Calling methods

The dot operator is also used to call methods:

```
> jane.describe()  // call method `describe`
'Person named Jane'
```

Setting properties

You can use the assignment operator (=) to set the value of a property referred to via the dot notation. For example:

```
> jane.name = 'John';  // set property `name`
> jane.describe()
'Person named John'
```

If a property doesn't exist yet, setting it automatically creates it. If a property already exists, setting it changes its value.

Deleting properties

The `delete` operator lets you completely remove a property (the whole key-value pair) from an object. For example:

```
> var obj = { hello: 'world' };
> delete obj.hello
true
> obj.hello
undefined
```

If you merely set a property to `undefined`, the property still exists and the object still contains its key:

```
> var obj = { foo: 'a', bar: 'b' };

> obj.foo = undefined;
> Object.keys(obj)
[ 'foo', 'bar' ]
```

If you delete the property, its key is gone, too:

```
> delete obj.foo
true
> Object.keys(obj)
[ 'bar' ]
```

`delete` affects only the direct ("own," noninherited) properties of an object. Its prototypes are not touched (see "Deleting an inherited property" on page 217).

 Use the `delete` operator sparingly. Most modern JavaScript engines optimize the performance of instances created by constructors if their "shape" doesn't change (roughly: no properties are removed or added). Deleting a property prevents that optimization.

The return value of delete

`delete` returns `false` if the property is an own property, but cannot be deleted. It returns `true` in all other cases. Following are some examples.

As a preparation, we create one property that can be deleted and another one that can't be deleted ("Getting and Defining Properties via Descriptors" on page 224 explains `Object.defineProperty()`):

```
var obj = {};
Object.defineProperty(obj, 'canBeDeleted', {
    value: 123,
    configurable: true
});
Object.defineProperty(obj, 'cannotBeDeleted', {
    value: 456,
```

```
    configurable: false
});
```

`delete` returns `false` for own properties that can't be deleted:

```
> delete obj.cannotBeDeleted
false
```

`delete` returns `true` in all other cases:

```
> delete obj.doesNotExist
true
> delete obj.canBeDeleted
true
```

`delete` returns `true` even if it doesn't change anything (inherited properties are never removed):

```
> delete obj.toString
true
> obj.toString // still there
[Function: toString]
```

Unusual Property Keys

While you can't use reserved words (such as `var` and `function`) as variable names, you can use them as property keys:

```
> var obj = { var: 'a', function: 'b' };
> obj.var
'a'
> obj.function
'b'
```

Numbers can be used as property keys in object literals, but they are interpreted as strings. The dot operator can only access properties whose keys are identifiers. Therefore, you need the bracket operator (shown in the following example) to access properties whose keys are numbers:

```
> var obj = { 0.7: 'abc' };
> Object.keys(obj)
[ '0.7' ]
> obj['0.7']
'abc'
```

Object literals also allow you to use arbitrary strings (that are neither identifiers nor numbers) as property keys, but you must quote them. Again, you need the bracket operator to access the property values:

```
> var obj = { 'not an identifier': 123 };
> Object.keys(obj)
[ 'not an identifier' ]
```

```
> obj['not an identifier']
123
```

Bracket Operator ([]): Accessing Properties via Computed Keys

While the dot operator works with fixed property keys, the bracket operator allows you to refer to a property via an expression.

Getting properties via the bracket operator

The bracket operator lets you compute the key of a property, via an expression:

```
> var obj = { someProperty: 'abc' };

> obj['some' + 'Property']
'abc'

> var propKey = 'someProperty';
> obj[propKey]
'abc'
```

That also allows you to access properties whose keys are not identifiers:

```
> var obj = { 'not an identifier': 123 };
> obj['not an identifier']
123
```

Note that the bracket operator coerces its interior to string. For example:

```
> var obj = { '6': 'bar' };
> obj[3+3]   // key: the string '6'
'bar'
```

Calling methods via the bracket operator

Calling methods works as you would expect:

```
> var obj = { myMethod: function () { return true } };
> obj['myMethod']()
true
```

Setting properties via the bracket operator

Setting properties works analogously to the dot operator:

```
> var obj = {};
> obj['anotherProperty'] = 'def';
> obj.anotherProperty
'def'
```

Deleting properties via the bracket operator

Deleting properties also works similarly to the dot operator:

```
> var obj = { 'not an identifier': 1, prop: 2 };
> Object.keys(obj)
[ 'not an identifier', 'prop' ]
> delete obj['not an identifier']
true
> Object.keys(obj)
[ 'prop' ]
```

Converting Any Value to an Object

It's not a frequent use case, but sometimes you need to convert an arbitrary value to an object. `Object()`, used as a function (not as a constructor), provides that service. It produces the following results:

Value	Result
(Called with no parameters)	`{}`
`undefined`	`{}`
`null`	`{}`
A boolean `bool`	`new Boolean(bool)`
A number `num`	`new Number(num)`
A string `str`	`new String(str)`
An object `obj`	`obj` (unchanged, nothing to convert)

Here are some examples:

```
> Object(null) instanceof Object
true

> Object(false) instanceof Boolean
true

> var obj = {};
> Object(obj) === obj
true
```

Tthe following function checks whether `value` is an object:

```
function isObject(value) {
    return value === Object(value);
}
```

Note that the preceding function creates an object if `value` isn't an object. You can implement the same function without doing that, via `typeof` (see "Pitfall: typeof null" on page 93).

You can also invoke `Object` as a constructor, which produces the same results as calling it as a function:

```
> var obj = {};
> new Object(obj) === obj
true

> new Object(123) instanceof Number
true
```

 Avoid the constructor; an empty object literal is almost always a better choice:

```
var obj = new Object(); // avoid
var obj = {}; // prefer
```

this as an Implicit Parameter of Functions and Methods

When you call a function, this is always an (implicit) parameter:

Normal functions in sloppy mode
Even though normal functions have no use for this, it still exists as a special variable
whose value is always the global object (window in browsers; see "The Global Object" on page 188):

```
> function returnThisSloppy() { return this }
> returnThisSloppy() === window
true
```

Normal functions in strict mode
this is always undefined:

```
> function returnThisStrict() { 'use strict'; return this }
> returnThisStrict() === undefined
true
```

Methods
this refers to the object on which the method has been invoked:

```
> var obj = { method: returnThisStrict };
> obj.method() === obj
true
```

In the case of methods, the value of this is called the *receiver* of the method call.

Calling Functions While Setting this: call(), apply(), and bind()

Remember that functions are also objects. Thus, each function has methods of its own.
Three of them are introduced in this section and help with calling functions. These three
methods are used in the following sections to work around some of the pitfalls of calling
functions. The upcoming examples all refer to the following object, jane:

```
var jane = {
    name: 'Jane',
    sayHelloTo: function (otherName) {
        'use strict';
        console.log(this.name+' says hello to '+otherName);
    }
};
```

Function.prototype.call(thisValue, arg1?, arg2?, ...)

The first parameter is the value that this will have inside the invoked function; the remaining parameters are handed over as arguments to the invoked function. The following three invocations are equivalent:

```
jane.sayHelloTo('Tarzan');

jane.sayHelloTo.call(jane, 'Tarzan');

var func = jane.sayHelloTo;
func.call(jane, 'Tarzan');
```

For the second invocation, you need to repeat jane, because call() doesn't know how you got the function that it is invoked on.

Function.prototype.apply(thisValue, argArray)

The first parameter is the value that this will have inside the invoked function; the second parameter is an array that provides the arguments for the invocation. The following three invocations are equivalent:

```
jane.sayHelloTo('Tarzan');

jane.sayHelloTo.apply(jane, ['Tarzan']);

var func = jane.sayHelloTo;
func.apply(jane, ['Tarzan']);
```

For the second invocation, you need to repeat jane, because apply() doesn't know how you got the function that it is invoked on.

"apply() for Constructors" on page 206 explains how to use apply() with constructors.

Function.prototype.bind(thisValue, arg1?, ..., argN?)

This method performs *partial function application*—meaning it creates a new function that calls the receiver of bind() in the following manner: the value of this is thisValue and the arguments start with arg1 until argN, followed by the arguments of the new function. In other words, the new function appends its arguments to arg1, ..., argN when it calls the original function. Let's look at an example:

```
function func() {
    console.log('this: '+this);
    console.log('arguments: '+Array.prototype.slice.call(arguments));
}
var bound = func.bind('abc', 1, 2);
```

The array method `slice` is used to convert `arguments` to an array, which is necessary for logging it (this operation is explained in "Array-Like Objects and Generic Methods" on page 262). bound is a new function. Here's the interaction:

```
> bound(3)
this: abc
arguments: 1,2,3
```

The following three invocations of `sayHelloTo` are all equivalent:

```
jane.sayHelloTo('Tarzan');

var func1 = jane.sayHelloTo.bind(jane);
func1('Tarzan');

var func2 = jane.sayHelloTo.bind(jane, 'Tarzan');
func2();
```

apply() for Constructors

Let's pretend that JavaScript has a triple dot operator (...) that turns arrays into actual parameters. Such an operator would allow you to use `Math.max()` (see "Other Functions" on page 330) with arrays. In that case, the following two expressions would be equivalent:

```
Math.max(...[13, 7, 30])
Math.max(13, 7, 30)
```

For functions, you can achieve the effect of the triple dot operator via `apply()`:

```
> Math.max.apply(null, [13, 7, 30])
30
```

The triple dot operator would also make sense for constructors:

```
new Date(...[2011, 11, 24]) // Christmas Eve 2011
```

Alas, here `apply()` does not work, because it helps only with function or method calls, not with constructor invocations.

Manually simulating an apply() for constructors

We can simulate `apply()` in two steps.

Step 1

Pass the arguments to `Date` via a method call (they are not in an array—yet):

```
new (Date.bind(null, 2011, 11, 24))
```

The preceding code uses bind() to create a constructor without parameters and invokes it via new.

Step 2

Use apply() to hand an array to bind(). Because bind() is a method call, we can use apply():

```
new (Function.prototype.bind.apply(
        Date, [null, 2011, 11, 24]))
```

The preceding array still has one element too many, null. We can use concat() to prepend it:

```
var arr = [2011, 11, 24];
new (Function.prototype.bind.apply(
        Date, [null].concat(arr)))
```

A library method

The preceding manual workaround is inspired by a library method (*http://mzl.la/1oOf7sK*) published by Mozilla. The following is a slightly edited version of it:

```
if (!Function.prototype.construct) {
    Function.prototype.construct = function(argArray) {
        if (! Array.isArray(argArray)) {
            throw new TypeError("Argument must be an array");
        }
        var constr = this;
        var nullaryFunc = Function.prototype.bind.apply(
            constr, [null].concat(argArray));
        return new nullaryFunc();
    };
}
```

Here is the method in use:

```
> Date.construct([2011, 11, 24])
Sat Dec 24 2011 00:00:00 GMT+0100 (CET)
```

An alternative approach

An alternative to the previous approach is to create an uninitialized instance via Object.create() and then call the constructor (as a function) via apply(). That means that you are effectively reimplementing the new operator (some checks are omitted):

```
Function.prototype.construct = function(argArray) {
    var constr = this;
    var inst = Object.create(constr.prototype);
    var result = constr.apply(inst, argArray); // (1)

    // Check: did the constructor return an object
```

```
    // and prevent `this` from being the result?
    return result ? result : inst;
};
```

 The preceding code does not work for most built-in constructors, which always produce new instances when called as functions. In other words, the step in line (1) doesn't set up inst as desired.

Pitfall: Losing this When Extracting a Method

If you extract a method from an object, it becomes a true function again. Its connection with the object is severed, and it usually doesn't work properly anymore. Take, for example, the following object, counter:

```
var counter = {
    count: 0,
    inc: function () {
        this.count++;
    }
}
```

Extracting inc and calling it (as a function!) fails:

```
> var func = counter.inc;
> func()
> counter.count   // didn't work
0
```

Here's the explanation: we have called the value of counter.inc as a function. Hence, this is the global object and we have performed window.count++. window.count does not exist and is undefined. Applying the ++ operator to it sets it to NaN:

```
> count   // global variable
NaN
```

How to get a warning

If method inc() is in strict mode, you get a warning:

```
> counter.inc = function () { 'use strict'; this.count++ };
> var func2 = counter.inc;
> func2()
TypeError: Cannot read property 'count' of undefined
```

The reason is that when we call the strict mode function func2, this is undefined, resulting in an error.

How to properly extract a method

Thanks to `bind()`, we can make sure that `inc` doesn't lose the connection with `counter`:

```
> var func3 = counter.inc.bind(counter);
> func3()
> counter.count   // it worked!
1
```

Callbacks and extracted methods

In JavaScript, there are many functions and methods that accept callbacks. Examples in browsers are `setTimeout()` and event handling. If we pass in `counter.inc` as a callback, it is also invoked as a function, resulting in the same problem just described. To illustrate this phenomenon, let's use a simple callback-invoking function:

```
function callIt(callback) {
    callback();
}
```

Executing `counter.count` via `callIt` triggers a warning (due to strict mode):

```
> callIt(counter.inc)
TypeError: Cannot read property 'count' of undefined
```

As before, we fix things via `bind()`:

```
> callIt(counter.inc.bind(counter))
> counter.count   // one more than before
2
```

 Each call to `bind()` creates a new function. That has consequences when you're registering and unregistering callbacks (e.g., for event handling). You need to store the value you registered somewhere and use it for unregistering, too.

Pitfall: Functions Inside Methods Shadow this

You often nest function definitions in JavaScript, because functions can be parameters (e.g., callbacks) and because they can be created in place, via function expressions. This poses a problem when a method contains a normal function and you want to access the former's `this` inside the latter, because the method's `this` is shadowed by the normal function's `this` (which doesn't even have any use for its own `this`). In the following example, the function at (1) tries to access the method's `this` at (2):

```
var obj = {
    name: 'Jane',
    friends: [ 'Tarzan', 'Cheeta' ],
    loop: function () {
        'use strict';
```

```
        this.friends.forEach(
            function (friend) {  // (1)
                console.log(this.name+' knows '+friend);  // (2)
            }
        );
    }
};
```

Obviously, this fails, because the function at (1) has its own `this`, which is `undefined` here:

```
> obj.loop();
TypeError: Cannot read property 'name' of undefined
```

There are three ways to work around this problem.

Workaround 1: that = this

We assign `this` to a variable that won't be shadowed inside the nested function:

```
loop: function () {
    'use strict';
    var that = this;
    this.friends.forEach(function (friend) {
        console.log(that.name+' knows '+friend);
    });
}
```

Here's the interaction:

```
> obj.loop();
Jane knows Tarzan
Jane knows Cheeta
```

Workaround 2: bind()

We can use `bind()` to give the callback a fixed value for `this`—namely, the method's `this` (line (1)):

```
loop: function () {
    'use strict';
    this.friends.forEach(function (friend) {
        console.log(this.name+' knows '+friend);
    }.bind(this));  // (1)
}
```

Workaround 3: a thisValue for forEach()

A workaround that is specific to `forEach()` (see "Examination Methods" on page 291) is to provide a second parameter after the callback that becomes the `this` of the callback:

```
loop: function () {
    'use strict';
    this.friends.forEach(function (friend) {
```

```
        console.log(this.name+' knows '+friend);
    }, this);
}
```

Layer 2: The Prototype Relationship Between Objects

The prototype relationship between two objects is about inheritance: every object can have another object as its prototype. Then the former object inherits all of its prototype's properties. An object specifies its prototype via the internal property [[Prototype]]. Every object has this property, but it can be null. The chain of objects connected by the [[Prototype]] property is called the *prototype chain* (Figure 17-1).

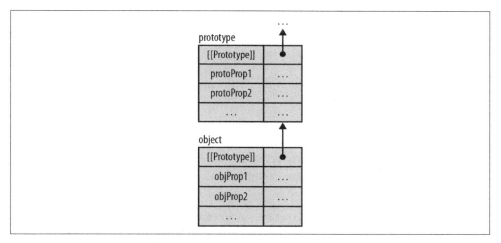

Figure 17-1. A prototype chain.

To see how prototype-based (or *prototypal*) inheritance works, let's look at an example (with invented syntax for specifying the [[Prototype]] property):

```
var proto = {
    describe: function () {
        return 'name: '+this.name;
    }
};
var obj = {
    [[Prototype]]: proto,
    name: 'obj'
};
```

The object obj inherits the property describe from proto. It also has a so-called *own* (noninherited, direct) property, name.

Inheritance

obj inherits the property `describe`; you can access it as if the object itself had that property:

```
> obj.describe
[Function]
```

Whenever you access a property via `obj`, JavaScript starts the search for it in that object and continues with its prototype, the prototype's prototype, and so on. That's why we can access `proto.describe` via `obj.describe`. The prototype chain behaves as if it were a single object. That illusion is maintained when you call a method: the value of `this` is always the object where the search for the method began, not where the method was found. That allows the method to access all of the properties of the prototype chain. For example:

```
> obj.describe()
'name: obj'
```

Inside `describe()`, `this` is `obj`, which allows the method to access `obj.name`.

Overriding

In a prototype chain, a property in an object *overrides* a property with the same key in a "later" object: the former property is found first. It hides the latter property, which can't be accessed anymore. As an example, let's override the method `proto.de scribe()` in `obj`:

```
> obj.describe = function () { return 'overridden' };
> obj.describe()
'overridden'
```

That is similar to how overriding of methods works in class-based languages.

Sharing Data Between Objects via a Prototype

Prototypes are great for sharing data between objects: several objects get the same prototype, which holds all shared properties. Let's look at an example. The objects `jane` and `tarzan` both contain the same method, `describe()`. That is something that we would like to avoid by using sharing:

```
var jane = {
    name: 'Jane',
    describe: function () {
        return 'Person named '+this.name;
    }
};
var tarzan = {
    name: 'Tarzan',
    describe: function () {
```

```
        return 'Person named '+this.name;
    }
};
```

Both objects are persons. Their name property is different, but we could have them share the method describe. We do that by creating a common prototype called PersonPro to and putting describe into it (Figure 17-2).

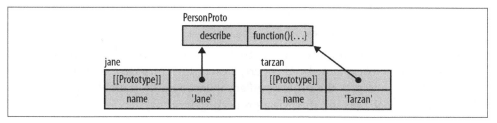

Figure 17-2. The objects jane and tarzan share the prototype PersonProto and thus the property describe.

The following code creates objects jane and tarzan that share the prototype Person Proto:

```
var PersonProto = {
    describe: function () {
        return 'Person named '+this.name;
    }
};
var jane = {
    [[Prototype]]: PersonProto,
    name: 'Jane'
};
var tarzan = {
    [[Prototype]]: PersonProto,
    name: 'Tarzan'
};
```

And here is the interaction:

```
> jane.describe()
Person named Jane
> tarzan.describe()
Person named Tarzan
```

This is a common pattern: the data resides in the first object of a prototype chain, while methods reside in later objects. JavaScript's flavor of prototypal inheritance is designed to support this pattern: setting a property affects only the first object in a prototype chain, whereas getting a property considers the complete chain (see "Setting and Deleting Affects Only Own Properties" on page 216).

Getting and Setting the Prototype

So far, we have pretended that you can access the internal property [[Prototype]] from JavaScript. But the language does not let you do that. Instead, there are functions for reading the prototype and for creating a new object with a given prototype.

Creating a new object with a given prototype

This invocation:

```
Object.create(proto, propDescObj?)
```

creates an object whose prototype is proto. Optionally, properties can be added via descriptors (which are explained in "Property Descriptors" on page 223). In the following example, object jane gets the prototype PersonProto and a mutable property name whose value is 'Jane' (as specified via a property descriptor):

```
var PersonProto = {
    describe: function () {
        return 'Person named '+this.name;
    }
};
var jane = Object.create(PersonProto, {
    name: { value: 'Jane', writable: true }
});
```

Here is the interaction:

```
> jane.describe()
'Person named Jane'
```

But you frequently just create an empty object and then manually add properties, because descriptors are verbose:

```
var jane = Object.create(PersonProto);
jane.value = 'Jane';
```

Reading the prototype of an object

This method call:

```
Object.getPrototypeOf(obj)
```

returns the prototype of obj. Continuing the preceding example:

```
> Object.getPrototypeOf(jane) === PersonProto
true
```

Checking whether one object a prototype of another one

This syntax:

```
Object.prototype.isPrototypeOf(obj)
```

checks whether the receiver of the method is a (direct or indirect) prototype of `obj`. In other words: are the receiver and `obj` in the same prototype chain, and does `obj` come before the receiver? For example:

```
> var A = {};
> var B = Object.create(A);
> var C = Object.create(B);
> A.isPrototypeOf(C)
true
> C.isPrototypeOf(A)
false
```

Finding the object where a property is defined

The following function iterates over the property chain of an object `obj`. It returns the first object that has an own property with the key `propKey`, or `null` if there is no such object:

```
function getDefiningObject(obj, propKey) {
    obj = Object(obj); // make sure it's an object
    while (obj && !{}.hasOwnProperty.call(obj, propKey)) {
        obj = Object.getPrototypeOf(obj);
        // obj is null if we have reached the end
    }
    return obj;
}
```

In the preceding code, we called the method `Object.prototype.hasOwnProperty` generically (see "Generic Methods: Borrowing Methods from Prototypes" on page 260).

The Special Property __proto__

Some JavaScript engines have a special property for getting and setting the prototype of an object: `__proto__`. It brings direct access to `[[Prototype]]` to the language:

```
> var obj = {};

> obj.__proto__ === Object.prototype
true

> obj.__proto__ = Array.prototype
> Object.getPrototypeOf(obj) === Array.prototype
true
```

There are several things you need to know about `__proto__`:

- `__proto__` is pronounced "dunder proto," an abbreviation of "double underscore proto." That pronunciation has been borrowed from the Python programming language (as suggested by Ned Batchelder (*http://bit.ly/1fwlzN8*) in 2006). Special variables with double underscores are quite frequent in Python.

- __proto__ is not part of the ECMAScript 5 standard. Therefore, you must not use it if you want your code to conform to that standard and run reliably across current JavaScript engines.

- However, more and more engines are adding support for __proto__ and it will be part of ECMAScript 6.

- The following expression checks whether an engine supports __proto__ as a special property:

  ```
  Object.getPrototypeOf({ __proto__: null }) === null
  ```

Setting and Deleting Affects Only Own Properties

Only getting a property considers the complete prototype chain of an object. Setting and deleting ignores inheritance and affects only own properties.

Setting a property

Setting a property creates an own property, even if there is an inherited property with that key. For example, given the following source code:

```
var proto = { foo: 'a' };
var obj = Object.create(proto);
```

obj inherits foo from proto:

```
> obj.foo
'a'
> obj.hasOwnProperty('foo')
false
```

Setting foo has the desired result:

```
> obj.foo = 'b';
> obj.foo
'b'
```

However, we have created an own property and not changed proto.foo:

```
> obj.hasOwnProperty('foo')
true
> proto.foo
'a'
```

The rationale is that prototype properties are meant to be shared by several objects. This approach allows us to nondestructively "change" them—only the current object is affected.

Deleting an inherited property

You can only delete own properties. Let's again set up an object, obj, with a prototype, proto:

```
var proto = { foo: 'a' };
var obj = Object.create(proto);
```

Deleting the inherited property foo has no effect:

```
> delete obj.foo
true
> obj.foo
'a'
```

For more information on the delete operator, consult "Deleting properties" on page 200.

Changing properties anywhere in the prototype chain

If you want to change an inherited property, you first have to find the object that owns it (see "Finding the object where a property is defined" on page 215) and then perform the change on that object. For example, let's delete the property foo from the previous example:

```
> delete getDefiningObject(obj, 'foo').foo;
true
> obj.foo
undefined
```

Iteration and Detection of Properties

Operations for iterating over and detecting properties are influenced by:

Inheritance (own properties versus inherited properties)
An own property of an object is stored directly in that object. An inherited property is stored in one of its prototypes.

Enumerability (enumerable properties versus nonenumerable properties)
The enumerability of a property is an *attribute* (see "Property Attributes and Property Descriptors" on page 222), a flag that can be true or false. Enumerability rarely matters and can normally be ignored (see "Enumerability: Best Practices" on page 228).

You can list own property keys, list all enumerable property keys, and check whether a property exists. The following subsections show how.

Listing Own Property Keys

You can either list all own property keys, or only enumerable ones:

- `Object.getOwnPropertyNames(obj)` returns the keys of all own properties of `obj`.
- `Object.keys(obj)` returns the keys of all enumerable own properties of `obj`.

Note that properties are normally enumerable (see "Enumerability: Best Practices" on page 228), so you can use `Object.keys()`, especially for objects that you have created.

Listing All Property Keys

If you want to list all properties (both own and inherited ones) of an object, then you have two options.

Option 1 is to use the loop:

```
for («variable» in «object»)
    «statement»
```

to iterate over the keys of all enumerable properties of `object`. See "for-in" on page 148 for a more thorough description.

Option 2 is to implement a function yourself that iterates over all properties (not just enumerable ones). For example:

```
function getAllPropertyNames(obj) {
    var result = [];
    while (obj) {
        // Add the own property names of `obj` to `result`
        Array.prototype.push.apply(result, Object.getOwnPropertyNames(obj));
        obj = Object.getPrototypeOf(obj);
    }
    return result;
}
```

Checking Whether a Property Exists

You can check whether an object has a property, or whether a property exists directly inside an object:

`propKey in obj`
> Returns `true` if `obj` has a property whose key is `propKey`. Inherited properties are included in this test.

`Object.prototype.hasOwnProperty(propKey)`
> Returns `true` if the receiver (`this`) has an own (noninherited) property whose key is `propKey`.

Avoid invoking hasOwnProperty() directly on an object, as it may be overridden (e.g., by an own property whose key is hasOwnProperty):

```
> var obj = { hasOwnProperty: 1, foo: 2 };
> obj.hasOwnProperty('foo')  // unsafe
TypeError: Property 'hasOwnProperty' is not a function
```

Instead, it is better to call it generically (see "Generic Methods: Borrowing Methods from Prototypes" on page 260):

```
> Object.prototype.hasOwnProperty.call(obj, 'foo')  // safe
true
> {}.hasOwnProperty.call(obj, 'foo')  // shorter
true
```

Examples

The following examples are based on these definitions:

```
var proto = Object.defineProperties({}, {
    protoEnumTrue: { value: 1, enumerable: true },
    protoEnumFalse: { value: 2, enumerable: false }
});
var obj = Object.create(proto, {
    objEnumTrue: { value: 1, enumerable: true },
    objEnumFalse: { value: 2, enumerable: false }
});
```

Object.defineProperties() is explained in "Getting and Defining Properties via Descriptors" on page 224, but it should be fairly obvious how it works: proto has the own properties protoEnumTrue and protoEnumFalse and obj has the own properties objEnumTrue and objEnumFalse (and inherits all of proto's properties).

Note that objects (such as proto in the preceding example) normally have at least the prototype Object.prototype (where standard methods such as toString() and hasOwnProperty() are defined):

```
> Object.getPrototypeOf({}) === Object.prototype
true
```

The effects of enumerability

Among property-related operations, enumerability only influences the for-in loop and Object.keys() (it also influences JSON.stringify(), see "JSON.stringify(value, replacer?, space?)" on page 337).

The for-in loop iterates over the keys of all enumerable properties, including inherited ones (note that none of the nonenumerable properties of Object.prototype show up):

```
> for (var x in obj) console.log(x);
objEnumTrue
protoEnumTrue
```

`Object.keys()` returns the keys of all own (noninherited) enumerable properties:

```
> Object.keys(obj)
[ 'objEnumTrue' ]
```

If you want the keys of all own properties, you need to use `Object.getOwnProperty Names()`:

```
> Object.getOwnPropertyNames(obj)
[ 'objEnumTrue', 'objEnumFalse' ]
```

The effects of inheritance

Only the `for-in` loop (see the previous example) and the `in` operator consider inheritance:

```
> 'toString' in obj
true
> obj.hasOwnProperty('toString')
false
> obj.hasOwnProperty('objEnumFalse')
true
```

Computing the number of own properties of an object

Objects don't have a method such as `length` or `size`, so you have to use the following workaround:

```
Object.keys(obj).length
```

Best Practices: Iterating over Own Properties

To iterate over property keys:

- Combine `for-in` with `hasOwnProperty()`, in the manner described in "for-in" on page 148. This works even on older JavaScript engines. For example:

```
for (var key in obj) {
    if (Object.prototype.hasOwnProperty.call(obj, key)) {
        console.log(key);
    }
}
```

- Combine `Object.keys()` or `Object.getOwnPropertyNames()` with `forEach()` array iteration:

```
var obj = { first: 'John', last: 'Doe' };
// Visit non-inherited enumerable keys
Object.keys(obj).forEach(function (key) {
```

```
        console.log(key);
    });
```

To iterate over property values or over (key, value) pairs:

- Iterate over the keys, and use each key to retrieve the corresponding value. Other languages make this simpler, but not JavaScript.

Accessors (Getters and Setters)

ECMAScript 5 lets you write methods whose invocations look like you are getting or setting a property. That means that a property is virtual and not storage space. You could, for example, forbid setting a property and always compute the value returned when reading it.

Defining Accessors via an Object Literal

The following example uses an object literal to define a setter and a getter for property foo:

```
var obj = {
    get foo() {
        return 'getter';
    },
    set foo(value) {
        console.log('setter: '+value);
    }
};
```

Here's the interaction:

```
> obj.foo = 'bla';
setter: bla
> obj.foo
'getter'
```

Defining Accessors via Property Descriptors

An alternate way to specify getters and setters is via property descriptors (see "Property Descriptors" on page 223). The following code defines the same object as the preceding literal:

```
var obj = Object.create(
    Object.prototype, { // object with property descriptors
        foo: { // property descriptor
            get: function () {
                return 'getter';
            },
```

```
                set: function (value) {
                    console.log('setter: '+value);
                }
            }
        }
    );
```

Accessors and Inheritance

Getters and setters are inherited from prototypes:

```
> var proto = { get foo() { return 'hello' } };
> var obj = Object.create(proto);

> obj.foo
'hello'
```

Property Attributes and Property Descriptors

 Property attributes and property descriptors are an advanced topic. You normally don't need to know how they work.

In this section, we'll look at the internal structure of properties:

- *Property attributes* are the atomic building blocks of properties.
- A *property descriptor* is a data structure for working programmatically with attributes.

Property Attributes

All of a property's state, both its data and its metadata, is stored in *attributes*. They are fields that a property has, much like an object has properties. Attribute keys are often written in double brackets. Attributes matter for normal properties and for accessors (getters and setters).

The following attributes are specific to normal properties:

- [[Value]] holds the property's value, its data.
- [[Writable]] holds a boolean indicating whether the value of a property can be changed.

The following attributes are specific to accessors:

- `[[Get]]` holds the getter, a function that is called when a property is read. The function computes the result of the read access.

- `[[Set]]` holds the setter, a function that is called when a property is set to a value. The function receives that value as a parameter.

All properties have the following attributes:

- `[[Enumerable]]` holds a boolean. Making a property nonenumerable hides it from some operations (see "Iteration and Detection of Properties" on page 217).

- `[[Configurable]]` holds a boolean. If it is `false`, you cannot delete a property, change any of its attributes (except `[[Value]]`), or convert it from a data property to an accessor property or vice versa. In other words, `[[Configurable]]` controls the writability of a property's metadata. There is one exception to this rule—JavaScript allows you to change an unconfigurable property from writable to read-only, for historic reasons (*http://bit.ly/1fwlIQI*); the property `length` of arrays has always been writable and unconfigurable. Without this exception, you wouldn't be able to freeze (see "Freezing" on page 230) arrays.

Default values

If you don't specify attributes, the following defaults are used:

Attribute key	Default value
`[[Value]]`	undefined
`[[Get]]`	undefined
`[[Set]]`	undefined
`[[Writable]]`	false
`[[Enumerable]]`	false
`[[Configurable]]`	false

These defaults are important when you are creating properties via property descriptors (see the following section).

Property Descriptors

A property descriptor is a data structure for working programmatically with attributes. It is an object that encodes the attributes of a property. Each of a descriptor's properties corresponds to an attribute. For example, the following is the descriptor of a read-only property whose value is 123:

```
{
    value: 123,
```

```
    writable: false,
    enumerable: true,
    configurable: false
}
```

You can achieve the same goal, immutability, via accessors. Then the descriptor looks as follows:

```
{
    get: function () { return 123 },
    enumerable: true,
    configurable: false
}
```

Getting and Defining Properties via Descriptors

Property descriptors are used for two kinds of operations:

Getting a property
    All attributes of a property are returned as a descriptor.

Defining a property
    Defining a property means something different depending on whether a property already exists:

- If a property does not exist, create a new property whose attributes are as specified by the descriptor. If an attribute has no corresponding property in the descriptor, then use the default value. The defaults are dictated by what the attribute names mean. They are the opposite of the values that are used when creating a property via assignment (then the property is writable, enumerable, and configurable). For example:

```
> var obj = {};
> Object.defineProperty(obj, 'foo', { configurable: true });
> Object.getOwnPropertyDescriptor(obj, 'foo')
{ value: undefined,
  writable: false,
  enumerable: false,
  configurable: true }
```

    I usually don't rely on the defaults and explicitly state all attributes, to be completely clear.

- If a property already exists, update the attributes of the property as specified by the descriptor. If an attribute has no corresponding property in the descriptor, then don't change it. Here is an example (continued from the previous one):

```
> Object.defineProperty(obj, 'foo', { writable: true });
> Object.getOwnPropertyDescriptor(obj, 'foo')
{ value: undefined,
  writable: true,
```

```
    enumerable: false,
    configurable: true }
```

The following operations allow you to get and set a property's attributes via property descriptors:

`Object.getOwnPropertyDescriptor(obj, propKey)`

Returns the descriptor of the own (noninherited) property of `obj` whose key is `propKey`. If there is no such property, `undefined` is returned:

```
> Object.getOwnPropertyDescriptor(Object.prototype, 'toString')
{ value: [Function: toString],
  writable: true,
  enumerable: false,
  configurable: true }

> Object.getOwnPropertyDescriptor({}, 'toString')
undefined
```

`Object.defineProperty(obj, propKey, propDesc)`

Create or change a property of `obj` whose key is `propKey` and whose attributes are specified via `propDesc`. Return the modified object. For example:

```
var obj = Object.defineProperty({}, 'foo', {
    value: 123,
    enumerable: true
    // writable: false (default value)
    // configurable: false (default value)
});
```

`Object.defineProperties(obj, propDescObj)`

The batch version of `Object.defineProperty()`. Each property of `propDescObj` holds a property descriptor. The keys of the properties and their values tell `Object.defineProperties` what properties to create or change on `obj`. For example:

```
var obj = Object.defineProperties({}, {
    foo: { value: 123, enumerable: true },
    bar: { value: 'abc', enumerable: true }
});
```

`Object.create(proto, propDescObj?)`

First, create an object whose prototype is `proto`. Then, if the optional parameter `propDescObj` has been specified, add properties to it—in the same manner as `Object.defineProperties`. Finally, return the result. For example, the following code snippet produces the same result as the previous snippet:

```
var obj = Object.create(Object.prototype, {
    foo: { value: 123, enumerable: true },
    bar: { value: 'abc', enumerable: true }
});
```

Copying an Object

To create an identical copy of an object, you need to get two things right:

1. The copy must have the same prototype (see "Layer 2: The Prototype Relationship Between Objects" on page 211) as the original.

2. The copy must have the same properties, with the same attributes as the original.

The following function performs such a copy:

```
function copyObject(orig) {
    // 1. copy has same prototype as orig
    var copy = Object.create(Object.getPrototypeOf(orig));

    // 2. copy has all of orig's properties
    copyOwnPropertiesFrom(copy, orig);

    return copy;
}
```

The properties are copied from `orig` to `copy` via this function:

```
function copyOwnPropertiesFrom(target, source) {
    Object.getOwnPropertyNames(source)  // (1)
    .forEach(function(propKey) {  // (2)
        var desc = Object.getOwnPropertyDescriptor(source, propKey); // (3)
        Object.defineProperty(target, propKey, desc);  // (4)
    });
    return target;
};
```

These are the steps involved:

1. Get an array with the keys of all own properties of `source`.

2. Iterate over those keys.

3. Retrieve a property descriptor.

4. Use that property descriptor to create an own property in `target`.

Note that this function is very similar to the function `_.extend()` (*http://underscor ejs.org/#extend*) in the Underscore.js library.

Properties: Definition Versus Assignment

The following two operations are very similar:

- Defining a property via `defineProperty()` and `defineProperties()` (see "Getting and Defining Properties via Descriptors" on page 224).

- Assigning to a property via =.

There are, however, a few subtle differences:

- *Defining a property* means creating a new own property or updating the attributes of an existing own property. In both cases, the prototype chain is completely ignored.
- *Assigning to a property* prop means changing an existing property. The process is as follows:
  — If prop is a setter (own or inherited), call that setter.
  — Otherwise, if prop is read-only (own or inherited), throw an exception (in strict mode) or do nothing (in sloppy mode). The next section explains this (slightly unexpected) phenomenon in more detail.
  — Otherwise, if prop is own (and writable), change the value of that property.
  — Otherwise, there either is no property prop, or it is inherited and writable. In both cases, define an own property prop that is writable, configurable, and enumerable. In the latter case, we have just overridden an inherited property (nondestructively changed it). In the former case, a missing property has been defined automatically. This kind of autodefining is problematic, because typos in assignments can be hard to detect.

Inherited Read-Only Properties Can't Be Assigned To

If an object, obj, inherits a property, foo, from a prototype and foo is not writable, then you can't assign to obj.foo:

```
var proto = Object.defineProperty({}, 'foo', {
    value: 'a',
    writable: false
});
var obj = Object.create(proto);
```

obj inherits the read-only property foo from proto. In sloppy mode, setting the property has no effect:

```
> obj.foo = 'b';
> obj.foo
'a'
```

In strict mode, you get an exception:

```
> (function () { 'use strict'; obj.foo = 'b' }());
TypeError: Cannot assign to read-only property 'foo'
```

This fits with the idea that assignment changes inherited properties, but nondestructively. If an inherited property is read-only, you want to forbid all changes, even nondestructive ones.

Note that you can circumvent this protection by defining an own property (see the previous subsection for the difference between definition and assignment):

```
> Object.defineProperty(obj, 'foo', { value: 'b' });
> obj.foo
'b'
```

Enumerability: Best Practices

The general rule is that properties created by the system are nonenumerable, while properties created by users are enumerable:

```
> Object.keys([])
[]
> Object.getOwnPropertyNames([])
[ 'length' ]

> Object.keys(['a'])
[ '0' ]
```

This is especially true for the methods of the built-in instance prototypes:

```
> Object.keys(Object.prototype)
[]
> Object.getOwnPropertyNames(Object.prototype)
[ hasOwnProperty',
  'valueOf',
  'constructor',
  'toLocaleString',
  'isPrototypeOf',
  'propertyIsEnumerable',
  'toString' ]
```

The main purpose of enumerability is to tell the for-in loop which properties it should ignore. As we have seen just now when we looked at instances of built-in constructors, everything not created by the user is hidden from for-in.

The only operations affected by enumerability are:

- The for-in loop
- Object.keys() ("Listing Own Property Keys" on page 217)
- JSON.stringify() ("JSON.stringify(value, replacer?, space?)" on page 337)

Here are some best practices to keep in mind:

- For your own code, you can usually ignore enumerability and should avoid the `for-in` loop ("Best Practices: Iterating over Arrays" on page 295).
- You normally shouldn't add properties to built-in prototypes and objects. But if you do, you should make them nonenumerable to avoid breaking existing code.

Protecting Objects

There are three levels of protecting an object, listed here from weakest to strongest:

- Preventing extensions
- Sealing
- Freezing

Preventing Extensions

Preventing extensions via:

```
Object.preventExtensions(obj)
```

makes it impossible to add properties to `obj`. For example:

```
var obj = { foo: 'a' };
Object.preventExtensions(obj);
```

Now adding a property fails silently in sloppy mode:

```
> obj.bar = 'b';
> obj.bar
undefined
```

and throws an error in strict mode:

```
> (function () { 'use strict'; obj.bar = 'b' }());
TypeError: Can't add property bar, object is not extensible
```

You can still delete properties, though:

```
> delete obj.foo
true
> obj.foo
undefined
```

You check whether an object is extensible via:

```
Object.isExtensible(obj)
```

Sealing

Sealing via:

```
Object.seal(obj)
```

prevents extensions and makes all properties "unconfigurable." The latter means that the attributes (see "Property Attributes and Property Descriptors" on page 222) of properties can't be changed anymore. For example, read-only properties stay read-only forever.

The following example demonstrates that sealing makes all properties unconfigurable:

```
> var obj = { foo: 'a' };

> Object.getOwnPropertyDescriptor(obj, 'foo')  // before sealing
{ value: 'a',
  writable: true,
  enumerable: true,
  configurable: true }

> Object.seal(obj)

> Object.getOwnPropertyDescriptor(obj, 'foo')  // after sealing
{ value: 'a',
  writable: true,
  enumerable: true,
  configurable: false }
```

You can still change the property foo:

```
> obj.foo = 'b';
'b'
> obj.foo
'b'
```

but you can't change its attributes:

```
> Object.defineProperty(obj, 'foo', { enumerable: false });
TypeError: Cannot redefine property: foo
```

You check whether an object is sealed via:

```
Object.isSealed(obj)
```

Freezing

Freezing is performed via:

```
Object.freeze(obj)
```

It makes all properties nonwritable and seals obj. In other words, obj is not extensible and all properties are read-only, and there is no way to change that. Let's look at an example:

```
var point = { x: 17, y: -5 };
Object.freeze(point);
```

Once again, you get silent failures in sloppy mode:

```
> point.x = 2;   // no effect, point.x is read-only
> point.x
17

> point.z = 123;   // no effect, point is not extensible
> point
{ x: 17, y: -5 }
```

And you get errors in strict mode:

```
> (function () { 'use strict'; point.x = 2 }());
TypeError: Cannot assign to read-only property 'x'

> (function () { 'use strict'; point.z = 123 }());
TypeError: Can't add property z, object is not extensible
```

You check whether an object is frozen via:

```
Object.isFrozen(obj)
```

Pitfall: Protection Is Shallow

Protecting an object is *shallow*: it affects the own properties, but not the values of those properties. For example, consider the following object:

```
var obj = {
    foo: 1,
    bar: ['a', 'b']
};
Object.freeze(obj);
```

Even though you have frozen `obj`, it is not completely immutable—you can change the (mutable) value of property `bar`:

```
> obj.foo = 2; // no effect
> obj.bar.push('c'); // changes obj.bar

> obj
{ foo: 1, bar: [ 'a', 'b', 'c' ] }
```

Additionally, `obj` has the prototype `Object.prototype`, which is also mutable.

Layer 3: Constructors—Factories for Instances

A *constructor function* (short: *constructor*) helps with producing objects that are similar in some way. It is a normal function, but it is named, set up, and invoked differently.

This section explains how constructors work. They correspond to classes in other languages.

We have already seen an example of two objects that are similar (in "Sharing Data Between Objects via a Prototype" on page 212):

```
var PersonProto = {
    describe: function () {
        return 'Person named '+this.name;
    }
};
var jane = {
    [[Prototype]]: PersonProto,
    name: 'Jane'
};
var tarzan = {
    [[Prototype]]: PersonProto,
    name: 'Tarzan'
};
```

The objects jane and tarzan are both considered "persons" and share the prototype object PersonProto. Let's turn that prototype into a constructor Person that creates objects like jane and tarzan. The objects a constructor creates are called its *instances*. Such instances have the same structure as jane and tarzan, consisting of two parts:

1. Data is instance-specific and stored in the own properties of the instance objects (jane and tarzan in the preceding example).
2. Behavior is shared by all instances—they have a common prototype object with methods (PersonProto in the preceding example).

A constructor is a function that is invoked via the new operator. By convention, the names of constructors start with uppercase letters, while the names of normal functions and methods start with lowercase letters. The function itself sets up part 1:

```
function Person(name) {
    this.name = name;
}
```

The object in Person.prototype becomes the prototype of all instances of Person. It contributes part 2:

```
Person.prototype.describe = function () {
    return 'Person named '+this.name;
};
```

Let's create and use an instance of Person:

```
> var jane = new Person('Jane');
> jane.describe()
'Person named Jane'
```

We can see that `Person` is a normal function. It only becomes a constructor when it is invoked via `new`. The `new` operator performs the following steps:

- First the behavior is set up: a new object is created whose prototype is `Person.prototype`.
- Then the data is set up: `Person` receives that object as the implicit parameter `this` and adds instance properties.

Figure 17-3 shows what the instance `jane` looks like. The property `constructor` of `Person.prototype` points back to the constructor and is explained in "The constructor Property of Instances" on page 234.

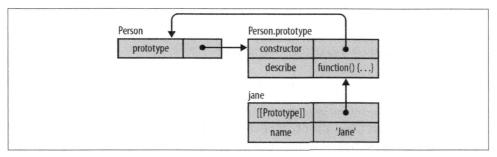

Figure 17-3. jane is an instance of the constructor Person; its prototype is the object Person.prototype.

The `instanceof` operator allows us to check whether an object is an instance of a given constructor:

```
> jane instanceof Person
true
> jane instanceof Date
false
```

The new Operator Implemented in JavaScript

If you were to manually implement the `new` operator, it would look roughly as follows:

```
function newOperator(Constr, args) {
    var thisValue = Object.create(Constr.prototype); // (1)
    var result = Constr.apply(thisValue, args);
    if (typeof result === 'object' && result !== null) {
        return result; // (2)
    }
    return thisValue;
}
```

In line (1), you can see that the prototype of an instance created by a constructor `Constr` is `Constr.prototype`.

Line (2) reveals another feature of the `new` operator: you can return an arbitrary object from a constructor and it becomes the result of the `new` operator. This is useful if you want a constructor to return an instance of a subconstructor (an example is given in "Returning arbitrary objects from a constructor" on page 240).

Terminology: The Two Prototypes

Unfortunately, the term *prototype* is used ambiguously in JavaScript:

Prototype 1: The prototype relationship
An object can be the prototype of another object:

```
> var proto = {};
> var obj = Object.create(proto);
> Object.getPrototypeOf(obj) === proto
true
```

In the preceding example, `proto` is the prototype of `obj`.

Prototype 2: The value of the property `prototype`
Each constructor `C` has a `prototype` property that refers to an object. That object becomes the prototype of all instances of `C`:

```
> function C() {}
> Object.getPrototypeOf(new C()) === C.prototype
true
```

Usually the context makes it clear which of the two prototypes is meant. Should disambiguation be necessary, then we are stuck with *prototype* to describe the relationship between objects, because that name has made it into the standard library via `getProto typeOf` and `isPrototypeOf`. We thus need to find a different name for the object referenced by the `prototype` property. One possibility is *constructor prototype*, but that is problematic because constructors have prototypes, too:

```
> function Foo() {}
> Object.getPrototypeOf(Foo) === Function.prototype
true
```

Thus, *instance prototype* is the best option.

The constructor Property of Instances

By default, each function `C` contains an instance prototype object `C.prototype` whose property `constructor` points back to `C`:

```
> function C() {}
> C.prototype.constructor === C
true
```

Because the `constructor` property is inherited from the prototype by each instance, you can use it to get the constructor of an instance:

```
> var o = new C();
> o.constructor
[Function: C]
```

Use cases for the constructor property

Switching over an object's constructor

In the following `catch` clause, we take different actions, depending on the constructor of the caught exception:

```
try {
    ...
} catch (e) {
    switch (e.constructor) {
        case SyntaxError:
            ...
            break;
        case CustomError:
            ...
            break;
        ...
    }
}
```

This approach detects only direct instances of a given constructor. In contrast, `instanceof` detects both direct instances and instances of all subconstructors.

Determining the name of an object's constructor

For example:

```
> function Foo() {}
> var f = new Foo();
> f.constructor.name
'Foo'
```

Not all JavaScript engines support the property `name` for functions.

Creating similar objects

This is how you create a new object, y, that has the same constructor as an existing object, x:

```
function Constr() {}
var x = new Constr();

var y = new x.constructor();
console.log(y instanceof Constr); // true
```

This trick is handy for a method that must work for instances of subconstructors and wants to create a new instance that is similar to this. Then you can't use a fixed constructor:

```
SuperConstr.prototype.createCopy = function () {
    return new this.constructor(...);
};
```

Referring to a superconstructor

Some inheritance libraries assign the superprototype to a property of a subconstructor. For example, the YUI framework provides subclassing via Y.extend (*http://yuilibrary.com/yui/docs/yui/yui-extend.html*):

```
function Super() {
}
function Sub() {
    Sub.superclass.constructor.call(this); // (1)
}
Y.extend(Sub, Super);
```

The call in line (1) works, because extend sets Sub.superclass to Super.proto type. Thanks to the constructor property, you can call the superconstructor as a method.

 The instanceof operator (see "The instanceof Operator" on page 237) does not rely on the property constructor.

Best practice

Make sure that for each constructor C, the following assertion holds:

```
C.prototype.constructor === C
```

By default, every function f already has a property prototype that is set up correctly:

```
> function f() {}
> f.prototype.constructor === f
true
```

You should thus avoid replacing this object and only add properties to it:

```
// Avoid:
C.prototype = {
    method1: function (...) { ... },
    ...
};

// Prefer:
C.prototype.method1 = function (...) { ... };
...
```

If you do replace it, you should manually assign the correct value to `constructor`:

```
C.prototype = {
    constructor: C,
    method1: function (...) { ... },
    ...
};
```

Note that nothing crucial in JavaScript depends on the `constructor` property; but it is good style to set it up, because it enables the techniques mentioned in this section.

The instanceof Operator

The `instanceof` operator:

```
value instanceof Constr
```

determines whether `value` has been created by the constructor `Constr` or a subconstructor. It does so by checking whether `Constr.prototype` is in the prototype chain of `value`. Therefore, the following two expressions are equivalent:

```
value instanceof Constr
Constr.prototype.isPrototypeOf(value)
```

Here are some examples:

```
> {} instanceof Object
true

> [] instanceof Array  // constructor of []
true
> [] instanceof Object  // super-constructor of []
true

> new Date() instanceof Date
true
> new Date() instanceof Object
true
```

As expected, `instanceof` is always `false` for primitive values:

```
> 'abc' instanceof Object
false
> 123 instanceof Number
false
```

Finally, instanceof throws an exception if its right side isn't a function:

```
> [] instanceof 123
TypeError: Expecting a function in instanceof check
```

Pitfall: objects that are not instances of Object

Almost all objects are instances of Object, because Object.prototype is in their prototype chain. But there are also objects where that is not the case. Here are two examples:

```
> Object.create(null) instanceof Object
false
> Object.prototype instanceof Object
false
```

The former object is explained in more detail in "The dict Pattern: Objects Without Prototypes Are Better Maps" on page 269. The latter object is where most prototype chains end (and they must end somewhere). Neither object has a prototype:

```
> Object.getPrototypeOf(Object.create(null))
null
> Object.getPrototypeOf(Object.prototype)
null
```

But typeof correctly classifies them as objects:

```
> typeof Object.create(null)
'object'
> typeof Object.prototype
'object'
```

This pitfall is not a deal-breaker for most use cases for instanceof, but you have to be aware of it.

Pitfall: crossing realms (frames or windows)

In web browsers, each frame and window has its own *realm* with separate global variables. That prevents instanceof from working for objects that cross realms. To see why, look at the following code:

```
if (myvar instanceof Array) ...  // Doesn't always work
```

If myvar is an array from a different realm, then its prototype is the Array.prototype from that realm. Therefore, instanceof will not find the Array.prototype of the current realm in the prototype chain of myvar and will return false. ECMAScript 5 has the function Array.isArray(), which always works:

```
<head>
    <script>
        function test(arr) {
            var iframe = frames[0];

            console.log(arr instanceof Array); // false
            console.log(arr instanceof iframe.Array); // true
            console.log(Array.isArray(arr)); // true
        }
    </script>
</head>
<body>
    <iframe srcdoc="<script>window.parent.test([])</script>">
    </iframe>
</body>
```

Obviously, this is also an issue with non-built-in constructors.

Apart from using `Array.isArray()`, there are several things you can do to work around this problem:

- Avoid objects crossing realms. Browsers have the `postMessage()` (*http://mzl.la/ 1fwmNrL*) method, which can copy an object to another realm instead of passing a reference.

- Check the name of the constructor of an instance (only works on engines that support the property `name` for functions):

    ```
    someValue.constructor.name === 'NameOfExpectedConstructor'
    ```

- Use a prototype property to mark instances as belonging to a type T. There are several ways in which you can do so. The checks for whether `value` is an instance of T look as follows:

    — `value.isT()`: The prototype of T instances must return `true` from this method; a common superconstructor should return the default value, `false`.

    — `'T' in value`: You must tag the prototype of T instances with a property whose key is `'T'` (or something more unique).

    — `value.TYPE_NAME === 'T'`: Every relevant prototype must have a `TYPE_NAME` property with an appropriate value.

Tips for Implementing Constructors

This section gives a few tips for implementing constructors.

Protection against forgetting new: strict mode

If you forget new when you use a constructor, you are calling it as a function instead of as a constructor. In sloppy mode, you don't get an instance and global variables are created. Unfortunately, all of this happens without a warning:

```
function SloppyColor(name) {
    this.name = name;
}
var c = SloppyColor('green'); // no warning!

// No instance is created:
console.log(c); // undefined
// A global variable is created:
console.log(name); // green
```

In strict mode, you get an exception:

```
function StrictColor(name) {
    'use strict';
    this.name = name;
}
var c = StrictColor('green');
// TypeError: Cannot set property 'name' of undefined
```

Returning arbitrary objects from a constructor

In many object-oriented languages, constructors can produce only direct instances. For example, consider Java: let's say you want to implement a class Expression that has the subclasses Addition and Multiplication. Parsing produces direct instances of the latter two classes. You can't implement it as a constructor of Expression, because that constructor can produce only direct instances of Expression. As a workaround, static factory methods are used in Java:

```
class Expression {
    // Static factory method:
    public static Expression parse(String str) {
        if (...) {
            return new Addition(...);
        } else if (...) {
            return new Multiplication(...);
        } else {
            throw new ExpressionException(...);
        }
    }
}
...
Expression expr = Expression.parse(someStr);
```

In JavaScript, you can simply return whatever object you need from a constructor. Thus, the JavaScript version of the preceding code would look like:

```
function Expression(str) {
    if (...) {
        return new Addition(..);
    } else if (...) {
        return new Multiplication(...);
    } else {
        throw new ExpressionException(...);
    }
}
...
var expr = new Expression(someStr);
```

That is good news: JavaScript constructors don't lock you in, so you can always change your mind as to whether a constructor should return a direct instance or something else.

Data in Prototype Properties

This section explains that in most cases, you should not put data in prototype properties. There are, however, a few exceptions to that rule.

Avoid Prototype Properties with Initial Values for Instance Properties

Prototypes contain properties that are shared by several objects. Hence, they work well for methods. Additionally, with a technique that is described next, you can also use them to provide initial values for instance properties. I'll later explain why that is not recommended.

A constructor usually sets instance properties to initial values. If one such value is a default, then you don't need to create an instance property. You only need a prototype property with the same key whose value is the default. For example:

```
/**
 * Anti-pattern: don't do this
 *
 * @param data an array with names
 */
function Names(data) {
    if (data) {
        // There is a parameter
        // => create instance property
        this.data = data;
    }
}
Names.prototype.data = [];
```

The parameter `data` is optional. If it is missing, the instance does not get a property `data`, but inherits `Names.prototype.data` instead.

This approach mostly works: you can create an instance n of Names. Getting n.data reads Names.prototype.data. Setting n.data creates a new own property in n and preserves the shared default value in the prototype. We only have a problem if we *change* the default value (instead of replacing it with a new value):

```
> var n1 = new Names();
> var n2 = new Names();

> n1.data.push('jane'); // changes default value
> n1.data
[ 'jane' ]

> n2.data
[ 'jane' ]
```

In the preceding example, push() changed the array in Names.prototype.data. Since that array is shared by all instances without an own property data, n2.data's initial value has changed, too.

Best practice: don't share default values

Given what we've just discussed, it is better to not share default values and to always create new ones:

```
function Names(data) {
    this.data = data || [];
}
```

Obviously, the problem of modifying a shared default value does not arise if that value is immutable (as all primitives are; see "Primitive Values" on page 69). But for consistency's sake, it's best to stick to a single way of setting up properties. I also prefer to maintain the usual separation of concerns (see "Layer 3: Constructors—Factories for Instances" on page 231): the constructor sets up the instance properties, and the prototype contains the methods.

ECMAScript 6 will make this even more of a best practice, because constructor parameters can have default values and you can define prototype methods via classes, but not prototype properties with data.

Creating instance properties on demand

Occasionally, creating a property value is an expensive operation (computationally or storage-wise). In that case, you can create an instance property on demand:

```
function Names(data) {
    if (data) this.data = data;
}
Names.prototype = {
    constructor: Names, // (1)
    get data() {
```

```
// Define, don't assign
// => avoid calling the (nonexistent) setter
Object.defineProperty(this, 'data', {
    value: [],
    enumerable: true,
    configurable: false,
    writable: false
});
return this.data;
    }
};
```

We can't add the property `data` to the instance via assignment, because JavaScript would complain about a missing setter (which it does when it only finds a getter). Therefore, we add it via `Object.defineProperty()`. Consult "Properties: Definition Versus Assignment" on page 226 to review the differences between defining and assigning. In line (1), we are ensuring that the property `constructor` is set up properly (see "The constructor Property of Instances" on page 234).

Obviously, that is quite a bit of work, so you have to be sure it is worth it.

Avoid Nonpolymorphic Prototype Properties

If the same property (same key, same semantics, generally different values), exists in several prototypes, it is called *polymorphic*. Then the result of reading the property via an instance is dynamically determined via that instance's prototype. Prototype properties that are not used polymorphically can be replaced by variables (which better reflects their nonpolymorphic nature).

For example, you can store a constant in a prototype property and access it via `this`:

```
function Foo() {}
Foo.prototype.FACTOR = 42;
Foo.prototype.compute = function (x) {
    return x * this.FACTOR;
};
```

This constant is not polymorphic. Therefore, you can just as well access it via a variable:

```
// This code should be inside an IIFE or a module
function Foo() {}
var FACTOR = 42;
Foo.prototype.compute = function (x) {
    return x * FACTOR;
};
```

Polymorphic Prototype Properties

Here is an example of polymorphic prototype properties with immutable data. Tagging instances of a constructor via prototype properties enables you to tell them apart from instances of a different constructor:

```
function ConstrA() { }
ConstrA.prototype.TYPE_NAME = 'ConstrA';

function ConstrB() { }
ConstrB.prototype.TYPE_NAME = 'ConstrB';
```

Thanks to the polymorphic "tag" TYPE_NAME, you can distinguish the instances of Con
strA and ConstrB even when they cross realms (then instanceof does not work; see
"Pitfall: crossing realms (frames or windows)" on page 238).

Keeping Data Private

JavaScript does not have dedicated means for managing private data for an object. This section will describe three techniques for working around that limitation:

- Private data in the environment of a constructor
- Private data in properties with marked keys
- Private data in properties with reified keys

Additionally, I will explain how to keep global data private via IIFEs.

Private Data in the Environment of a Constructor (Crockford Privacy Pattern)

When a constructor is invoked, two things are created: the constructor's instance and an environment (see "Environments: Managing Variables" on page 190). The instance is to be initialized by the constructor. The environment holds the constructor's parameters and local variables. Every function (which includes methods) created inside the constructor will retain a reference to the environment—the environment in which it was created. Thanks to that reference, it will always have access to the environment, even after the constructor is finished. This combination of function and environment is called a *closure* ("Closures: Functions Stay Connected to Their Birth Scopes" on page 193). The constructor's environment is thus data storage that is independent of the instance and related to it only because the two are created at the same time. To properly connect them, we must have functions that live in both worlds. Using Douglas Crockford's terminology (*http://www.crockford.com/javascript/private.html*), an instance can have three kinds of values associated with it (see Figure 17-4):

Public properties

> Values stored in properties (either in the instance or in its prototype) are publicly accessible.

Private values

> Data and functions stored in the environment are *private*—only accessible to the constructor and to the functions it created.

Privileged methods

> Private functions can access public properties, but public methods in the prototype can't access private data. We thus need *privileged* methods—public methods in the instance. Privileged methods are public and can be called by everyone, but they also have access to private values, because they were created in the constructor.

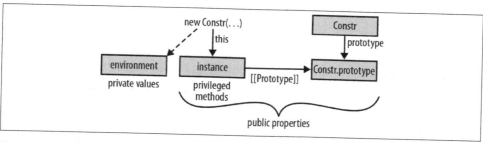

Figure 17-4. When a constructor Constr is invoked, two data structures are created: an environment for parameters and local variables and an instance to be initialized.

The following sections explain each kind of value in more detail.

Public properties

Remember that given a constructor `Constr`, there are two kinds of properties that are *public*, accessible to everyone. First, *prototype properties* are stored in `Constr.proto type` and shared by all instances. Prototype properties are usually methods:

```
Constr.prototype.publicMethod = ...;
```

Second, *instance properties* are unique to each instance. They are added in the constructor and usually hold data (not methods):

```
function Constr(...) {
    this.publicData = ...;
    ...
}
```

Private values

The constructor's environment consists of the parameters and local variables. They are accessible only from inside the constructor and thus private to the instance:

```
function Constr(...) {
    ...
    var that = this; // make accessible to private functions

    var privateData = ...;

    function privateFunction(...) {
        // Access everything
        privateData = ...;

        that.publicData = ...;
        that.publicMethod(...);
    }
    ...
}
```

Privileged methods

Private data is so safe from outside access that prototype methods can't access it. But then how else would you use it after leaving the constructor? The answer is *privileged methods*: functions created in the constructor are added as instance methods. That means that, on one hand, they can access private data; on the other hand, they are public and therefore seen by prototype methods. In other words, they serve as mediators between private data and the public (including prototype methods):

```
function Constr(...) {
    ...
    this.privilegedMethod = function (...) {
        // Access everything
        privateData = ...;
        privateFunction(...);

        this.publicData = ...;
        this.publicMethod(...);
    };
}
```

An example

The following is an implementation of a `StringBuilder`, using the Crockford privacy pattern:

```
function StringBuilder() {
    var buffer = [];
    this.add = function (str) {
        buffer.push(str);
    };
```

```
      this.toString = function () {
          return buffer.join('');
      };
}
// Can't put methods in the prototype!
```

Here is the interaction:

```
> var sb = new StringBuilder();
> sb.add('Hello');
> sb.add(' world!');
> sb.toString()
'Hello world!'
```

The pros and cons of the Crockford privacy pattern

Here are some points to consider when you are using the Crockford privacy pattern:

It's not very elegant

Mediating access to private data via privileged methods introduces an unnecessary indirection. Privileged methods and private functions both destroy the separation of concerns between the constructor (setting up instance data) and the instance prototype (methods).

It's completely secure

There is no way to access the environment's data from outside, which makes this solution secure if you need that (e.g., for security-critical code). On the other hand, private data not being accessible to the outside can also be an inconvenience. Sometimes you want to unit-test private functionality. And some temporary quick fixes depend on the ability to access private data. This kind of quick fix cannot be predicted, so no matter how good your design is, the need can arise.

It may be slower

Accessing properties in the prototype chain is highly optimized in current JavaScript engines. Accessing values in the closure may be slower. But these things change constantly, so you'll have to measure should this really matter for your code.

It consumes more memory

Keeping the environment around and putting privileged methods in instances costs memory. Again, be sure it really matters for your code and measure.

Private Data in Properties with Marked Keys

For most non-security-critical applications, privacy is more like a hint to clients of an API: "You don't need to see this." That's the key benefit of encapsulation—hiding complexity. Even though more is going on under the hood, you only need to understand the public part of an API. The idea of a naming convention is to let clients know about privacy by marking the key of a property. A prefixed underscore is often used for this purpose.

Let's rewrite the previous `StringBuilder` example so that the buffer is kept in a property `_buffer`, which is private, but by convention only:

```
function StringBuilder() {
    this._buffer = [];
}
StringBuilder.prototype = {
    constructor: StringBuilder,
    add: function (str) {
        this._buffer.push(str);
    },
    toString: function () {
        return this._buffer.join('');
    }
};
```

Here are some pros and cons of privacy via marked property keys:

It offers a more natural coding style
>   Being able to access private and public data in the same manner is more elegant than using environments for privacy.

It pollutes the namespace of properties
>   Properties with marked keys can be seen everywhere. The more people use IDEs, the more it will be a nuisance that they are shown alongside public properties, in places where they should be hidden. IDEs could, in theory, adapt by recognizing naming conventions and by hiding private properties where possible.

Private properties can be accessed from "outside"
>   That can be useful for unit tests and quick fixes. Additionally, subconstructors and helper functions (so-called "friend functions") can profit from easier access to private data. The environment approach doesn't offer this kind of flexibility; private data can be accessed only from within the constructor.

It can lead to key clashes
>   Keys of private properties can clash. This is already an issue for subconstructors, but it is even more problematic if you work with multiple inheritance (as enabled by some libraries). With the environment approach, there are never any clashes.

Private Data in Properties with Reified Keys

One problem with a naming convention for private properties is that keys might clash (e.g., a key from a constructor with a key from a subconstructor, or a key from a mixin with a key from a constructor). You can make such clashes less likely by using longer keys, that, for example, include the name of the constructor. Then, in the previous case, the private property _buffer would be called _StringBuilder_buffer. If such a key is too long for your taste, you have the option of *reifying it*, of storing it in a variable:

```
var KEY_BUFFER = '_StringBuilder_buffer';
```

We now access the private data via this[KEY_BUFFER]:

```
var StringBuilder = function () {
    var KEY_BUFFER = '_StringBuilder_buffer';

    function StringBuilder() {
        this[KEY_BUFFER] = [];
    }
    StringBuilder.prototype = {
        constructor: StringBuilder,
        add: function (str) {
            this[KEY_BUFFER].push(str);
        },
        toString: function () {
            return this[KEY_BUFFER].join('');
        }
    };
    return StringBuilder;
}();
```

We have wrapped an IIFE around StringBuilder so that the constant KEY_BUFFER stays local and doesn't pollute the global namespace.

Reified property keys enable you to use UUIDs (universally unique identifiers) in keys. For example, via Robert Kieffer's node-uuid (*https://github.com/broofa/node-uuid*):

```
var KEY_BUFFER = '_StringBuilder_buffer_' + uuid.v4();
```

KEY_BUFFER has a different value each time the code runs. It may, for example, look like this:

```
_StringBuilder_buffer_110ec58a-a0f2-4ac4-8393-c866d813b8d1
```

Long keys with UUIDs make key clashes virtually impossible.

Keeping Global Data Private via IIFEs

This subsection explains how to keep global data private to singleton objects, constructors, and methods, via IIFEs (see "Introducing a New Scope via an IIFE" on page 183). Those IIFEs create new environments (refer back to "Environments: Managing Variables" on page 190), which is where you put the private data.

Attaching private global data to a singleton object

You don't need a constructor to associate an object with private data in an environment. The following example shows how to use an IIFE for the same purpose, by wrapping it around a singleton object:

```
var obj = function () {  // open IIFE

    // public
    var self = {
        publicMethod: function (...) {
            privateData = ...;
            privateFunction(...);
        },
        publicData: ...
    };

    // private
    var privateData = ...;
    function privateFunction(...) {
        privateData = ...;
        self.publicData = ...;
        self.publicMethod(...);
    }

    return self;
}(); // close IIFE
```

Keeping global data private to all of a constructor

Some global data is relevant only for a constructor and the prototype methods. By wrapping an IIFE around both, you can hide it from public view. "Private Data in Properties with Reified Keys" on page 248 gave an example: the constructor StringBuild er and its prototype methods use the constant KEY_BUFFER, which contains a property key. That constant is stored in the environment of an IIFE:

```
var StringBuilder = function () { // open IIFE
    var KEY_BUFFER = '_StringBuilder_buffer_' + uuid.v4();

    function StringBuilder() {
        this[KEY_BUFFER] = [];
    }
    StringBuilder.prototype = {
        // Omitted: methods accessing this[KEY_BUFFER]
    };
    return StringBuilder;
}(); // close IIFE
```

Note that if you are using a module system (see Chapter 31), you can achieve the same effect with cleaner code by putting the constructor plus methods in a module.

Attaching global data to a method

Sometimes you only need global data for a single method. You can keep it private by putting it in the environment of an IIFE that you wrap around the method. For example:

```
var obj = {
    method: function () {  // open IIFE
```

```
        // method-private data
        var invocCount = 0;

        return function () {
            invocCount++;
            console.log('Invocation #'+invocCount);
            return 'result';
        };
    }() // close IIFE
};
```

Here is the interaction:

```
> obj.method()
Invocation #1
'result'
> obj.method()
Invocation #2
'result'
```

Layer 4: Inheritance Between Constructors

In this section, we examine how constructors can be inherited from: given a constructor Super, how can we write a new constructor, Sub, that has all the features of Super plus some features of its own? Unfortunately, JavaScript does not have a built-in mechanism for performing this task. Hence, we'll have to do some manual work.

Figure 17-5 illustrates the idea: the subconstructor Sub should have all of the properties of Super (both prototype properties and instance properties) in addition to its own. Thus, we have a rough idea of what Sub should look like, but don't know how to get there. There are several things we need to figure out, which I'll explain next:

- Inheriting instance properties.

- Inheriting prototype properties.

- Ensuring that instanceof works: if sub is an instance of Sub, we also want sub instanceof Super to be true.

- Overriding a method to adapt one of Super's methods in Sub.

- Making supercalls: if we have overridden one of Super's methods, we may need to call the original method from Sub.

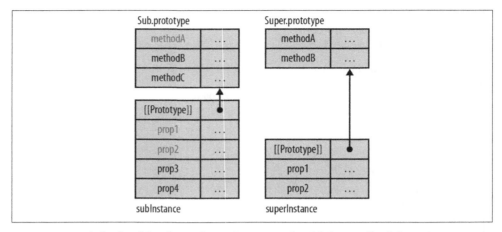

Figure 17-5. Sub should inherit from Super: it should have all of Super's prototype properties and all of Super's instance properties in addition to its own. Note that methodB overrides Super's methodB.

Inheriting Instance Properties

Instance properties are set up in the constructor itself, so inheriting the superconstructor's instance properties involves calling that constructor:

```
function Sub(prop1, prop2, prop3, prop4) {
    Super.call(this, prop1, prop2);  // (1)
    this.prop3 = prop3;  // (2)
    this.prop4 = prop4;  // (3)
}
```

When Sub is invoked via new, its implicit parameter this refers to a fresh instance. It first passes that instance on to Super (1), which adds its instance properties. Afterward, Sub sets up its own instance properties (2,3). The trick is not to invoke Super via new, because that would create a fresh superinstance. Instead, we call Super as a function and hand in the current (sub)instance as the value of this.

Inheriting Prototype Properties

Shared properties such as methods are kept in the instance prototype. Thus, we need to find a way for Sub.prototype to inherit all of Super.prototype's properties. The solution is to give Sub.prototype the prototype Super.prototype.

Confused by the two kinds of prototypes?

Yes, JavaScript terminology is confusing here. If you feel lost, consult "Terminology: The Two Prototypes" on page 234, which explains how they differ.

This is the code that achieves that:

```
Sub.prototype = Object.create(Super.prototype);
Sub.prototype.constructor = Sub;
Sub.prototype.methodB = ...;
Sub.prototype.methodC = ...;
```

`Object.create()` produces a fresh object whose prototype is `Super.prototype`. Afterward, we add Sub's methods. As explained in "The constructor Property of Instances" on page 234, we also need to set up the property `constructor`, because we have replaced the original instance prototype where it had the correct value.

Figure 17-6 shows how Sub and Super are related now. Sub's structure does resemble what I have sketched in Figure 17-5. The diagram does not show the instance properties, which are set up by the function call mentioned in the diagram.

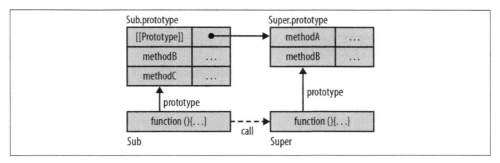

Figure 17-6. The constructor Sub inherits the constructor Super by calling it and by making Sub.prototype a prototypee of Super.prototype.

Ensuring That instanceof Works

"Ensuring that `instanceof` works" means that every instance of Sub must also be an instance of Super. Figure 17-7 shows what the prototype chain of `subInstance`, an instance of Sub, looks like: its first prototype is `Sub.prototype`, and its second prototype is `Super.prototype`.

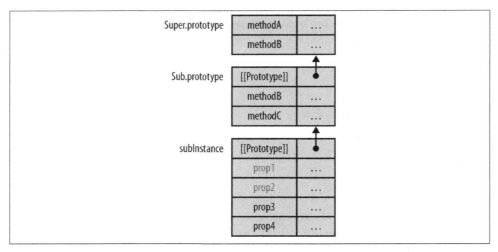

Figure 17-7. subInstance has been created by the constructor Sub. It has the two proto-types Sub.prototype and Super.prototype.

Let's start with an easier question: is subInstance an instance of Sub? Yes, it is, because the following two assertions are equivalent (the latter can be considered the definition of the former):

```
subInstance instanceof Sub
Sub.prototype.isPrototypeOf(subInstance)
```

As mentioned before, Sub.prototype is one of the prototypes of subInstance, so both assertions are true. Similarly, subInstance is also an instance of Super, because the following two assertions hold:

```
subInstance instanceof Super
Super.prototype.isPrototypeOf(subInstance)
```

Overriding a Method

We override a method in Super.prototype by adding a method with the same name to Sub.prototype. methodB is an example and in Figure 17-7, we can see why it works: the search for methodB begins in subInstance and finds Sub.prototype.methodB before Super.prototype.methodB.

Making a Supercall

To understand supercalls, you need to know the term *home object*. The home object of a method is the object that owns the property whose value is the method. For example, the home object of Sub.prototype.methodB is Sub.prototype. Supercalling a method foo involves three steps:

---

1. Start your search "after" (in the prototype of) the home object of the current method.

2. Look for a method whose name is foo.

3. Invoke that method with the current this. The rationale is that the supermethod must work with the same instance as the current method; it must be able to access the same instance properties.

Therefore, the code of the submethod looks as follows. It supercalls itself, it calls the method it has overridden:

```
Sub.prototype.methodB = function (x, y) {
    var superResult = Super.prototype.methodB.call(this, x, y); // (1)
    return this.prop3 + ' ' + superResult;
}
```

One way of reading the supercall at (1) is as follows: refer to the supermethod directly and call it with the current this. However, if we split it into three parts, we find the aforementioned steps:

1. Super.prototype: Start your search in Super.prototype, the prototype of Sub.prototype (the home object of the current method Sub.prototype.methodB).

2. methodB: Look for a method with the name methodB.

3. call(this, ...): Call the method found in the previous step, and maintain the current this.

Avoiding Hardcoding the Name of the Superconstructor

Until now, we have always referred to supermethods and superconstructors by mentioning the superconstructor name. This kind of hardcoding makes your code less flexible. You can avoid it by assigning the superprototype to a property of Sub:

```
Sub._super = Super.prototype;
```

Then calling the superconstructor and a supermethod looks as follows:

```
function Sub(prop1, prop2, prop3, prop4) {
    Sub._super.constructor.call(this, prop1, prop2);
    this.prop3 = prop3;
    this.prop4 = prop4;
}
Sub.prototype.methodB = function (x, y) {
    var superResult = Sub._super.methodB.call(this, x, y);
    return this.prop3 + ' ' + superResult;
}
```

Setting up `Sub._super` is usually handled by a utility function that also connects the subprototype to the superprototype. For example:

```
function subclasses(SubC, SuperC) {
    var subProto = Object.create(SuperC.prototype);
    // Save `constructor` and, possibly, other methods
    copyOwnPropertiesFrom(subProto, SubC.prototype);
    SubC.prototype = subProto;
    SubC._super = SuperC.prototype;
};
```

This code uses the helper function `copyOwnPropertiesFrom()`, which is shown and explained in "Copying an Object" on page 226.

 Read "subclasses" as a verb: SubC *subclasses* SuperC. Such a utility function can take some of the pain out of creating a subconstructor: there are fewer things to do manually, and the name of the superconstructor is never mentioned redundantly. The following example demonstrates how it simplifies code.

Example: Constructor Inheritance in Use

As a concrete example, let's assume that the constructor `Person` already exists:

```
function Person(name) {
    this.name = name;
}
Person.prototype.describe = function () {
    return 'Person called '+this.name;
};
```

We now want to create the constructor `Employee` as a subconstructor of `Person`. We do so manually, which looks like this:

```
function Employee(name, title) {
    Person.call(this, name);
    this.title = title;
}
Employee.prototype = Object.create(Person.prototype);
Employee.prototype.constructor = Employee;
Employee.prototype.describe = function () {
    return Person.prototype.describe.call(this)+' ('+this.title+')';
};
```

Here is the interaction:

```
> var jane = new Employee('Jane', 'CTO');
> jane.describe()
Person called Jane (CTO)
> jane instanceof Employee
true
```

```
> jane instanceof Person
true
```

The utility function `subclasses()` from the previous section makes the code of `Employee` slightly simpler and avoids hardcoding the superconstructor `Person`:

```
function Employee(name, title) {
    Employee._super.constructor.call(this, name);
    this.title = title;
}
Employee.prototype.describe = function () {
    return Employee._super.describe.call(this)+' ('+this.title+')';
};
subclasses(Employee, Person);
```

Example: The Inheritance Hierarchy of Built-in Constructors

Built-in constructors use the same subclassing approach described in this section. For example, `Array` is a subconstructor of `Object`. Therefore, the prototype chain of an instance of `Array` looks like this:

```
> var p = Object.getPrototypeOf

> p([]) === Array.prototype
true
> p(p([])) === Object.prototype
true
> p(p(p([]))) === null
true
```

Antipattern: The Prototype Is an Instance of the Superconstructor

Before ECMAScript 5 and `Object.create()`, an often-used solution was to create the subprototype by invoking the superconstructor:

```
Sub.prototype = new Super();  // Don't do this
```

This is not recommended under ECMAScript 5. The prototype will have all of `Super`'s instance properties, which it has no use for. Therefore, it is better to use the aforementioned pattern (involving `Object.create()`).

Methods of All Objects

Almost all objects have `Object.prototype` in their prototype chain:

```
> Object.prototype.isPrototypeOf({})
true
> Object.prototype.isPrototypeOf([])
true
```

```
> Object.prototype.isPrototypeOf(/xyz/)
true
```

The following subsections describe the methods that `Object.prototype` provides for its prototypees.

Conversion to Primitive

The following two methods are used to convert an object to a primitive value:

`Object.prototype.toString()`
>   Returns a string representation of an object:

```
> ({ first: 'John', last: 'Doe' }.toString())
'[object Object]'
> [ 'a', 'b', 'c' ].toString()
'a,b,c'
```

`Object.prototype.valueOf()`
>   This is the preferred way of converting an object to a number. The default implementation returns `this`:

```
> var obj = {};
> obj.valueOf() === obj
true
```

>   `valueOf` is overridden by wrapper constructors to return the wrapped primitive:

```
> new Number(7).valueOf()
7
```

The conversion to number and string (whether implicit or explicit) builds on the conversion to primitive (for details, see "Algorithm: ToPrimitive()—Converting a Value to a Primitive" on page 79). That is why you can use the aforementioned two methods to configure those conversions. `valueOf()` is preferred by the conversion to number:

```
> 3 * { valueOf: function () { return 5 } }
15
```

`toString()` is preferred by the conversion to string:

```
> String({ toString: function () { return 'ME' } })
'Result: ME'
```

The conversion to boolean is not configurable; objects are always considered to be `true` (see "Converting to Boolean" on page 97).

Object.prototype.toLocaleString()

This method returns a locale-specific string representation of an object. The default implementation calls `toString()`. Most engines don't go beyond this support for this method. However, the ECMAScript Internationalization API (see "The ECMAScript

Internationalization API" on page 406), which is supported by many modern engines, overrides it for several built-in constructors.

Prototypal Inheritance and Properties

The following methods help with prototypal inheritance and properties:

`Object.prototype.isPrototypeOf(obj)`

Returns `true` if the receiver is part of the prototype chain of `obj`:

```
> var proto = { };
> var obj = Object.create(proto);
> proto.isPrototypeOf(obj)
true
> obj.isPrototypeOf(obj)
false
```

`Object.prototype.hasOwnProperty(key)`

Returns `true` if `this` owns a property whose key is `key`. "Own" means that the property exists in the object itself and not in one of its prototypes.

 You normally should invoke this method generically (not directly), especially on objects whose properties you don't know statically. Why and how is explained in "Iteration and Detection of Properties" on page 217:

```
> var proto = { foo: 'abc' };
> var obj = Object.create(proto);
> obj.bar = 'def';

> Object.prototype.hasOwnProperty.call(obj, 'foo')
false
> Object.prototype.hasOwnProperty.call(obj, 'bar')
true
```

`Object.prototype.propertyIsEnumerable(propKey)`

Returns `true` if the receiver has a property with the key `propKey` that is enumerable and `false` otherwise:

```
> var obj = { foo: 'abc' };
> obj.propertyIsEnumerable('foo')
true
> obj.propertyIsEnumerable('toString')
false
> obj.propertyIsEnumerable('unknown')
false
```

Generic Methods: Borrowing Methods from Prototypes

Sometimes instance prototypes have methods that are useful for more objects than those that inherit from them. This section explains how to use the methods of a prototype without inheriting from it. For example, the instance prototype `Wine.prototype` has the method `incAge()`:

```
function Wine(age) {
    this.age = age;
}
Wine.prototype.incAge = function (years) {
    this.age += years;
}
```

The interaction is as follows:

```
> var chablis = new Wine(3);
> chablis.incAge(1);
> chablis.age
4
```

The method `incAge()` works for any object that has the property `age`. How can we invoke it on an object that is not an instance of `Wine`? Let's look at the preceding method call:

```
chablis.incAge(1)
```

There are actually two arguments:

1. `chablis` is the receiver of the method call, passed to `incAge` via `this`.

2. `1` is an argument, passed to `incAge` via `years`.

We can't replace the former with an arbitrary object—the receiver must be an instance of `Wine`. Otherwise, the method `incAge` is not found. But the preceding method call is equivalent to (refer back to "Calling Functions While Setting this: call(), apply(), and bind()" on page 204):

```
Wine.prototype.incAge.call(chablis, 1)
```

With the preceding pattern, we can make an object the receiver (first argument of `call`) that is not an instance of `Wine`, because the receiver isn't used to find the method `Wine.prototype.incAge`. In the following example, we apply the method `incAge()` to the object `john`:

```
> var john = { age: 51 };
> Wine.prototype.incAge.call(john, 3)
> john.age
54
```

A function that can be used in this manner is called a *generic method*; it must be prepared for this not being an instance of "its" constructor. Thus, not all methods are generic; the ECMAScript language specification explicitly states which ones are (see "A List of All Generic Methods" on page 264).

Accessing Object.prototype and Array.prototype via Literals

Calling a method generically is quite verbose:

```
Object.prototype.hasOwnProperty.call(obj, 'propKey')
```

You can make this shorter by accessing hasOwnProperty via an instance of Object, as created by an empty object literal {}:

```
{}.hasOwnProperty.call(obj, 'propKey')
```

Similarly, the following two expressions are equivalent:

```
Array.prototype.join.call(str, '-')
[].join.call(str, '-')
```

The advantage of this pattern is that it is less verbose. But it is also less self-explanatory. Performance should not be an issue (at least long term), as engines can statically determine that the literals should not create objects.

Examples of Calling Methods Generically

These are a few examples of generic methods in use:

- Use apply()(see "Function.prototype.apply(thisValue, argArray)" on page 205) to push an array (instead of individual elements; see "Adding and Removing Elements (Destructive)" on page 286):

```
> var arr1 = [ 'a', 'b' ];
> var arr2 = [ 'c', 'd' ];

> [].push.apply(arr1, arr2)
4
> arr1
[ 'a', 'b', 'c', 'd' ]
```

This example is about turning an array into arguments, not about borrowing a method from another constructor.

- Apply the array method join() to a string (which is not an array):

```
> Array.prototype.join.call('abc', '-')
'a-b-c'
```

- Apply the array method `map()` to a string:[1]

```
> [].map.call('abc', function (x) { return x.toUpperCase() })
[ 'A', 'B', 'C' ]
```

Using `map()` generically is more efficient than using `split('')`, which creates an intermediate array:

```
> 'abc'.split('').map(function (x) { return x.toUpperCase() })
[ 'A', 'B', 'C' ]
```

- Apply a string method to nonstrings. `toUpperCase()` converts the receiver to a string and uppercases the result:

```
> String.prototype.toUpperCase.call(true)
'TRUE'
> String.prototype.toUpperCase.call(['a','b','c'])
'A,B,C'
```

Using generic array methods on plain objects gives you insight into how they work:

- Invoke an array method on a fake array:

```
> var fakeArray = { 0: 'a', 1: 'b', length: 2 };
> Array.prototype.join.call(fakeArray, '-')
'a-b'
```

- See how an array method transforms an object that it treats like an array:

```
> var obj = {};
> Array.prototype.push.call(obj, 'hello');
1
> obj
{ '0': 'hello', length: 1 }
```

Array-Like Objects and Generic Methods

There are some objects in JavaScript that feel like an array, but actually aren't. That means that while they have indexed access and a `length` property, they don't have any of the array methods (`forEach()`, `push`, `concat()`, etc.). This is unfortunate, but as we will see, generic array methods enable a workaround. Examples of array-like objects include:

- The special variable `arguments` (see "All Parameters by Index: The Special Variable arguments" on page 171), which is an important array-like object, because it is such a fundamental part of JavaScript. `arguments` looks like an array:

```
> function args() { return arguments }
> var arrayLike = args('a', 'b');
```

---

1. Using `map()` in this manner is a tip by Brandon Benvie (@benvie).

```
> arrayLike[0]
'a'
> arrayLike.length
2
```

But none of the array methods are available:

```
> arrayLike.join('-')
TypeError: object has no method 'join'
```

That's because `arrayLike` is not an instance of `Array` (and `Array.prototype` is not in the prototype chain):

```
> arrayLike instanceof Array
false
```

• Browser DOM node lists, which are returned by `document.getElementsBy*()` (e.g., `getElementsByTagName()`), `document.forms`, and so on:

```
> var elts = document.getElementsByTagName('h3');
> elts.length
3
> elts instanceof Array
false
```

• Strings, which are array-like, too:

```
> 'abc'[1]
'b'
> 'abc'.length
3
```

The term *array-like* can also be seen as a contract between generic array methods and objects. The objects have to fulfill certain requirements; otherwise, the methods won't work on them. The requirements are:

• The elements of an array-like object must be accessible via square brackets and integer indices starting at 0. All methods need read access, and some methods additionally need write access. Note that all objects support this kind of indexing: an index in brackets is converted to a string and used as a key to look up a property value:

```
> var obj = { '0': 'abc' };
> obj[0]
'abc'
```

• An array-like object must have a `length` property whose value is the number of its elements. Some methods require `length` to be mutable (for example, `reverse()`). Values whose lengths are immutable (for example, strings) cannot be used with those methods.

Patterns for working with array-like objects

The following patterns are useful for working with array-like objects:

- Turn an array-like object into an array:

```
var arr = Array.prototype.slice.call(arguments);
```

  The method slice() (see "Concatenating, Slicing, Joining (Nondestructive)" on page 289) without any arguments creates a copy of an array-like receiver:

```
var copy = [ 'a', 'b' ].slice();
```

- To iterate over all elements of an array-like object, you can use a simple for loop:

```
function logArgs() {
    for (var i=0; i<arguments.length; i++) {
        console.log(i+'. '+arguments[i]);
    }
}
```

  But you can also borrow Array.prototype.forEach():

```
function logArgs() {
    Array.prototype.forEach.call(arguments, function (elem, i) {
        console.log(i+'. '+elem);
    });
}
```

In both cases, the interaction looks as follows:

```
> logArgs('hello', 'world');
0. hello
1. world
```

A List of All Generic Methods

The following list includes all methods that are generic, as mentioned in the ECMA-Script language specification:

- Array.prototype (see "Array Prototype Methods" on page 286):
  — concat
  — every
  — filter
  — forEach
  — indexOf
  — join
  — lastIndexOf

- — map
- — pop
- — push
- — reduce
- — reduceRight
- — reverse
- — shift
- — slice
- — some
- — sort
- — splice
- — toLocaleString
- — toString
- — unshift

- `Date.prototype` (see "Date Prototype Methods" on page 319)

  - — toJSON

- `Object.prototype` (see "Methods of All Objects" on page 257)

  - — (All `Object` methods are automatically generic—they have to work for all objects.)

- `String.prototype` (see "String Prototype Methods" on page 139)

  - — charAt
  - — charCodeAt
  - — concat
  - — indexOf
  - — lastIndexOf
  - — localeCompare
  - — match
  - — replace
  - — search
  - — slice
  - — split

— substring

— toLocaleLowerCase

— toLocaleUpperCase

— toLowerCase

— toUpperCase

— trim

Pitfalls: Using an Object as a Map

Since JavaScript has no built-in data structure for maps, objects are often used as maps from strings to values. Alas, that is more error-prone than it seems. This section explains three pitfalls that are involved in this task.

Pitfall 1: Inheritance Affects Reading Properties

The operations that read properties can be partitioned into two kinds:

- Some operations consider the whole prototype chain and see inherited properties.
- Other operations access only the *own* (noninherited) properties of an object.

You need to choose carefully between these kinds of operations when you read the entries of an object-as-map. To see why, consider the following example:

```
var proto = { protoProp: 'a' };
var obj = Object.create(proto);
obj.ownProp = 'b';
```

obj is an object with one own property whose prototype is proto, which also has one own property. proto has the prototype Object.prototype, like all objects that are created by object literals. Thus, obj inherits properties from both proto and Object. prototype.

We want obj to be interpreted as a map with the single entry:

```
ownProp: 'b'
```

That is, we want to ignore inherited properties and only consider own properties. Let's see which read operations interpret obj in this manner and which don't. Note that for objects-as-maps, we normally want to use arbitrary property keys, stored in variables. That rules out dot notation.

Checking whether a property exists

The `in` operator checks whether an object has a property with a given key, but it considers inherited properties:

```
> 'ownProp' in obj  // ok
true
> 'unknown' in obj  // ok
false
> 'toString' in obj  // wrong, inherited from Object.prototype
true
> 'protoProp' in obj  // wrong, inherited from proto
true
```

We need the check to ignore inherited properties. `hasOwnProperty()` does what we want:

```
> obj.hasOwnProperty('ownProp')  // ok
true
> obj.hasOwnProperty('unknown')  // ok
false
> obj.hasOwnProperty('toString')  // ok
false
> obj.hasOwnProperty('protoProp')  // ok
false
```

Collecting property keys

What operations can we use to find all of the keys of `obj`, while honoring our interpretation of it as a map? `for-in` looks like it might work. But, alas, it doesn't:

```
> for (propKey in obj) console.log(propKey)
ownProp
protoProp
```

It considers inherited enumerable properties. The reason that no properties of `Object.prototype` show up here is that all of them are nonenumerable.

In contrast, `Object.keys()` lists only own properties:

```
> Object.keys(obj)
[ 'ownProp' ]
```

This method returns only enumerable own properties; `ownProp` has been added via assignment and is thus enumerable by default. If you want to list all own properties, you need to use `Object.getOwnPropertyNames()`.

Getting a property value

For reading the value of a property, we can only choose between the dot operator and the bracket operator. We can't use the former, because we have arbitrary keys, stored in variables. That leaves us with the bracket operator, which considers inherited properties:

```
> obj['toString']
[Function: toString]
```

This is not what we want. There is no built-in operation for reading only own properties, but you can easily implement one yourself:

```
function getOwnProperty(obj, propKey) {
    // Using hasOwnProperty() in this manner is problematic
    // (explained and fixed later)
    return (obj.hasOwnProperty(propKey)
            ? obj[propKey] : undefined);
}
```

With that function, the inherited property toString is ignored:

```
> getOwnProperty(obj, 'toString')
undefined
```

Pitfall 2: Overriding Affects Invoking Methods

The function getOwnProperty() invoked the method hasOwnProperty() on obj. Normally, that is fine:

```
> getOwnProperty({ foo: 123 }, 'foo')
123
```

However, if you add a property to obj whose key is hasOwnProperty, then that property overrides the method Object.prototype.hasOwnProperty() and getOwnProperty() ceases to work:

```
> getOwnProperty({ hasOwnProperty: 123 }, 'foo')
TypeError: Property 'hasOwnProperty' is not a function
```

You can fix this problem by directly referring to hasOwnProperty(). This avoids going through obj to find it:

```
function getOwnProperty(obj, propKey) {
    return (Object.prototype.hasOwnProperty.call(obj, propKey)
            ? obj[propKey] : undefined);
}
```

We have called hasOwnProperty() generically (see "Generic Methods: Borrowing Methods from Prototypes" on page 260).

Pitfall 3: The Special Property __proto__

In many JavaScript engines, the property __proto__ (see "The Special Property __proto__" on page 215) is special: getting it retrieves the prototype of an object, and setting it changes the prototype of an object. This is why the object can't store map data in a property whose key is '__proto__'. If you want to allow the map key '__proto__', you must escape it before using it as a property key:

```
function get(obj, key) {
    return obj[escapeKey(key)];
}
function set(obj, key, value) {
    obj[escapeKey(key)] = value;
}
// Similar: checking if key exists, deleting an entry

function escapeKey(key) {
    if (key.indexOf('__proto__') === 0) {  // (1)
        return key+'%';
    } else {
        return key;
    }
}
```

We also need to escape the escaped version of '__proto__' (etc.) to avoid clashes; that is, if we escape the key '__proto__' as '__proto__%', then we also need to escape the key '__proto__%' so that it doesn't replace a '__proto__' entry. That's what happens in line (1).

Mark S. Miller mentions the real-world implications of this pitfall in an email (*http://mzl.la/1fwnd1l*):

> Think this exercise is academic and doesn't arise in real systems? As observed at a support thread, until recently, on all non-IE browsers, if you typed "__proto__" at the beginning of a new Google Doc, your Google Doc would hang. This was tracked down to such a buggy use of an object as a string map.

The dict Pattern: Objects Without Prototypes Are Better Maps

You create an object without a prototype like this:

```
var dict = Object.create(null);
```

Such an object is a better map (dictionary) than a normal object, which is why this pattern is sometimes called the *dict pattern* (*dict* for *dictionary*). Let's first examine normal objects and then find out why prototype-less objects are better maps.

Normal objects

Usually, each object you create in JavaScript has at least Object.prototype in its prototype chain. The prototype of Object.prototype is null, so that's where most prototype chains end:

```
> Object.getPrototypeOf({}) === Object.prototype
true
> Object.getPrototypeOf(Object.prototype)
null
```

Prototype-less objects

Prototype-less objects have two advantages as maps:

- Inherited properties (pitfall #1) are not an issue anymore, simply because there are none. Therefore, you can now freely use the in operator to detect whether a property exists and brackets to read properties.
- Soon, __proto__ will be disabled. In ECMAScript 6, the special property __proto__ will be disabled if Object.prototype is not in the prototype chain of an object. You can expect JavaScript engines to slowly migrate to this behavior, but it is not yet very common.

The only disadvantage is that you'll lose the services provided by Object.prototype. For example, a dict object can't be automatically converted to a string anymore:

```
> console.log('Result: '+obj)
TypeError: Cannot convert object to primitive value
```

But that is not a real disadvantage, because it isn't safe to directly invoke methods on a dict object anyway.

Recommendation

Use the dict pattern for quick hacks and as a foundation for libraries. In (nonlibrary) production code, a library is preferable, because you can be sure to avoid all pitfalls. The next section lists a few such libraries.

Best Practices

There are many applications for using objects as maps. If all property keys are known statically (at development time), then you just need to make sure that you ignore inheritance and look only at own properties. If arbitrary keys can be used, you should turn to a library to avoid the pitfalls mentioned in this section. Here are two examples:

- StringMap.js (*http://bit.ly/1fwnp0E*) by Google's es-lab (*http://code.google.com/p/es-lab/*)
- stringmap.js (*https://github.com/olov/stringmap*) by Olov Lassus

Cheat Sheet: Working with Objects

This section is a quick reference with pointers to more thorough explanations.

- Object literals (see "Object Literals" on page 198):

```
var jane = {
    name: 'Jane',
```

```
    'not an identifier': 123,

    describe: function () { // method
        return 'Person named '+this.name;
    },
};
// Call a method:
console.log(jane.describe()); // Person named Jane
```

- Dot operator (.) (see "Dot Operator (.): Accessing Properties via Fixed Keys" on page 199):

```
obj.propKey
obj.propKey = value
delete obj.propKey
```

- Bracket operator ([]) (see "Bracket Operator ([]): Accessing Properties via Computed Keys" on page 202):

```
obj['propKey']
obj['propKey'] = value
delete obj['propKey']
```

- Getting and setting the prototype (see "Getting and Setting the Prototype" on page 214):

```
Object.create(proto, propDescObj?)
Object.getPrototypeOf(obj)
```

- Iteration and detection of properties (see "Iteration and Detection of Properties" on page 217):

```
Object.keys(obj)
Object.getOwnPropertyNames(obj)

Object.prototype.hasOwnProperty.call(obj, propKey)
propKey in obj
```

- Getting and defining properties via descriptors (see "Getting and Defining Properties via Descriptors" on page 224):

```
Object.defineProperty(obj, propKey, propDesc)
Object.defineProperties(obj, propDescObj)
Object.getOwnPropertyDescriptor(obj, propKey)
Object.create(proto, propDescObj?)
```

- Protecting objects (see "Protecting Objects" on page 229):

```
Object.preventExtensions(obj)
Object.isExtensible(obj)

Object.seal(obj)
Object.isSealed(obj)
```

```
Object.freeze(obj)
Object.isFrozen(obj)
```

- Methods of all objects (see "Methods of All Objects" on page 257):

```
Object.prototype.toString()
Object.prototype.valueOf()

Object.prototype.toLocaleString()

Object.prototype.isPrototypeOf(obj)
Object.prototype.hasOwnProperty(key)
Object.prototype.propertyIsEnumerable(propKey)
```

CHAPTER 18

Arrays

An array is a map from indices (natural numbers, starting at zero) to arbitrary values. The values (the range of the map) are called the array's *elements*. The most convenient way of creating an array is via an array literal. Such a literal enumerates the array elements; an element's position implicitly specifies its index.

In this chapter, I will first cover basic array mechanisms, such as indexed access and the length property, and then go over array methods.

Overview

This section provides a quick overview of arrays. Details are explained later.

As a first example, we create an array arr via an array literal (see "Creating Arrays" on page 274) and access elements (see "Array Indices" on page 276):

```
> var arr = [ 'a', 'b', 'c' ]; // array literal
> arr[0]  // get element 0
'a'
> arr[0] = 'x';  // set element 0
> arr
[ 'x', 'b', 'c' ]
```

We can use the array property length (see "length" on page 279) to remove and append elements:

```
> var arr = [ 'a', 'b', 'c' ];
> arr.length
3
> arr.length = 2;  // remove an element
> arr
[ 'a', 'b' ]
> arr[arr.length] = 'd';  // append an element
```

```
> arr
[ 'a', 'b', 'd' ]
```

The array method push( ) provides another way of appending an element:

```
> var arr = [ 'a', 'b' ];
> arr.push('d')
3
> arr
[ 'a', 'b', 'd' ]
```

Arrays Are Maps, Not Tuples

The ECMAScript standard specifies arrays as maps (dictionaries) from indices to values. In other words, arrays may not be contiguous and can have holes in them. For
example:

```
> var arr = [];
> arr[0] = 'a';
'a'
> arr[2] = 'b';
'b'
> arr
[ 'a', , 'b' ]
```

The preceding array has a hole: there is no element at index 1. "Holes in Arrays" on page
282 explains holes in more detail.

Note that most JavaScript engines optimize arrays without holes internally and store
them contiguously.

Arrays Can Also Have Properties

Arrays are still objects and can have object properties. Those are not considered part of
the actual array; that is, they are not considered array elements:

```
> var arr = [ 'a', 'b' ];
> arr.foo = 123;
> arr
[ 'a', 'b' ]
> arr.foo
123
```

Creating Arrays

You create an array via an array literal:

```
var myArray = [ 'a', 'b', 'c' ];
```

Trailing commas in arrays are ignored:

```
> [ 'a', 'b' ].length
2
> [ 'a', 'b', ].length
2
> [ 'a', 'b', ,].length  // hole + trailing comma
3
```

The Array Constructor

There are two ways to use the constructor `Array`: you can create an empty array with a given length or an array whose elements are the given values. For this constructor, `new` is optional: invoking it as a normal function (without `new`) does the same as invoking it as a constructor.

Creating an empty array with a given length

An empty array with a given length has only holes in it! Thus, it rarely makes sense to use this version of the constructor:

```
> var arr = new Array(2);
> arr.length
2
> arr  // two holes plus trailing comma (ignored!)
[ , ,]
```

Some engines may preallocate contiguous memory when you call `Array()` in this manner, which may slightly improve performance. However, be sure that the increased verbosity and redundancy is worth it!

Initializing an array with elements (avoid!)

This way of invoking `Array` is similar to an array literal:

```
// The same as ['a', 'b', 'c']:
var arr1 = new Array('a', 'b', 'c');
```

The problem is that you can't create arrays with a single number in them, because that is interpreted as creating an array whose `length` is the number:

```
> new Array(2)  // alas, not [ 2 ]
[ , ,]

> new Array(5.7)  // alas, not [ 5.7 ]
RangeError: Invalid array length

> new Array('abc')  // ok
[ 'abc' ]
```

Multidimensional Arrays

If you need multiple dimensions for elements, you must nest arrays. When you create such nested arrays, the innermost arrays can grow as needed. But if you want direct access to elements, you need to at least create the outer arrays. In the following example, I create a three-by-three matrix for Tic-tac-toe. The matrix is completely filled with data (as opposed to letting rows grow as needed):

```
// Create the Tic-tac-toe board
var rows = [];
for (var rowCount=0; rowCount < 3; rowCount++) {
    rows[rowCount] = [];
    for (var colCount=0; colCount < 3; colCount++) {
        rows[rowCount][colCount] = '.';
    }
}

// Set an X in the upper right corner
rows[0][2] = 'X';  // [row][column]

// Print the board
rows.forEach(function (row) {
    console.log(row.join(' '));
});
```

Here is the output:

```
. . X
. . .
. . .
```

I wanted the example to demonstrate the general case. Obviously, if a matrix is so small and has fixed dimensions, you can set it up via an array literal:

```
var rows = [ ['.','.','.'], ['.','.','.'], ['.','.','.'] ];
```

Array Indices

When you are working with array indices, you must keep in mind the following limits:

- Indices are numbers i in the range $0 \leq i < 2^{32}-1$.
- The maximum length is $2^{32}-1$.

Indices that are out of range are treated as normal property keys (strings!). They don't show up as array elements and they don't influence the property `length`. For example:

```
> var arr = [];

> arr[-1] = 'a';
> arr
```

```
[]
> arr['-1']
'a'

> arr[4294967296] = 'b';
> arr
[]
> arr['4294967296']
'b'
```

The in Operator and Indices

The in operator detects whether an object has a property with a given key. But it can also be used to determine whether a given element index exists in an array. For example:

```
> var arr = [ 'a', , 'b' ];
> 0 in arr
true
> 1 in arr
false
> 10 in arr
false
```

Deleting Array Elements

In addition to deleting properties, the delete operator also deletes array elements. Deleting elements creates holes (the length property is not updated):

```
> var arr = [ 'a', 'b' ];
> arr.length
2
> delete arr[1]  // does not update length
true
> arr
[ 'a',  ]
> arr.length
2
```

You can also delete trailing array elements by decreasing an array's length (see "length" on page 279 for details). To remove elements without creating holes (i.e., the indices of subsequent elements are decremented), you use Array.prototype.splice() (see "Adding and Removing Elements (Destructive)" on page 286). In this example, we remove two elements at index 1:

```
> var arr = ['a', 'b', 'c', 'd'];
> arr.splice(1, 2) // returns what has been removed
[ 'b', 'c' ]
> arr
[ 'a', 'd' ]
```

Array Indices in Detail

 This is an advanced section. You normally don't need to know the details explained here.

Array indices are not what they seem. Until now, I have pretended that array indices are numbers. And that is how JavaScript engines implement arrays, internally. However, the ECMAScript specification sees indices differently. Paraphrasing Section 15.4 (*http://bit.ly/1fwoCFg*):

- A property key P (a string) is an *array index* if and only if ToString(ToUint32(P)) is equal to P and ToUint32(P) is not equal to $2^{32}-1$. What this means is explained momentarily.
- An array property whose key is an array index is called an *element*.

In other words, in the world of the spec all values in brackets are converted to strings and interpreted as property keys, even numbers. The following interaction demonstrates this:

```
> var arr = ['a', 'b'];
> arr['0']
'a'
> arr[0]
'a'
```

To be an array index, a property key P (a string!) must be equal to the result of the following computation:

1. Convert P to a number.
2. Convert the number to a 32-bit unsigned integer.
3. Convert the integer to a string.

That means that an array index must be a stringified integer i in the 32-bit range $0 \leq i < 2^{32}-1$. The upper limit has been explicitly excluded in the spec (as quoted previously). It is reserved for the maximum length. To see how this definition works, let's use the function ToUint32() from "32-bit Integers via Bitwise Operators" on page 119.

First, a string that doesn't contain a number is always converted to 0, which, after stringification, is not equal to the string:

```
> ToUint32('xyz')
0
```

```
> ToUint32('?@#!')
0
```

Second, a stringified integer that is out of range is also converted to a completely different integer, which is not equal to the string, after stringification:

```
> ToUint32('-1')
4294967295
> Math.pow(2, 32)
4294967296
> ToUint32('4294967296')
0
```

Third, stringified noninteger numbers are converted to integers, which are, again, different:

```
> ToUint32('1.371')
1
```

Note that the specification also enforces that array indices don't have exponents:

```
> ToUint32('1e3')
1000
```

And that they don't have leading zeros:

```
> var arr = ['a', 'b'];
> arr['0']  // array index
'a'
> arr['00'] // normal property
undefined
```

length

The basic function of the length property is to track the highest index in an array:

```
> [ 'a', 'b' ].length
2
> [ 'a', , 'b' ].length
3
```

Thus, length does not count the number of elements, so you'd have to write your own function for doing so. For example:

```
function countElements(arr) {
    var elemCount = 0;
    arr.forEach(function () {
        elemCount++;
    });
    return elemCount;
}
```

To count elements (nonholes), we have used the fact that forEach skips holes. Here is the interaction:

```
> countElements([ 'a', 'b' ])
2
> countElements([ 'a', , 'b' ])
2
```

Manually Increasing the Length of an Array

Manually increasing the length of an array has remarkably little effect on an array; it only creates holes:

```
> var arr = [ 'a', 'b' ];
> arr.length = 3;
> arr  // one hole at the end
[ 'a', 'b', ,]
```

The last result has two commas at the end, because a trailing comma is optional and thus always ignored.

What we just did did not add any elements:

```
> countElements(arr)
2
```

However, the length property does act as a pointer indicating where to insert new elements. For example:

```
> arr.push('c')
4
> arr
[ 'a', 'b', , 'c' ]
```

Thus, setting the initial length of an array via the Array constructor creates an array that is completely empty:

```
> var arr = new Array(2);
> arr.length
2
> countElements(arr)
0
```

Decreasing the Length of an Array

If you decrease the length of an array, all elements at the new length and above are deleted:

```
> var arr = [ 'a', 'b', 'c' ];
> 1 in arr
true
> arr[1]
'b'

> arr.length = 1;
> arr
```

```
[ 'a' ]
> 1 in arr
false
> arr[1]
undefined
```

Clearing an array

If you set an array's length to 0, then it becomes empty. That allows you to clear an array for someone else. For example:

```
function clearArray(arr) {
    arr.length = 0;
}
```

Here's the interaction:

```
> var arr = [ 'a', 'b', 'c' ];
> clearArray(arr)
> arr
[]
```

Note, however, that this approach can be slow, because each array element is explicitly deleted. Ironically, creating a new empty array is often faster:

```
arr = [];
```

Clearing shared arrays

You need to be aware of the fact that setting an array's length to zero affects everybody who shares the array:

```
> var a1 = [1, 2, 3];
> var a2 = a1;
> a1.length = 0;

> a1
[]
> a2
[]
```

In contrast, assigning an empty array doesn't:

```
> var a1 = [1, 2, 3];
> var a2 = a1;
> a1 = [];

> a1
[]
> a2
[ 1, 2, 3 ]
```

The Maximum Length

The maximum array length is $2^{32}-1$:

```
> var arr1 = new Array(Math.pow(2, 32));   // not ok
RangeError: Invalid array length

> var arr2 = new Array(Math.pow(2, 32)-1);  // ok
> arr2.push('x');
RangeError: Invalid array length
```

Holes in Arrays

Arrays are maps from indices to values. That means that arrays can have *holes*, indices smaller than the length that are missing in the array. Reading an element at one of those indices returns undefined.

 It is recommended that you avoid holes in arrays. JavaScript handles them inconsistently (i.e., some methods ignore them, other don't). Thankfully, you normally don't need to know how holes are handled: they are rarely useful and affect performance negatively.

Creating Holes

You can create holes by assigning to array indices:

```
> var arr = [];
> arr[0] = 'a';
> arr[2] = 'c';
> 1 in arr   // hole at index 1
false
```

You can also create holes by omitting values in array literals:

```
> var arr = ['a',,'c'];
> 1 in arr   // hole at index 1
false
```

 You need two trailing commas to create a trailing hole, because the last comma is always ignored:

```
> [ 'a', ].length
1
> [ 'a', ,].length
2
```

Sparse Arrays Versus Dense Arrays

This section examines the differences between a hole and `undefined` as an element. Given that reading a hole returns `undefined`, both are very similar.

An array with holes is called *sparse*. An array without holes is called *dense*. Dense arrays are contiguous and have an element at each index—starting at zero, and ending at `length` − 1. Let's compare the following two arrays, a sparse array and a dense array. The two are very similar:

```
var sparse = [ , , 'c' ];
var dense  = [ undefined, undefined, 'c' ];
```

A hole is almost like having the element `undefined` at the same index. Both arrays have the same length:

```
> sparse.length
3
> dense.length
3
```

But the sparse array does not have an element at index 0:

```
> 0 in sparse
false
> 0 in dense
true
```

Iteration via `for` is the same for both arrays:

```
> for (var i=0; i<sparse.length; i++) console.log(sparse[i]);
undefined
undefined
c
> for (var i=0; i<dense.length; i++) console.log(dense[i]);
undefined
undefined
c
```

Iteration via `forEach` skips the holes, but not the undefined elements:

```
> sparse.forEach(function (x) { console.log(x) });
c
> dense.forEach(function (x) { console.log(x) });
undefined
undefined
c
```

Which Operations Ignore Holes, and Which Consider Them?

Some operations involving arrays ignore holes, while others consider them. This sections explains the details.

Array iteration methods

forEach() skips holes:

```
> ['a',, 'b'].forEach(function (x,i) { console.log(i+'.'+x) })
0.a
2.b
```

every() also skips holes (similarly: some()):

```
> ['a',, 'b'].every(function (x) { return typeof x === 'string' })
true
```

map() skips, but preserves holes:

```
> ['a',, 'b'].map(function (x,i) { return i+'.'+x })
[ '0.a', , '2.b' ]
```

filter() eliminates holes:

```
> ['a',, 'b'].filter(function (x) { return true })
[ 'a', 'b' ]
```

Other array methods

join() converts holes, undefineds, and nulls to empty strings:

```
> ['a',, 'b'].join('-')
'a--b'
> [ 'a', undefined, 'b' ].join('-')
'a--b'
```

sort() preserves holes while sorting:

```
> ['a',, 'b'].sort()  // length of result is 3
[ 'a', 'b', , ]
```

The for-in loop

The for-in loop correctly lists property keys (which are a superset of array indices):

```
> for (var key in ['a',, 'b']) { console.log(key) }
0
2
```

Function.prototype.apply()

apply() turns each hole into an argument whose value is undefined. The following interaction demonstrates this: function f() returns its arguments as an array. When we pass apply() an array with three holes in order to invoke f(), the latter receives three undefined arguments:

```
> function f() { return [].slice.call(arguments) }
> f.apply(null, [ , , ,])
[ undefined, undefined, undefined ]
```

That means that we can use `apply()` to create an array with undefineds:

```
> Array.apply(null, Array(3))
[ undefined, undefined, undefined ]
```

 `apply()` translates holes to undefineds in empty arrays, but it can't be used to plug holes in arbitrary arrays (which may or may not contain holes). Take, for example, the arbitrary array [2]:

```
> Array.apply(null, [2])
[ , ,]
```

The array does not contain any holes, so `apply()` should return the same array. Instead, it returns an empty array with length 2 (all it contains are two holes). That is because `Array()` interprets single numbers as array lengths, not as array elements.

Removing Holes from Arrays

As we have seen, `filter()` removes holes:

```
> ['a',, 'b'].filter(function (x) { return true })
[ 'a', 'b' ]
```

Use a custom function to convert holes to undefineds in arbitrary arrays:

```
function convertHolesToUndefineds(arr) {
    var result = [];
    for (var i=0; i < arr.length; i++) {
        result[i] = arr[i];
    }
    return result;
}
```

Using the function:

```
> convertHolesToUndefineds(['a',, 'b'])
[ 'a', undefined, 'b' ]
```

Array Constructor Method

`Array.isArray(obj)`
  Returns `true` if `obj` is an array. It correctly handles objects that cross *realms* (windows or frames)—as opposed to `instanceof` (see "Pitfall: crossing realms (frames or windows)" on page 238).

Array Prototype Methods

In the following sections, array prototype methods are grouped by functionality. For each of the subsections, I mention whether the methods are *destructive* (they change the arrays that they are invoked on) or *nondestructive* (they don't modify their receivers; such methods often return new arrays).

Adding and Removing Elements (Destructive)

All of the methods in this section are destructive:

`Array.prototype.shift()`
Removes the element at index 0 and returns it. The indices of subsequent elements are decremented by 1:

```
> var arr = [ 'a', 'b' ];
> arr.shift()
'a'
> arr
[ 'b' ]
```

`Array.prototype.unshift(elem1?, elem2?, ...)`
Prepends the given elements to the array. It returns the new length:

```
> var arr = [ 'c', 'd' ];
> arr.unshift('a', 'b')
4
> arr
[ 'a', 'b', 'c', 'd' ]
```

`Array.prototype.pop()`
Removes the last element of the array and returns it:

```
> var arr = [ 'a', 'b' ];
> arr.pop()
'b'
> arr
[ 'a' ]
```

`Array.prototype.push(elem1?, elem2?, ...)`
Adds the given elements to the end of the array. It returns the new length:

```
> var arr = [ 'a', 'b' ];
> arr.push('c', 'd')
4
> arr
[ 'a', 'b', 'c', 'd' ]
```

apply() (see "Function.prototype.apply(thisValue, argArray)" on page 205) enables you to destructively append an array arr2 to another array arr1:

```
> var arr1 = [ 'a', 'b' ];
> var arr2 = [ 'c', 'd' ];

> Array.prototype.push.apply(arr1, arr2)
4
> arr1
[ 'a', 'b', 'c', 'd' ]
```

`Array.prototype.splice(start, deleteCount?, elem1?, elem2?, ...)`

Starting at `start`, removes `deleteCount` elements and inserts the elements given. In other words, you are replacing the `deleteCount` elements at position `start` with `elem1`, `elem2`, and so on. The method returns the elements that have been removed:

```
> var arr = [ 'a', 'b', 'c', 'd' ];
> arr.splice(1, 2, 'X');
[ 'b', 'c' ]
> arr
[ 'a', 'X', 'd' ]
```

Special parameter values:

- `start` can be negative, in which case it is added to the length to determine the start index. Thus, `-1` refers the last element, and so on.

- `deleteCount` is optional. If it is omitted (along with all subsequent arguments), then all elements at and after index `start` are removed.

In this example, we remove all elements after and including the second-to-last index:

```
> var arr = [ 'a', 'b', 'c', 'd' ];
> arr.splice(-2)
[ 'c', 'd' ]
> arr
[ 'a', 'b' ]
```

Sorting and Reversing Elements (Destructive)

These methods are also destructive:

`Array.prototype.reverse()`

Reverses the order of the elements in the array and returns a reference to the original (modified) array:

```
> var arr = [ 'a', 'b', 'c' ];
> arr.reverse()
[ 'c', 'b', 'a' ]
> arr // reversing happened in place
[ 'c', 'b', 'a' ]
```

```
Array.prototype.sort(compareFunction?)
```
Sorts the array and returns it:

```
> var arr = ['banana', 'apple', 'pear', 'orange'];
> arr.sort()
[ 'apple', 'banana', 'orange', 'pear' ]
> arr  // sorting happened in place
[ 'apple', 'banana', 'orange', 'pear' ]
```

Keep in mind that sorting compares values by converting them to strings, which means that numbers are not sorted numerically:

```
> [-1, -20, 7, 50].sort()
[ -1, -20, 50, 7 ]
```

You can fix this by providing the optional parameter compareFunction, which controls how sorting is done. It has the following signature:

```
function compareFunction(a, b)
```

This function compares a and b and returns:

- An integer less than zero (e.g., -1) if a is less than b
- Zero if a is equal to b
- An integer greater than zero (e.g., 1) if a is greater than b

Comparing Numbers

For numbers, you can simply return a-b, but that can cause numeric overflow. To prevent that from happening, you need more verbose code:

```
function compareCanonically(a, b) {
    if (a < b) {
        return -1;
    } else if (a > b) {
        return 1;
    } else {
        return 0;
    }
}
```

I don't like nested conditional operators. But in this case, the code is so much less verbose that I'm tempted to recommend it:

```
function compareCanonically(a, b) {
    return return a < b ? -1 (a > b ? 1 : 0);
}
```

Using the function:

```
> [-1, -20, 7, 50].sort(compareCanonically)
[ -20, -1, 7, 50 ]
```

Comparing Strings

For strings, you can use `String.prototype.localeCompare` (see "Comparing Strings" on page 136):

```
> ['c', 'a', 'b'].sort(function (a,b) { return a.localeCompare(b) })
[ 'a', 'b', 'c' ]
```

Comparing Objects

The parameter `compareFunction` is also useful for sorting objects:

```
var arr = [
    { name: 'Tarzan' },
    { name: 'Cheeta' },
    { name: 'Jane' } ];

function compareNames(a,b) {
    return a.name.localeCompare(b.name);
}
```

With `compareNames` as the compare function, `arr` is sorted by `name`:

```
> arr.sort(compareNames)
[ { name: 'Cheeta' },
  { name: 'Jane' },
  { name: 'Tarzan' } ]
```

Concatenating, Slicing, Joining (Nondestructive)

The following methods perform various nondestructive operations on arrays:

`Array.prototype.concat(arr1?, arr2?, ...)`
    Creates a new array that contains all the elements of the receiver, followed by all the elements of the array `arr1`, and so on. If one of the parameters is not an array, then it is added to the result as an element (for example, the first argument, `'c'`, here):

```
> var arr = [ 'a', 'b' ];
> arr.concat('c', ['d', 'e'])
[ 'a', 'b', 'c', 'd', 'e' ]
```

The array that `concat()` is invoked on is not changed:

```
> arr
[ 'a', 'b' ]
```

`Array.prototype.slice(begin?, end?)`

Copies array elements into a new array, starting at `begin`, until and excluding the element at `end`:

```
> [ 'a', 'b', 'c', 'd' ].slice(1, 3)
[ 'b', 'c' ]
```

If `end` is missing, the array length is used:

```
> [ 'a', 'b', 'c', 'd' ].slice(1)
[ 'b', 'c', 'd' ]
```

If both indices are missing, the array is copied:

```
> [ 'a', 'b', 'c', 'd' ].slice()
[ 'a', 'b', 'c', 'd' ]
```

If either of the indices is negative, the array length is added to it. Thus, -1 refers to the last element, and so on:

```
> [ 'a', 'b', 'c', 'd' ].slice(1, -1)
[ 'b', 'c' ]
> [ 'a', 'b', 'c', 'd' ].slice(-2)
[ 'c', 'd' ]
```

`Array.prototype.join(separator?)`

Creates a string by applying `toString()` to all array elements and putting the string in `separator` between the results. If `separator` is omitted, `','` is used:

```
> [3, 4, 5].join('-')
'3-4-5'
> [3, 4, 5].join()
'3,4,5'
> [3, 4, 5].join('')
'345'
```

`join()` converts `undefined` and `null` to empty strings:

```
> [undefined, null].join('#')
'#'
```

Holes in arrays are also converted to empty strings:

```
> ['a',, 'b'].join('-')
'a--b'
```

Searching for Values (Nondestructive)

The following methods search for values in arrays:

```
Array.prototype.indexOf(searchValue, startIndex?)
```
Searches the array for `searchValue`, starting at `startIndex`. It returns the index of the first occurrence or –1 if nothing is found. If `startIndex` is negative, the array length is added to it; if it is missing, the whole array is searched:

```
> [ 3, 1, 17, 1, 4 ].indexOf(1)
1
> [ 3, 1, 17, 1, 4 ].indexOf(1, 2)
3
```

Strict equality (see"Equality Operators: === Versus ==" on page 83) is used for the search, which means that `indexOf()` can't find NaN:

```
> [NaN].indexOf(NaN)
-1
```

```
Array.prototype.lastIndexOf(searchElement, startIndex?)
```
Searches the array for `searchElement`, starting at `startIndex`, backward. It returns the index of the first occurrence or –1 if nothing is found. If `startIndex` is negative, the array length is added to it; if it is missing, the whole array is searched. Strict equality (see "Equality Operators: === Versus ==" on page 83) is used for the search:

```
> [ 3, 1, 17, 1, 4 ].lastIndexOf(1)
3
> [ 3, 1, 17, 1, 4 ].lastIndexOf(1, -3)
1
```

Iteration (Nondestructive)

Iteration methods use a function to iterate over an array. I distinguish three kinds of iteration methods, all of which are nondestructive: *examination methods* mainly observe the content of an array; *transformation methods* derive a new array from the receiver; and *reduction methods* compute a result based on the receiver's elements.

Examination Methods

Each method described in this section looks like this:

```
arr.examinationMethod(callback, thisValue?)
```

Such a method takes the following parameters:

- `callback` is its first parameter, a function that it calls. Depending on the examination method, the callback returns a boolean or nothing. It has the following signature:

  ```
  function callback(element, index, array)
  ```

element is an array element for `callback` to process, `index` is the element's index, and `array` is the array that `examinationMethod` has been invoked on.

- `thisValue` allows you to configure the value of `this` inside `callback`.

And now for the examination methods whose signatures I have just described:

`Array.prototype.forEach(callback, thisValue?)`
Iterates over the elements of an array:

```
var arr = [ 'apple', 'pear', 'orange' ];
arr.forEach(function (elem) {
    console.log(elem);
});
```

`Array.prototype.every(callback, thisValue?)`
Returns `true` if the callback returns `true` for every element. It stops iteration as soon as the callback returns `false`. Note that not returning a value leads to an implicit return of `undefined`, which `every()` interprets as `false`. `every()` works like the universal quantifier ("for all").

This example checks whether every number in the array is even:

```
> function isEven(x) { return x % 2 === 0 }
> [ 2, 4, 6 ].every(isEven)
true
> [ 2, 3, 4 ].every(isEven)
false
```

If the array is empty, the result is `true` (and `callback` is not called):

```
> [].every(function () { throw new Error() })
true
```

`Array.prototype.some(callback, thisValue?)`
Returns `true` if the callback returns `true` for at least one element. It stops iteration as soon as the callback returns `true`. Note that not returning a value leads to an implicit return of `undefined`, which `some` interprets as `false`. `some()` works like the existential quantifier ("there exists").

This example checks whether there is an even number in the array:

```
> function isEven(x) { return x % 2 === 0 }
> [ 1, 3, 5 ].some(isEven)
false
> [ 1, 2, 3 ].some(isEven)
true
```

If the array is empty, the result is `false` (and `callback` is not called):

```
> [].some(function () { throw new Error() })
false
```

One potential pitfall of forEach() is that it does not support break or something similar to prematurely abort the loop. If you need to do that, you can use some():

```
function breakAtEmptyString(strArr) {
    strArr.some(function (elem) {
        if (elem.length === 0) {
            return true; // break
        }
        console.log(elem);
        // implicit: return undefined (interpreted as false)
    });
}
```

some() returns true if a break happened, and false otherwise. This allows you to react differently depending on whether iterating finished successfully (something that is slightly tricky with for loops).

Transformation Methods

Transformation methods take an input array and produce an output array, while the callback controls how the output is produced. The callback has the same signature as for examination:

```
function callback(element, index, array)
```

There are two transformation methods:

Array.prototype.map(callback, thisValue?)
> Each output array element is the result of applying callback to an input element. For example:

```
> [ 1, 2, 3 ].map(function (x) { return 2 * x })
[ 2, 4, 6 ]
```

Array.prototype.filter(callback, thisValue?)
> The output array contains only those input elements for which callback returns true. For example:

```
> [ 1, 0, 3, 0 ].filter(function (x) { return x !== 0 })
[ 1, 3 ]
```

Reduction Methods

For reducing, the callback has a different signature:

```
function callback(previousValue, currentElement, currentIndex, array)
```

The parameter previousValue is the value previously returned by the callback. When the callback is first called, there are two possibilities (the descriptions are for Array.prototype.reduce(); differences with reduceRight() are mentioned in parentheses):

- An explicit `initialValue` has been provided. Then `previousValue` is `initialVal ue`, and `currentElement` is the first array element (`reduceRight`: the last array element).

- No explicit `initialValue` has been provided. Then `previousValue` is the first array element, and `currentElement` is the second array element (`reduceRight`: the last array element and second-to-last array element).

There are two reduction methods:

`Array.prototype.reduce(callback, initialValue?)`
Iterates from left to right and invokes the callback as previously sketched. The result of the method is the last value returned by the callback. This example computes the sum of all array elements:

```
function add(prev, cur) {
    return prev + cur;
}
console.log([10, 3, -1].reduce(add)); // 12
```

If you invoke `reduce` on an array with a single element, that element is returned:

```
> [7].reduce(add)
7
```

If you invoke `reduce` on an empty array, you must specify `initialValue`, otherwise you get an exception:

```
> [].reduce(add)
TypeError: Reduce of empty array with no initial value
> [].reduce(add, 123)
123
```

`Array.prototype.reduceRight(callback, initialValue?)`
Works the same as `reduce()`, but iterates from right to left.

 In many functional programming languages, `reduce` is known as `fold` or `foldl` (left fold) and `reduceRight` is known as `foldr` (right fold).

Another way to look at the `reduce` method is that it implements an n-ary operator `OP`:

$$OP_{1 \le i \le n}\ x_i$$

via a series of applications of a binary operator `op2`:

$$(...(x_1\ op2\ x_2)\ op2\ ...)\ op2\ x_n$$

That's what happened in the previous code example: we implemented an n-ary sum operator for arrays via JavaScript's binary plus operator.

As an example, let's examine the two iteration directions via the following function:

```
function printArgs(prev, cur, i) {
    console.log('prev:'+prev+', cur:'+cur+', i:'+i);
    return prev + cur;
}
```

As expected, `reduce()` iterates from left to right:

```
> ['a', 'b', 'c'].reduce(printArgs)
prev:a, cur:b, i:1
prev:ab, cur:c, i:2
'abc'
> ['a', 'b', 'c'].reduce(printArgs, 'x')
prev:x, cur:a, i:0
prev:xa, cur:b, i:1
prev:xab, cur:c, i:2
'xabc'
```

And `reduceRight()` iterates from right to left:

```
> ['a', 'b', 'c'].reduceRight(printArgs)
prev:c, cur:b, i:1
prev:cb, cur:a, i:0
'cba'
> ['a', 'b', 'c'].reduceRight(printArgs, 'x')
prev:x, cur:c, i:2
prev:xc, cur:b, i:1
prev:xcb, cur:a, i:0
'xcba'
```

Pitfall: Array-Like Objects

Some objects in JavaScript look like an array, but they aren't one. That usually means that they have indexed access and a `length` property, but none of the array methods. Examples include the special variable `arguments`, DOM node lists, and strings. "Array-Like Objects and Generic Methods" on page 262 gives tips for working with array-like objects.

Best Practices: Iterating over Arrays

To iterate over an array `arr`, you have two options:

- A simple `for` loop (see "for" on page 147):

```
for (var i=0; i<arr.length; i++) {
    console.log(arr[i]);
}
```

- One of the array iteration methods (see "Iteration (Nondestructive)" on page 291). For example, forEach():

```
arr.forEach(function (elem) {
    console.log(elem);
});
```

Do not use the for-in loop (see "for-in" on page 148) to iterate over arrays. It iterates over indices, not over values. And it includes the keys of normal properties while doing so, including inherited ones.

CHAPTER 19

Regular Expressions

This chapter gives an overview of the JavaScript API for regular expressions. It assumes that you are roughly familiar with how they work. If you are not, there are many good tutorials on the Web. Two examples are:

- Regular-Expressions.info (*http://www.regular-expressions.info/*) by Jan Goyvaerts
- JavaScript Regular Expression Enlightenment (*http://bit.ly/1fwoQMs*) by Cody Lindley

Regular Expression Syntax

The terms used here closely reflect the grammar in the ECMAScript specification. I sometimes deviate to make things easier to understand.

Atoms: General

The syntax for general atoms is as follows:

Special characters
   All of the following characters have special meaning:

   ```
   \ ^ $ . * + ? ( ) [ ] { } |
   ```

   You can escape them by prefixing a backslash. For example:

   ```
   > /^(ab)$/.test('(ab)')
   false
   > /^\(ab\)$/.test('(ab)')
   true
   ```

   Additional special characters are:

   - Inside a character class [...]:

- Inside a group that starts with a question mark (?...):

    : = ! < >

  The angle brackets are used only by the XRegExp library (see Chapter 30), to name groups.

Pattern characters

    All characters except the aforementioned special ones match themselves.

. (dot)

    Matches any JavaScript character (UTF-16 code unit) except line terminators (newline, carriage return, etc.). To really match any character, use [\s\S]. For example:

```
> /./.test('\n')
false
> /[\s\S]/.test('\n')
true
```

Character escapes (match single characters)

- Specific control characters include \f (form feed), \n (line feed, newline), \r (carriage return), \t (horizontal tab), and \v (vertical tab).
- \0 matches the NUL character (\u0000).
- Any control character: \cA – \cZ.
- Unicode character escapes: \u0000 – \xFFFF (Unicode code units; see Chapter 24).
- Hexadecimal character escapes: \x00 – \xFF.

Character class escapes (match one of a set of characters)

- Digits: \d matches any digit (same as [0-9]); \D matches any nondigit (same as [^0-9]).
- Alphanumeric characters: \w matches any Latin alphanumeric character plus underscore (same as [A-Za-z0-9_]); \W matches all characters not matched by \w.
- Whitespace: \s matches whitespace characters (space, tab, line feed, carriage return, form feed, all Unicode spaces, etc.); \S matches all nonwhitespace characters.

Atoms: Character Classes

The syntax for character classes is as follows:

- [«charSpecs»] matches any single character that matches at least one of the charSpecs.

- [^«charSpecs»] matches any single character that does not match any of the charSpecs.

The following constructs are all character specifications:

- Source characters match themselves. Most characters are source characters (even many characters that are special elsewhere). Only three characters are not:

  \ ] -

As usual, you escape via a backslash. If you want to match a dash without escaping it, it must be the first character after the opening bracket or the right side of a range, as described shortly.

- Class escapes: Any of the character escapes and character class escapes listed previously are allowed. There is one additional escape:

  — Backspace (\b): Outside a character class, \b matches word boundaries. Inside a character class, it matches the control character *backspace*.

- Ranges comprise a source character or a class escape, followed by a dash (-), followed by a source character or a class escape.

To demonstrate using character classes, this example parses a date formatted in the ISO 8601 standard:

```
function parseIsoDate(str) {
    var match = /^([0-9]{4})-([0-9]{2})-([0-9]{2})$/.exec(str);

    // Other ways of writing the regular expression:
    // /^([0-9][0-9][0-9][0-9])-([0-9][0-9])-([0-9][0-9])$/
    // /^(\d\d\d\d)-(\d\d)-(\d\d)$/

    if (!match) {
        throw new Error('Not an ISO date: '+str);
    }
    console.log('Year: '  + match[1]);
    console.log('Month: ' + match[2]);
    console.log('Day: '   + match[3]);
}
```

And here is the interaction:

```
> parseIsoDate('2001-12-24')
Year: 2001
Month: 12
Day: 24
```

Atoms: Groups

The syntax for groups is as follows:

- (*«pattern»*) is a capturing group. Whatever is matched by pattern can be accessed via backreferences or as the result of a match operation.
- (?:*«pattern»*) is a noncapturing group. pattern is still matched against the input, but not saved as a capture. Therefore, the group does not have a number you can refer to (e.g., via a backreference).

\1, \2, and so on are known as *backreferences*; they refer back to a previously matched group. The number after the backslash can be any integer greater than or equal to 1, but the first digit must not be 0.

In this example, a backreference guarantees the same amount of a's before and after the dash:

```
> /^(a+)-\1$/.test('a-a')
true
> /^(a+)-\1$/.test('aaa-aaa')
true
> /^(a+)-\1$/.test('aa-a')
false
```

This example uses a backreference to match an HTML tag (obviously, you should normally use a proper parser to process HTML):

```
> var tagName = /<([^>]+)>[^<]*<\/\1>/;
> tagName.exec('<b>bold</b>')[1]
'b'
> tagName.exec('<strong>text</strong>')[1]
'strong'
> tagName.exec('<strong>text</stron>')
null
```

Quantifiers

Any atom (including character classes and groups) can be followed by a quantifier:

- ? means match never or once.
- * means match zero or more times.
- + means match one or more times.
- {n} means match exactly n times.
- {n,} means match n or more times.
- {n,m} means match at least n, at most m, times.

By default, quantifiers are *greedy*; that is, they match as much as possible. You can get *reluctant* matching (as little as possible) by suffixing any of the preceding quantifiers (including the ranges in curly braces) with a question mark (?). For example:

```
> '<a> <strong>'.match(/^<(.*)>/)[1]   // greedy
'a> <strong'
> '<a> <strong>'.match(/^<(.*?)>/)[1]  // reluctant
'a'
```

Thus, .*? is a useful pattern for matching everything until the next occurrence of the following atom. For example, the following is a more compact version of the regular expression for HTML tags just shown (which used [^<]* instead of .*?):

```
/<(.+?)>.*?<\/\1>/
```

Assertions

Assertions, shown in the following list, are checks about the current position in the input:

^	Matches only at the beginning of the input.
$	Matches only at the end of the input.
\b	Matches only at a word boundary. Don't confuse with [\b], which matches a backspace.
\B	Matches only if not at a word boundary.
(?=«pattern»)	Positive lookahead: Matches only if pattern matches what comes next. pattern is used only to look ahead, but otherwise ignored.
(?!«pattern»)	Negative lookahead: Matches only if pattern does not match what comes next. pattern is used only to look ahead, but otherwise ignored.

This example matches a word boundary via \b:

```
> /\bell\b/.test('hello')
false
> /\bell\b/.test('ello')
false
> /\bell\b/.test('ell')
true
```

This example matches the inside of a word via \B:

```
> /\Bell\B/.test('ell')
false
> /\Bell\B/.test('hell')
false
> /\Bell\B/.test('hello')
true
```

Lookbehind is not supported. "Manually Implementing Lookbehind" on page 313 explains how to implement it manually.

Disjunction

A disjunction operator (|) separates two alternatives; either of the alternatives must match for the disjunction to match. The alternatives are atoms (optionally including quantifiers).

The operator binds very weakly, so you have to be careful that the alternatives don't extend too far. For example, the following regular expression matches all strings that either start with aa or end with bb:

```
> /^aa|bb$/.test('aaxx')
true
> /^aa|bb$/.test('xxbb')
true
```

In other words, the disjunction binds more weakly than even ^ and $ and the two alternatives are ^aa and bb$. If you want to match the two strings 'aa' and 'bb', you need parentheses:

```
/^(aa|bb)$/
```

Similarly, if you want to match the strings 'aab' and 'abb':

```
/^a(a|b)b$/
```

Unicode and Regular Expressions

JavaScript's regular expressions have only very limited support for Unicode. Especially when it comes to code points in the astral planes, you have to be careful. Chapter 24 explains the details.

Creating a Regular Expression

You can create a regular expression via either a literal or a constructor and configure how it works via flags.

Literal Versus Constructor

There are two ways to create a regular expression: you can use a literal or the constructor RegExp:

Literal	`/xyz/i`	Compiled at load time
Constructor (second argument is optional)	`new RegExp('xyz', 'i')`	Compiled at runtime

A literal and a constructor differ in when they are compiled:

- The literal is compiled at load time. The following code will cause an exception when it is evaluated:

```
function foo() {
    /[/;
}
```

- The constructor compiles the regular expression when it is called. The following code will not cause an exception, but calling foo() will:

```
function foo() {
    new RegExp('[');
}
```

Thus, you should normally use literals, but you need the constructor if you want to dynamically assemble a regular expression.

Flags

Flags are a suffix of regular expression literals and a parameter of regular expression constructors; they modify the matching behavior of regular expressions. The following flags exist:

Short name	Long name	Description
g	global	The given regular expression is matched multiple times. Influences several methods, especially `replace()`.
i	ignoreCase	Case is ignored when trying to match the given regular expression.
m	multiline	In multiline mode, the begin operator ^ and the end operator $ match each line, instead of the complete input string.

The short name is used for literal prefixes and constructor parameters (see examples in the next section). The long name is used for properties of a regular expression that indicate what flags were set during its creation.

Instance Properties of Regular Expressions

Regular expressions have the following instance properties:

- Flags: boolean values indicating what flags are set:
  - global: Is flag /g set?
  - ignoreCase: Is flag /i set?

— `multiline`: Is flag /m set?

- Data for matching multiple times (flag /g is set):

  — `lastIndex` is the index where to continue the search next time.

The following is an example of accessing the instance properties for flags:

```
> var regex = /abc/i;
> regex.ignoreCase
true
> regex.multiline
false
```

Examples of Creating Regular Expressions

In this example, we create the same regular expression first with a literal, then with a constructor, and use the `test()` method to determine whether it matches a string:

```
> /abc/.test('ABC')
false
> new RegExp('abc').test('ABC')
false
```

In this example, we create a regular expression that ignores case (flag /i):

```
> /abc/i.test('ABC')
true
> new RegExp('abc', 'i').test('ABC')
true
```

RegExp.prototype.test: Is There a Match?

The `test()` method checks whether a regular expression, `regex`, matches a string, `str`:

```
regex.test(str)
```

`test()` operates differently depending on whether the flag /g is set or not.

If the flag /g is not set, then the method checks whether there is a match somewhere in `str`. For example:

```
> var str = '_x_x';

> /x/.test(str)
true
> /a/.test(str)
false
```

If the flag /g is set, then the method returns `true` as many times as there are matches for `regex` in `str`. The property `regex.lastIndex` contains the index after the last match:

```
> var regex = /x/g;
> regex.lastIndex
0

> regex.test(str)
true
> regex.lastIndex
2

> regex.test(str)
true
> regex.lastIndex
4

> regex.test(str)
false
```

String.prototype.search: At What Index Is There a Match?

The search() method looks for a match with regex within str:

```
str.search(regex)
```

If there is a match, the index where it was found is returned. Otherwise, the result is -1. The properties global and lastIndex of regex are ignored as the search is performed (and lastIndex is not changed).

For example:

```
> 'abba'.search(/b/)
1
> 'abba'.search(/x/)
-1
```

If the argument of search() is not a regular expression, it is converted to one:

```
> 'aaab'.search('^a+b+$')
0
```

RegExp.prototype.exec: Capture Groups

The following method call captures groups while matching regex against str:

```
var matchData = regex.exec(str);
```

If there was no match, matchData is null. Otherwise, matchData is a *match result*, an array with two additional properties:

Array elements
- Element 0 is the match for the complete regular expression (group 0, if you will).

- Element *n* > 1 is the capture of group *n*.

Properties
- input is the complete input string.
- index is the index where the match was found.

First Match (Flag /g Not Set)

If the flag /g is not set, only the first match is returned:

```
> var regex = /a(b+)/;
> regex.exec('_abbb_ab_')
[ 'abbb',
  'bbb',
  index: 1,
  input: '_abbb_ab_' ]
> regex.lastIndex
0
```

All Matches (Flag /g Set)

If the flag /g is set, all matches are returned if you invoke exec() repeatedly. The return value null signals that there are no more matches. The property lastIndex indicates where matching will continue next time:

```
> var regex = /a(b+)/g;
> var str = '_abbb_ab_';

> regex.exec(str)
[ 'abbb',
  'bbb',
  index: 1,
  input: '_abbb_ab_' ]
> regex.lastIndex
6

> regex.exec(str)
[ 'ab',
  'b',
  index: 7,
  input: '_abbb_ab_' ]
> regex.lastIndex
10

> regex.exec(str)
null
```

Here we loop over matches:

```
var regex = /a(b+)/g;
var str = '_abbb_ab_';
var match;
while (match = regex.exec(str)) {
    console.log(match[1]);
}
```

and we get the following output:

```
bbb
b
```

String.prototype.match: Capture Groups or Return All Matching Substrings

The following method call matches `regex` against `str`:

```
var matchData = str.match(regex);
```

If the flag `/g` of `regex` is not set, this method works like `RegExp.prototype.exec()`:

```
> 'abba'.match(/a/)
[ 'a', index: 0, input: 'abba' ]
```

If the flag is set, then the method returns an array with all matching substrings in `str` (i.e., group 0 of every match) or `null` if there is no match:

```
> 'abba'.match(/a/g)
[ 'a', 'a' ]
> 'abba'.match(/x/g)
null
```

String.prototype.replace: Search and Replace

The `replace()` method searches a string, `str`, for matches with `search` and replaces them with `replacement`:

```
str.replace(search, replacement)
```

There are several ways in which the two parameters can be specified:

search
    Either a string or a regular expression:

    • String: To be found literally in the input string. Be warned that only the first
      occurrence of a string is replaced. If you want to replace multiple occurrences,
      you must use a regular expression with a /g flag. This is unexpected and a major
      pitfall.

- Regular expression: To be matched against the input string. Warning: Use the global flag, otherwise only one attempt is made to match the regular expression.

replacement
Either a string or a function:

- String: Describes how to replace what has been found.
- Function: Computes a replacement and is given matching information via parameters.

Replacement Is a String

If replacement is a string, its content is used verbatim to replace the match. The only exception is the special character dollar sign ($), which starts so-called *replacement directives*:

- Groups: $n inserts group n from the match. n must be at least 1 ($0 has no special meaning).
- The matching substring:
  — $` (backtick) inserts the text before the match.
  — $& inserts the complete match.
  — $' (apostrophe) inserts the text after the match.
- $$ inserts a single $.

This example refers to the matching substring and its prefix and suffix:

```
> 'axb cxd'.replace(/x/g, "[$`,$&,$']")
'a[a,x,b cxd]b c[axb c,x,d]d'
```

This example refers to a group:

```
> '"foo" and "bar"'.replace(/"(.*?)"/g, '#$1#')
'#foo# and #bar#'
```

Replacement Is a Function

If replacement is a function, it computes the string that is to replace the match. This function has the following signature:

```
function (completeMatch, group_1, ..., group_n, offset, inputStr)
```

completeMatch is the same as $& previously, offset indicates where the match was found, and inputStr is what is being matched against. Thus, you can use the special variable `arguments` to access groups (group 1 via `arguments[1]`, and so on). For example:

```
> function replaceFunc(match) { return 2 * match }
> '3 apples and 5 oranges'.replace(/[0-9]+/g, replaceFunc)
'6 apples and 10 oranges'
```

Problems with the Flag /g

Regular expressions whose /g flag is set are problematic if a method invoked on them must be invoked multiple times to return all results. That's the case for two methods:

- `RegExp.prototype.test()`
- `RegExp.prototype.exec()`

Then JavaScript abuses the regular expression as an iterator, as a pointer into the sequence of results. That causes problems:

Problem 1: /g regular expressions can't be inlined
For example:

```
// Don't do that:
var count = 0;
while (/a/g.test('babaa')) count++;
```

The preceding loop is infinite, because a new regular expression is created for each loop iteration, which restarts the iteration over the results. Therefore, the code must be rewritten:

```
var count = 0;
var regex = /a/g;
while (regex.test('babaa')) count++;
```

Here is another example:

```
// Don't do that:
function extractQuoted(str) {
    var match;
    var result = [];
    while ((match = /"(.*?)"/g.exec(str)) != null) {
        result.push(match[1]);
    }
    return result;
}
```

Calling the preceding function will again result in an infinite loop. The correct version is (why `lastIndex` is set to 0 is explained shortly):

```
var QUOTE_REGEX = /"(.*?)"/g;
function extractQuoted(str) {
    QUOTE_REGEX.lastIndex = 0;
```

```
    var match;
    var result = [];
    while ((match = QUOTE_REGEX.exec(str)) != null) {
        result.push(match[1]);
    }
    return result;
}
```

Using the function:

```
> extractQuoted('"hello", "world"')
[ 'hello', 'world' ]
```

 It's a best practice not to inline anyway (then you can give regular expressions descriptive names). But you have to be aware that you can't do it, not even in quick hacks.

Problem 2: /g regular expressions as parameters

Code that wants to invoke `test()` and `exec()` multiple times must be careful with a regular expression handed to it as a parameter. Its flag /g must active and, to be safe, its `lastIndex` should be set to zero (an explanation is offered in the next example).

Problem 3: Shared /g regular expressions (e.g., constants)

Whenever you are referring to a regular expression that has not been freshly created, you should set its `lastIndex` property to zero, before using it as an iterator (an explanation is offered in the next example). As iteration depends on `lastIndex`, such a regular expression can't be used in more than one iteration at the same time.

The following example illustrates problem 2. It is a naive implementation of a function that counts how many matches there are for the regular expression `regex` in the string `str`:

```
// Naive implementation
function countOccurrences(regex, str) {
    var count = 0;
    while (regex.test(str)) count++;
    return count;
}
```

Here's an example of using this function:

```
> countOccurrences(/x/g, '_x_x')
2
```

The first problem is that this function goes into an infinite loop if the regular expression's /g flag is not set. For example:

```
countOccurrences(/x/, '_x_x') // never terminates
```

The second problem is that the function doesn't work correctly if `regex.lastIndex` isn't 0, because that property indicates where to start the search. For example:

```
> var regex = /x/g;
> regex.lastIndex = 2;
> countOccurrences(regex, '_x_x')
1
```

The following implementation fixes the two problems:

```
function countOccurrences(regex, str) {
    if (! regex.global) {
        throw new Error('Please set flag /g of regex');
    }
    var origLastIndex = regex.lastIndex;  // store
    regex.lastIndex = 0;

    var count = 0;
    while (regex.test(str)) count++;

    regex.lastIndex = origLastIndex;  // restore
    return count;
}
```

A simpler alternative is to use `match()`:

```
function countOccurrences(regex, str) {
    if (! regex.global) {
        throw new Error('Please set flag /g of regex');
    }
    return (str.match(regex) || []).length;
}
```

There's one possible pitfall: `str.match()` returns `null` if the `/g` flag is set and there are no matches. We avoid that pitfall in the preceding code by using `[]` if the result of `match()` isn't truthy.

Tips and Tricks

This section gives a few tips and tricks for working with regular expressions in JavaScript.

Quoting Text

Sometimes, when you assemble a regular expression manually, you want to use a given string verbatim. That means that none of the special characters (e.g., *, [) should be interpreted as such—all of them need to be escaped. JavaScript has no built-in means for this kind of quoting, but you can program your own function, `quoteText`, that would work as follows:

```
> console.log(quoteText('*All* (most?) aspects.'))
\*All\* \(most\?\) aspects\.
```

Such a function is especially handy if you need to do a search and replace with multiple occurrences. Then the value to search for must be a regular expression with the `global` flag set. With `quoteText()`, you can use arbitrary strings. The function looks like this:

```
function quoteText(text) {
    return text.replace(/[\\^$.*+?()[\]{}|=!<>:-]/g, '\\$&');
}
```

All special characters are escaped, because you may want to quote several characters inside parentheses or square brackets.

Pitfall: Without an Assertion (e.g., ^, $), a Regular Expression Is Found Anywhere

If you don't use assertions such as ^ and $, most regular expression methods find a pattern anywhere. For example:

```
> /aa/.test('xaay')
true
> /^aa$/.test('xaay')
false
```

Matching Everything or Nothing

It's a rare use case, but sometimes you need a regular expression that matches everything or nothing. For example, a function may have a parameter with a regular expression that is used for filtering. If that parameter is missing, you give it a default value, a regular expression that matches everything.

Matching everything

The empty regular expression matches everything. We can create an instance of `RegExp` based on that regular expression like this:

```
> new RegExp('').test('dfadsfdsa')
true
> new RegExp('').test('')
true
```

However, the empty regular expression literal would be `//`, which is interpreted as a comment by JavaScript. Therefore, the following is the closest you can get via a literal: `/(?:)/` (empty noncapturing group). The group matches everything, while not capturing anything, which the group from influencing the result returned by `exec()`. Even

JavaScript itself uses the preceding representation when displaying an empty regular expression:

```
> new RegExp('')
/(?:)/
```

Matching nothing

The empty regular expression has an inverse—the regular expression that matches nothing:

```
> var never = /.^/;
> never.test('abc')
false
> never.test('')
false
```

Manually Implementing Lookbehind

Lookbehind is an assertion. Similar to lookahead, a pattern is used to check something about the current position in the input, but otherwise ignored. In contrast to lookahead, the match for the pattern has to *end* at the current position (not start at it).

The following function replaces each occurrence of the string `'NAME'` with the value of the parameter `name`, but only if the occurrence is not preceded by a quote. We handle the quote by "manually" checking the character before the current match:

```
function insertName(str, name) {
    return str.replace(
        /NAME/g,
        function (completeMatch, offset) {
            if (offset === 0 ||
                (offset > 0 && str[offset-1] !== '"')) {
                return name;
            } else {
                return completeMatch;
            }
        }
    );
}
> insertName('NAME "NAME"', 'Jane')
'Jane "NAME"'
> insertName('"NAME" NAME', 'Jane')
'"NAME" Jane'
```

An alternative is to include the characters that may escape in the regular expression. Then you have to temporarily add a prefix to the string you are searching in; otherwise, you'd miss matches at the beginning of that string:

```
function insertName(str, name) {
    var tmpPrefix = ' ';
```

```
        str = tmpPrefix + str;
        str = str.replace(
            /([^"])NAME/g,
            function (completeMatch, prefix) {
                return prefix + name;
            }
        );
        return str.slice(tmpPrefix.length); // remove tmpPrefix
    }
```

Regular Expression Cheat Sheet

Atoms (see "Atoms: General" on page 297):

- . (dot) matches everything except line terminators (e.g., newlines). Use [\s\S] to really match everything.
- Character class escapes:
    - \d matches digits ([0-9]); \D matches nondigits ([^0-9]).
    - \w matches Latin alphanumeric characters plus underscore ([A-Za-z0-9_]); \W matches all other characters.
    - \s matches all whitespace characters (space, tab, line feed, etc.); \S matches all nonwhitespace characters.
- Character class (set of characters): [...] and [^...]
    - Source characters: [abc] (all characters except \ ] - match themselves)
    - Character class escapes (see previous): [\d\w]
    - Ranges: [A-Za-z0-9]
- Groups:
    - Capturing group: (...); backreference: \1
    - Noncapturing group: (?:...)

Quantifiers (see "Quantifiers" on page 300):

- Greedy:
    - ? * +
    - {n} {n,} {n,m}
- Reluctant: Put a ? after any of the greedy quantifiers.

Assertions (see "Assertions" on page 301):

- Beginning of input, end of input: ^ $

- At a word boundary, not at a word boundary: \b \B
- Positive lookahead: (?=...) (pattern must come next, but is otherwise ignored)
- Negative lookahead: (?!...) (pattern must not come next, but is otherwise ignored)

Disjunction: |

Creating a regular expression (see "Creating a Regular Expression" on page 302):

- Literal: /xyz/i (compiled at load time)
- Constructor: new RegExp('xzy', 'i') (compiled at runtime)

Flags (see "Flags" on page 303):

- global: /g (influences several regular expression methods)
- ignoreCase: /i
- multiline: /m (^ and $ match per line, as opposed to the complete input)

Methods:

- regex.test(str): Is there a match (see "RegExp.prototype.test: Is There a Match?" on page 304)?

  — /g is not set: Is there a match somewhere?

  — /g is set: Return true as many times as there are matches.

- str.search(regex): At what index is there a match (see "String.prototype.search: At What Index Is There a Match?" on page 305)?

- regex.exec(str): Capture groups (see the section "RegExp.prototype.exec: Capture Groups" on page 305)?

  — /g is not set: Capture groups of first match only (invoked once)

  — /g is set: Capture groups of all matches (invoked repeatedly; returns null if there are no more matches)

- str.match(regex): Capture groups or return all matching substrings (see "String.prototype.match: Capture Groups or Return All Matching Substrings" on page 307)

  — /g is not set: Capture groups

  — /g is set: Return all matching substrings in an array

- str.replace(search, replacement): Search and replace (see "String.prototype.replace: Search and Replace" on page 307)

— `search`: String or regular expression (use the latter, set `/g`!)

— `replacement`: String (with `$1`, etc.) or function (`arguments[1]` is group 1, etc.) that returns a string

For tips on using the flag `/g`, see "Problems with the Flag `/g`" on page 309.

Acknowledgments

Mathias Bynens (@mathias) and Juan Ignacio Dopazo (@juandopazo) recommended using `match()` and `test()` for counting occurrences, and Šime Vidas (@simevidas) warned me about being careful with `match()` if there are no matches. The pitfall of the global flag causing infinite loops comes from a talk by Andrea Giammarchi (*http://bit.ly/1fwpdXv*) (@webreflection). Claude Pache told me to escape more characters in `quoteText()`.

CHAPTER 20

Dates

JavaScript's `Date` constructor helps with parsing, managing, and displaying dates. This chapter describes how it works.

The date API uses the term *UTC* (Coordinated Universal Time). For most purposes, UTC is a synonym for GMT (Greenwich Mean Time) and roughly means the time zone of London, UK.

The Date Constructor

There are four ways of invoking the constructor of `Date`:

`new Date(year, month, date?, hours?, minutes?, seconds?, milliseconds?)`
> Constructs a new date from the given data. The time is interpreted relative to the current time zone. `Date.UTC()` provides similar functionality, but relative to UTC. The parameters have the following ranges:
>
> - year: For $0 \leq year \leq 99$, 1900 is added.
> - month: 0–11 (0 is January, 1 is February, etc.)
> - date: 1–31
> - hours: 0–23
> - minutes: 0–59
> - seconds: 0–59
> - milliseconds: 0–999
>
> Here are some examples:
>
> ```
> > new Date(2001, 1, 27, 14, 55)
> Date {Tue Feb 27 2001 14:55:00 GMT+0100 (CET)}
> ```

```
> new Date(01, 1, 27, 14, 55)
Date {Wed Feb 27 1901 14:55:00 GMT+0100 (CET)}
```

As an aside, JavaScript has inherited the slightly weird convention of interpreting 0 as January, 1 as February, and so on, from Java.

`new Date(dateTimeStr)`

This is a date time string that is converted into a number, with which `new Date(number)` is invoked. "Date Time Formats" on page 324 explains the date time formats. For example:

```
> new Date('2004-08-29')
Date {Sun Aug 29 2004 02:00:00 GMT+0200 (CEST)}
```

Illegal date time strings lead to NaN being passed to `new Date(number)`.

`new Date(timeValue)`

Creates a date as specified in the number of milliseconds since 1 January 1970 00:00:00 UTC. For example:

```
> new Date(0)
Date {Thu Jan 01 1970 01:00:00 GMT+0100 (CET)}
```

The inverse of this constructor is the `getTime()` method, which returns the milliseconds:

```
> new Date(123).getTime()
123
```

You can use NaN as an argument, which produces a special instance of `Date`, an "invalid date":

```
> var d = new Date(NaN);
> d.toString()
'Invalid Date'
> d.toJSON()
null
> d.getTime()
NaN
> d.getYear()
NaN
```

`new Date()`

Creates an object for the current date and time; it works the same as `new Date(Date.now())`.

Date Constructor Methods

The constructor `Date` has the following methods:

```
Date.now()
```
Returns the current date and time in milliseconds (since 1 January 1970, 00:00:00 UTC). It produces the same result as `new Date().getTime()`.

```
Date.parse(dateTimeString)
```
Converts `dateTimeString` to milliseconds since 1 January 1970, 00:00:00 UTC. "Date Time Formats" on page 324 explains the format of `dateTimeString`. The result can be used to invoke `new Date(number)`. Here are some examples:

```
> Date.parse('1970-01-01')
0
> Date.parse('1970-01-02')
86400000
```

If it can't parse a string, this method returns `NaN`:

```
> Date.parse('abc')
NaN
```

```
Date.UTC(year, month, date?, hours?, minutes?, seconds?, milliseconds?)
```
Converts the given data to milliseconds since 1 January 1970 00:00:00 UTC. It differs from the `Date` constructor with the same arguments in two ways:

- It returns a number, not a new date object.
- It interprets the arguments as UTC, rather than as local time.

Date Prototype Methods

This section covers the methods of `Date.prototype`.

Time Unit Getters and Setters

Time unit getters and setters are available with the following signatures:

- Local time:
  - `Date.prototype.get«Unit»()` returns `Unit`, according to local time.
  - `Date.prototype.set«Unit»(number)` sets `Unit`, according to local time.
- Universal time:
  - `Date.prototype.getUTC«Unit»()` returns `Unit`, according to universal time.
  - `Date.prototype.setUTC«Unit»(number)` sets `Unit`, according to universal time.

`Unit` is one of the following words:

- `FullYear`: Usually four digits
- `Month`: Month (0–11)
- `Date`: Day of the month (1–31)
- `Day` (getter only): Day of the week (0–6); 0 is Sunday
- `Hours`: Hour (0–23)
- `Minutes`: Minutes (0–59)
- `Seconds`: Seconds (0–59)
- `Milliseconds`: Milliseconds (0–999)

For example:

```
> var d = new Date('1968-11-25');
Date {Mon Nov 25 1968 01:00:00 GMT+0100 (CET)}
> d.getDate()
25
> d.getDay()
1
```

Various Getters and Setters

The following methods enable you to get and set the time in milliseconds since 1 January 1970 and more:

- `Date.prototype.getTime()` returns the milliseconds since 1 January 1970 00:00:00 UTC (see "Time Values: Dates as Milliseconds Since 1970-01-01" on page 324).
- `Date.prototype.setTime(timeValue)` sets the date as specified in milliseconds since 1 January 1970 00:00:00 UTC (see "Time Values: Dates as Milliseconds Since 1970-01-01" on page 324).
- `Date.prototype.valueOf()` is the same as `getTime()`. This method is called when a date is converted to a number.
- `Date.prototype.getTimezoneOffset()` returns the difference between local time and UTC time in minutes.

The unit `Year` has been deprecated in favor of `FullYear`:

- `Date.prototype.getYear()` is deprecated; use `getFullYear()` instead.
- `Date.prototype.setYear(number)` is deprecated; use `setFullYear()` instead.

Convert a Date to a String

Note that conversion to a string is highly implementation-dependent. The following date is used to compute the output in the following examples (in Firefox, which had the most complete support when this book was written):

```
new Date(2001,9,30, 17,43,7, 856);
```

Time (human-readable)

- `Date.prototype.toTimeString()`:

  ```
  17:43:07 GMT+0100 (CET)
  ```

  The time, in the current time zone.

- `Date.prototype.toLocaleTimeString()`:

  ```
  17:43:07
  ```

  The time in a locale-specific format. This method is provided by the ECMA-Script Internationalization API (see "The ECMAScript Internationalization API" on page 406) and does not make much sense without it.

Date (human-readable)

- `Date.prototype.toDateString()`:

  ```
  Tue Oct 30 2001
  ```

  The date.

- `Date.prototype.toLocaleDateString()`:

  ```
  10/30/2001
  ```

  The date, in a locale-specific format. This method is provided by the ECMA-Script Internationalization API (see "The ECMAScript Internationalization API" on page 406) and does not make much sense without it.

Date and time (human-readable)

- `Date.prototype.toString()`:

  ```
  Tue Oct 30 2001 17:43:07 GMT+0100 (CET)
  ```

  Date and time, in the current time zone. For any `Date` instance that has no milliseconds (i.e., the second is full), the following expression is true:

  ```
  Date.parse(d.toString()) === d.valueOf()
  ```

- `Date.prototype.toLocaleString()`:

  ```
  Tue Oct 30 17:43:07 2001
  ```

  Date and time in a locale-specific format. This method is provided by the EC-MAScript Internationalization API (see "The ECMAScript Internationalization API" on page 406) and does not make much sense without it.

- `Date.prototype.toUTCString()`:

    Tue, 30 Oct 2001 16:43:07 GMT

    Date and time, in UTC.

- `Date.prototype.toGMTString()`:

    Deprecated; use `toUTCString()` instead.

Date and time (machine-readable)
- `Date.prototype.toISOString()`:

    2001-10-30T16:43:07.856Z

    All internal properties show up in the returned string. The format is in accordance with "Date Time Formats" on page 324; the time zone is always Z.

- `Date.prototype.toJSON()`:

    This method internally calls `toISOString()`. It is used by `JSON.stringify()` (see "JSON.stringify(value, replacer?, space?)" on page 337) to convert date objects to JSON strings.

Date Time Formats

This section describes formats for expressing points in time as strings. There are many ways of doing so: indicating just the date, including a time of day, omitting the time zone, specifying the time zone, and more. In its support for date time formats, ECMA-Script 5 closely follows the standard ISO 8601 Extended Format. JavaScript engines implement the ECMAScript specification relatively completely, but there are still some variations, so you have to be vigilant.

The longest date time format is:

YYYY-MM-DDTHH:mm:ss.sssZ

Each part stands for several decimal digits of date time data. For example, YYYY means that the format starts with a four-digit year. The following subsections explain what each part means. Formats are relevant for the following methods:

- `Date.parse()` can parse the formats.
- `new Date()` can parse the formats.
- `Date.prototype.toISOString()` creates a string in the aforementioned "full" format:

    ```
    > new Date().toISOString()
    '2014-09-12T23:05:07.414Z'
    ```

Date Formats (No Time)

The following date formats are available:

```
YYYY-MM-DD
YYYY-MM
YYYY
```

They include the following parts:

- YYYY refers to year (Gregorian calendar).

- MM refers to month, from 01 to 12.

- DD refers to day, from 01 to 31.

For example:

```
> new Date('2001-02-22')
Date {Thu Feb 22 2001 01:00:00 GMT+0100 (CET)}
```

Time Formats (No Date)

The following time formats are available. As you can see, time zone information Z is optional:

```
THH:mm:ss.sss
THH:mm:ss.sssZ

THH:mm:ss
THH:mm:ssZ

THH:mm
THH:mmZ
```

They include the following parts:

- T is the prefix of the time part of a format (a literal T, not a digit).

- HH refers to hour, from 00 to 23. You can use 24 as a value for HH (which refers to hour 00 of the following day), but then all remaining parts must be 0.

- mm indicates the minute, from 00 to 59.

- ss indicates the second, from 00 to 59.

- sss indicates the millisecond, from 000 to 999.

- Z refers to time zone, either of the following two:

  — "Z" for UTC

  — "+" or "-" followed by a time "hh:mm"

Some JavaScript engines allow you to specify only a time (others require a date):

```
> new Date('T13:17')
Date {Thu Jan 01 1970 13:17:00 GMT+0100 (CET)}
```

Date Time Formats

Date formats and time formats can also be combined. In date time formats, you can use a date or a date and a time (or, in some engines, just the time). For example:

```
> new Date('2001-02-22T13:17')
Date {Thu Feb 22 2001 13:17:00 GMT+0100 (CET)}
```

Time Values: Dates as Milliseconds Since 1970-01-01

What the date API calls `time` is called a *time value* by the ECMAScript specification. It is a primitive number that encodes a date as milliseconds since 1 January 1970 00:00:00 UTC. Each date object stores its state as a time value, in the internal property [[Primi tiveValue]] (the same property that instances of the wrapper constructors `Boolean`, `Number`, and `String` use to store their wrapped primitive values).

 Leap seconds are ignored in time values.

The following methods work with time values:

- `new Date(timeValue)` uses a time value to create a date.
- `Date.parse(dateTimeString)` parses a string with a date time string and returns a time value.
- `Date.now()` returns the current date time as a time value.
- `Date.UTC(year, month, date?, hours?, minutes?, seconds?, millisec onds?)` interprets the parameters relative to UTC and returns a time value.
- `Date.prototype.getTime()` returns the time value stored in the receiver.
- `Date.prototype.setTime(timeValue)` changes the date as specified via a time value.
- `Date.prototype.valueOf()` returns the time value stored in the receiver. This method determines how dates are converted to primitives, as explained in the next subsection.

The range of JavaScript integers (53 bits plus a sign) is large enough that a time span can be represented that starts at approximately 285,616 years before 1970 and ends at approximately 285,616 years after 1970.

Here are a few examples of converting dates to time values:

```
> new Date('1970-01-01').getTime()
0
> new Date('1970-01-02').getTime()
86400000
> new Date('1960-01-02').getTime()
-315532800000
```

The `Date` constructor enables you to convert times values to dates:

```
> new Date(0)
Date {Thu Jan 01 1970 01:00:00 GMT+0100 (CET)}
> new Date(24 * 60 * 60 * 1000)  // 1 day in ms
Date {Fri Jan 02 1970 01:00:00 GMT+0100 (CET)}
> new Date(-315532800000)
Date {Sat Jan 02 1960 01:00:00 GMT+0100 (CET)}
```

Converting a Date to a Number

A date is converted to a number via `Date.prototype.valueOf()`, which returns a time value. This allows you to compare dates:

```
> new Date('1980-05-21') > new Date('1980-05-20')
true
```

You can also perform arithmetic, but beware that leap seconds are ignored:

```
> new Date('1980-05-21') - new Date('1980-05-20')
86400000
```

 Using the plus operator (+) to add a date to another date or a number results in a string, because the default for the conversion to primitive is to convert dates to strings (consult "The Plus Operator (+)" on page 88 for an explanation of how the plus operator works):

```
> new Date('2024-10-03') + 86400000
'Thu Oct 03 2024 02:00:00 GMT+0200 (CEST)86400000'
> new Date(Number(new Date('2024-10-03')) + 86400000)
Fri Oct 04 2024 02:00:00 GMT+0200 (CEST)
```

CHAPTER 21

Math

The `Math` object is used as a namespace for several math functions. This chapter provides an overview.

Math Properties

The properties of `Math` are as follows:

`Math.E`
Euler's constant (e)

`Math.LN2`
Natural logarithm of 2

`Math.LN10`
Natural logarithm of 10

`Math.LOG2E`
Base 2 logarithm of e

`Math.LOG10E`
Base 10 logarithm of e

`Math.PI`
The ratio of the circumference of a circle to its diameter (3.14159 ...), π

`Math.SQRT1_2`
The square root of one-half, $\sqrt{\frac{1}{2}}$

`Math.SQRT2`
The square root of two, $\sqrt{2}$

Numerical Functions

The numerical functions of `Math` include the following:

`Math.abs(x)`

Returns the absolute value of x.

`Math.ceil(x)`

Returns the smallest integer ≥ x:

```
> Math.ceil(3.999)
4
> Math.ceil(3.001)
4
> Math.ceil(-3.001)
-3
> Math.ceil(3.000)
3
```

For more on converting floating-point numbers to integers, see "Converting to Integer" on page 117.

`Math.exp(x)`

Returns e^x where e is Euler's constant (`Math.E`). This is the inverse of `Math.log()`.

`Math.floor(x)`

Returns the largest integer ≤ x:

```
> Math.floor(3.999)
3
> Math.floor(3.001)
3
> Math.floor(-3.001)
-4
> Math.floor(3.000)
3
```

For more on converting floating-point numbers to integers, see "Converting to Integer" on page 117.

`Math.log(x)`

Returns the natural (base is Euler's constant) logarithm ln(x) of x. This is the inverse of `Math.exp()`.

`Math.pow(x, y)`

Returns x^y, x raised to the power of y:

```
> Math.pow(9, 2)
81
> Math.pow(36, 0.5)
6
```

```
Math.round(x)
```

Returns x rounded to the nearest integer (the greater one if it is between two integers):

```
> Math.round(3.999)
4
> Math.round(3.001)
3
> Math.round(3.5)
4
> Math.round(-3.5)
-3
```

For more on converting floating-point numbers to integers, see "Converting to Integer" on page 117.

```
Math.sqrt(x)
```

Returns $\sqrt{x}$, the square root of x:

```
> Math.sqrt(256)
16
```

Trigonometric Functions

The trigonometric methods accept and return angles as radians. The following functions show you how you could implement conversions, should you need to:

- From degrees to radians:

```
function toRadians(degrees) {
    return degrees / 180 * Math.PI;
}
```

Here is the interaction:

```
> toRadians(180)
3.141592653589793
> toRadians(90)
1.5707963267948966
```

- From radians to degrees:

```
function toDegrees(radians) {
    return radians / Math.PI * 180;
}
```

Here is the interaction:

```
> toDegrees(Math.PI * 2)
360
> toDegrees(Math.PI)
180
```

The trigonometric methods are as follows:

`Math.acos(x)`
> Returns the arc cosine of x.

`Math.asin(x)`
> Returns the arc sine of x.

`Math.atan(x)`
> Returns the arc tangent of x.

`Math.atan2(y, x)`
> Returns the arc tangent of the quotient $\frac{y}{x}$.

`Math.cos(x)`
> Returns the cosine of x.

`Math.sin(x)`
> Returns the sine of x.

`Math.tan(x)`
> Returns the tangent of x.

Other Functions

Following are the remaining `Math` functions:

`min(x1?, x2?, ...)`
> Returns the smallest number among the parameters:

```
> Math.min()
Infinity
> Math.min(27)
27
> Math.min(27, -38)
-38
> Math.min(27, -38, -43)
-43
```

> Use it on arrays via `apply()` (see "func.apply(thisValue, argArray)" on page 170):

```
> Math.min.apply(null, [27, -38, -43])
-43
```

`max(x1?, x2?, ...)`
> Returns the largest number among the parameters:

```
> Math.max()
-Infinity
> Math.max(7)
7
```

```
> Math.max(7, 10)
10
> Math.max(7, 10, -333)
10
```

Use it on arrays via `apply()` (see "func.apply(thisValue, argArray)" on page 170):

```
> Math.max.apply(null, [7, 10, -333])
10
```

Math.random()

Returns a pseudorandom number r, $0 \le r < 1$. The following function uses `Math.random()` to compute a random integer:

```
/**
 * Compute a random integer within the given range.
 *
 * @param [lower] Optional lower bound. Default: zero.
 * @returns A random integer i, lower ≤ i < upper
 */
function getRandomInteger(lower, upper) {
    if (arguments.length === 1) {
        upper = lower;
        lower = 0;
    }
    return Math.floor(Math.random() * (upper - lower)) + lower;
}
```

CHAPTER 22

JSON

JSON (JavaScript Object Notation) is a plain-text format for data storage. It has become quite popular as a data interchange format for web services, for configuration files, and more. ECMAScript 5 has an API for converting from a string in JSON format to a JavaScript value (*parsing*) and vice versa (*stringifying*).

Background

This section explains what JSON is and how it was created.

Data Format

JSON stores data as plain text. Its grammar is a subset of the grammar of JavaScript expressions. For example:

```
{
    "first": "Jane",
    "last": "Porter",
    "married": true,
    "born": 1890,
    "friends": [ "Tarzan", "Cheeta" ]
}
```

JSON uses the following constructs from JavaScript expressions:

Compound
    Objects of JSON data and arrays of JSON data

Atomic
    Strings, numbers, booleans, and null

It adheres to these rules:

- Strings must always be double-quoted; string literals such as `'mystr'` are illegal.
- Property keys must be double-quoted.

History

Douglas Crockford discovered JSON in 2001. He gave it a name and put up a specification at *http://json.org*:

> I discovered JSON. I do not claim to have invented JSON, because it already existed in nature. What I did was I found it, I named it, I described how it was useful. I don't claim to be the first person to have discovered it; I know that there are other people who discovered it at least a year before I did. The earliest occurrence I've found was, there was someone at Netscape who was using JavaScript array literals for doing data communication as early as 1996, which was at least five years before I stumbled onto the idea.

Initially, Crockford wanted JSON to have the name *JavaScript Markup Language*, but the acronym JSML was already taken by the JSpeech Markup Language (*http://www.w3.org/TR/jsml/*).

The JSON specification has been translated to many human languages, and there are now libraries for many programming languages that support parsing and generating JSON.

Grammar

Douglas Crockford created a JSON business card with a logo on the front (see Figure 22-1) and the full grammar on the back (see Figure 22-2). That makes it visually obvious how positively simple JSON is.

Figure 22-1. The front side of the JSON business card shows a logo (source: Eric Miraglia (http://www.flickr.com/photos/equanimity/3762360637/)).

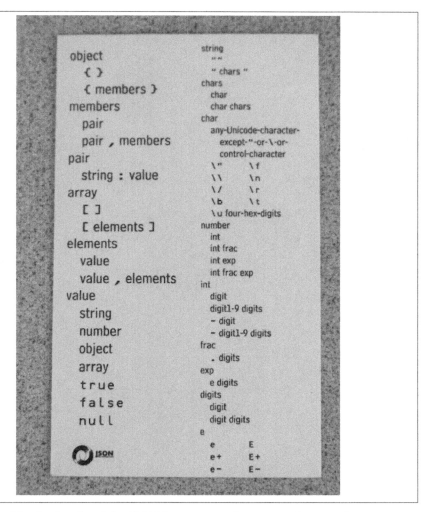

Figure 22-2. The back side of the JSON business card contains the complete grammar (source: Eric Miraglia (http://www.flickr.com/photos/equanimity/3763158824/)).

The grammar can be transcribed as follows:

object
    { }
    { members }

members
    pair

        pair , members

pair
        string : value

array
        [ ]

        [elements]

elements
        value

        value , elements

value
        string

        number

        object

        array

        true

        false

        null

string
        " "

        " chars "

chars
        char

        char chars

char
        any-Unicode-character-except-"-or-\-or-control-character

        \" \\ \/ \b \f \n \r \t

        \u four-hex-digits

number
        int

        int frac

        int exp

    int frac exp

int

    digit

    digit1-9 digits

    - digit

    - digit1-9 digits

frac

    . digits

exp

    e digits

digits

    digit

    digit digits

e

    e e+ e-

    E E+ E-

The global variable JSON serves as a namespace for functions that produce and parse strings with JSON data.

JSON.stringify(value, replacer?, space?)

JSON.stringify(value, replacer?, space?) translates the JavaScript value value to a string in JSON format. It has two optional arguments.

The optional parameter replacer is used to change the value before stringifying it. It can be:

- A *node visitor* (see "Transforming Data via Node Visitors" on page 341) that transforms the tree of values before it is stringified. For example:

```
function replacer(key, value) {
    if (typeof value === 'number') {
        value = 2 * value;
    }
    return value;
}
```

Using the replacer:

```
> JSON.stringify({ a: 5, b: [ 2, 8 ] }, replacer)
'{"a":10,"b":[4,16]}'
```

- A whitelist of property keys that hides all properties (of nonarray objects) whose keys are not in the list. For example:

```
> JSON.stringify({foo: 1, bar: {foo: 1, bar: 1}}, ['bar'])
'{"bar":{"bar":1}}'
```

The whitelist has no effect on arrays:

```
> JSON.stringify(['a', 'b'], ['0'])
'["a","b"]'
```

The optional parameter `space` influences the formatting of the output. Without this parameter, the result of `stringify` is a single line of text:

```
> console.log(JSON.stringify({a: 0, b: ['\n']}))
{"a":0,"b":["\n"]}
```

With it, newlines are inserted and each level of nesting via arrays and objects increases indentation. There are two ways to specify how to indent:

A number

Multiply the number by the level of indentation and indent the line by as many spaces. Numbers smaller than 0 are interpreted as 0; numbers larger than 10 are interpreted as 10:

```
> console.log(JSON.stringify({a: 0, b: ['\n']}, null, 2))
{
  "a": 0,
  "b": [
    "\n"
  ]
}
```

A string

To indent, repeat the given string once for each level of indentation. Only the first 10 characters of the string are used:

```
> console.log(JSON.stringify({a: 0, b: ['\n']}, null, '|--'))
{
|--"a": 0,
|--"b": [
|--|--"\n"
|--]
}
```

Therefore, the following invocation of `JSON.stringify()` prints an object as a nicely formatted tree:

```
JSON.stringify(data, null, 4)
```

Data Ignored by JSON.stringify()

In objects, `JSON.stringify()` only considers enumerable own properties (see "Property Attributes and Property Descriptors" on page 222). The following example demonstrates the nonenumerable own property `obj.foo` being ignored:

```
> var obj = Object.defineProperty({}, 'foo', { enumerable: false, value: 7 });
> Object.getOwnPropertyNames(obj)
[ 'foo' ]
> obj.foo
7
> JSON.stringify(obj)
'{}'
```

How `JSON.stringify()` handles values that are not supported by JSON (such as functions and `undefined`) depends on where it encounters them. An unsupported value itself leads to `stringify()` returning `undefined` instead of a string:

```
> JSON.stringify(function () {})
undefined
```

Properties whose values are unsupported are simply ignored:

```
> JSON.stringify({ foo: function () {} })
'{}'
```

Unsupported values in arrays are stringified as `null`s:

```
> JSON.stringify([ function () {} ])
'[null]'
```

The toJSON() Method

If `JSON.stringify()` encounters an object that has a `toJSON` method, it uses that method to obtain a value to be stringified. For example:

```
> JSON.stringify({ toJSON: function () { return 'Cool' } })
'"Cool"'
```

Dates already have a `toJSON` method that produces an ISO 8601 date string:

```
> JSON.stringify(new Date('2011-07-29'))
'"2011-07-28T22:00:00.000Z"'
```

The full signature of a `toJSON` method is as follows:

```
function (key)
```

The key parameter allows you to stringify differently, depending on context. It is always a string and indicates where your object was found in the parent object:

Root position
    The empty string

Property value
The property key

Array element
The element's index as a string

I'll demonstrate toJSON() via the following object:

```
var obj = {
    toJSON: function (key) {
        // Use JSON.stringify for nicer-looking output
        console.log(JSON.stringify(key));
        return 0;
    }
};
```

If you use JSON.stringify(), each occurrence of obj is replaced with 0. The toJ
SON() method is notified that obj was encountered at the property key 'foo' and at the
array index 0:

```
> JSON.stringify({ foo: obj, bar: [ obj ]})
"foo"
"0"
'{"foo":0,"bar":[0]}'
```

The built-in toJSON() methods are as follows:

- Boolean.prototype.toJSON()

- Number.prototype.toJSON()

- String.prototype.toJSON()

- Date.prototype.toJSON()

JSON.parse(text, reviver?)

JSON.parse(text, reviver?) parses the JSON data in text and returns a JavaScript
value. Here are some examples:

```
> JSON.parse("'String'") // illegal quotes
SyntaxError: Unexpected token ILLEGAL
> JSON.parse('"String"')
'String'
> JSON.parse('123')
123
> JSON.parse('[1, 2, 3]')
[ 1, 2, 3 ]
> JSON.parse('{ "hello": 123, "world": 456 }')
{ hello: 123, world: 456 }
```

The optional parameter `reviver` is a *node visitor* (see "Transforming Data via Node Visitors" on page 341) and can be used to transform the parsed data. In this example, we are translating date strings to date objects:

```
function dateReviver(key, value) {
    if (typeof value === 'string') {
        var x = Date.parse(value);
        if (!isNaN(x)) { // valid date string?
            return new Date(x);
        }
    }
    return value;
}
```

And here is the interaction:

```
> var str = '{ "name": "John", "birth": "2011-07-28T22:00:00.000Z" }';
> JSON.parse(str, dateReviver)
{ name: 'John', birth: Thu, 28 Jul 2011 22:00:00 GMT }
```

Transforming Data via Node Visitors

Both `JSON.stringify()` and `JSON.parse()` let you transform JavaScript data by passing in a function:

- `JSON.stringify()` lets you change the JavaScript data before turning it into JSON.

- `JSON.parse()` parses JSON and then lets you post-process the resulting JavaScript data.

The JavaScript data is a tree whose compound nodes are arrays and objects and whose leaves are primitive values (booleans, numbers, strings, `null`). Let's use the name *node visitor* for the transformation function that you pass in. The methods iterate over the tree and call the visitor for each node. It then has the option to replace or delete the node. The node visitor has the signature:

```
function nodeVisitor(key, value)
```

The parameters are:

`this`
> The parent of the current node.

`key`
> A key where the current node is located inside its parent. `key` is always a string.

`value`
> The current node.

The root node root has no parent. When root is visited, a pseudoparent is created for it and the parameters have the following values:

- this is { '': root }.
- key is ''.
- value is root.

The node visitor has three options for returning a value:

- Return value as it is. Then no change is performed.
- Return a different value. Then the current node is replaced with it.
- Return undefined. Then the node is removed.

The following is an example of a node visitor. It logs what values have been passed to it.

```
function nodeVisitor(key, value) {
    console.log([
        // Use JSON.stringify for nicer-looking output
        JSON.stringify(this), // parent
        JSON.stringify(key),
        JSON.stringify(value)
    ].join(' # '));
    return value; // don't change node
}
```

Let's use this function to examine how the JSON methods iterate over JavaScript data.

JSON.stringify()

The special root node comes first, in a prefix iteration (parent before children). The first node that is visited is always the pseudoroot. The last line that is displayed after each call is the string returned by stringify():

```
> JSON.stringify(['a','b'], nodeVisitor)
{"":["a","b"]} # "" # ["a","b"]
["a","b"] # "0" # "a"
["a","b"] # "1" # "b"
'["a","b"]'

> JSON.stringify({a:1, b:2}, nodeVisitor)
{"":{"a":1,"b":2}} # "" # {"a":1,"b":2}
{"a":1,"b":2} # "a" # 1
{"a":1,"b":2} # "b" # 2
'{"a":1,"b":2}'

> JSON.stringify('abc', nodeVisitor)
{"":"abc"} # "" # "abc"
'"abc"'
```

JSON.parse()

The leaves come first, in a postfix iteration (children before parent). The last node that is visited is always the pseudoroot. The last line that is displayed after each call is the JavaScript value returned by parse():

```
> JSON.parse('["a","b"]', nodeVisitor)
["a","b"] # "0" # "a"
["a","b"] # "1" # "b"
{"":["a","b"]} # "" # ["a","b"]
[ 'a', 'b' ]

> JSON.parse('{"a":1, "b":2}', nodeVisitor)
{"a":1,"b":2} # "a" # 1
{"a":1,"b":2} # "b" # 2
{"":{"a":1,"b":2}} # "" # {"a":1,"b":2}
{ a: 1, b: 2 }

> JSON.parse('"hello"', nodeVisitor)
{"":"hello"} # "" # "hello"
'hello'
```

Standard Global Variables

This chapter is a reference for the global variables standardized by the ECMAScript specification. Web browsers have more global variables, which are listed on MDN (*https://developer.mozilla.org/en-US/docs/Web/API/Window*). All global variables are (own or inherited) properties of the global object (`window` in browsers; see "The Global Object" on page 188).

Constructors

For details on the following constructors, see the sections indicated in parentheses:

- `Array` ("The Array Constructor" on page 275)
- `Boolean` ("Wrapper Objects for Primitives" on page 75)
- `Date` ("The Date Constructor" on page 317)
- `Function` ("Evaluating *Code* Using new Function()" on page 350)
- `Number` ("Wrapper Objects for *Primitives*" on page 75)
- `Object` ("Converting Any Value to an *Object*" on page 203)
- `RegExp` ("Creating a Regular Expression" on page *302*)
- `String` ("Wrapper Objects for Primitives" on page 75)

Error Constructors

For details on these constructors, see "Error Constructors" on page *161*:

- `Error`
- `EvalError`

- RangeError
- ReferenceError
- SyntaxError
- TypeError
- URIError

Nonconstructor Functions

Several global functions are not constructors. They are listed in this section.

Encoding and Decoding Text

The following functions handle several ways of URI encoding and decoding:

encodeURI(uri)
> Percent-encodes special characters in uri. Special characters are all Unicode characters except for the following ones:

> URI characters: ; , / ? : @ & = + $ #
>
> Not encoded either: a-z A-Z 0-9 - _ . ! ~ * ' ( )

> For example:

> ```
> > encodeURI('http://example.com/Für Elise/')
> 'http://example.com/F%C3%BCr%20Elise/'
> ```

encodeURIComponent(uriComponent)
> Percent-encodes all characters in uriComponent, except for:

> Not encoded: a-z A-Z 0-9 - _ . ! ~ * ' ( )

> In contrast to encodeURI, characters that are significant in URLs and filenames are encoded, too. You can thus use this function to turn any text into a legal filename or URL path segment. For example:

> ```
> > encodeURIComponent('http://example.com/Für Elise/')
> 'http%3A%2F%2Fexample.com%2FF%C3%BCr%20Elise%2F'
> ```

decodeURI(encodedURI)
> Decodes a percent-encoded URI that has been produced by encodeURI:

> ```
> > decodeURI('http://example.com/F%C3%BCr%20Elise/')
> 'http://example.com/Für Elise/'
> ```

> encodeURI does not encode URI characters and decodeURI does not decode them, *even* if they have been correctly encoded:

```
> decodeURI('%2F')
'%2F'
> decodeURIComponent('%2F')
'/'
```

decodeURIComponent(encodedURIComponent)

Decodes a percent-encoded URI component that has been produced by encodeUR
IComponent. In contrast to decodeURI, all percent-encoded characters are decoded:

```
> decodeURIComponent('http%3A%2F%2Fexample.com%2FF%C3%BCr%20Elise%2F')
'http://example.com/Für Elise/'
```

The following are deprecated:

- escape(str) percent-encodes str. It is deprecated because it does not handle non-ASCII characters properly. Use encodeURIComponent() instead.

- unescape(str) percent-decodes str. It is deprecated because it does not handle non-ASCII characters properly. Use decodeURIComponent() instead.

Categorizing and Parsing Numbers

The following methods help with categorizing and parsing numbers:

- isFinite(number) ("Checking for Infinity" on page 108)
- isNaN(value) ("Pitfall: checking whether a value is NaN" on page 107)
- parseFloat(string) ("parseFloat()" on page 105)
- parseInt(string, radix) ("Integers via parseInt()" on page 120)

Dynamically Evaluating JavaScript Code via eval() and new Function()

This section examines how one can dynamically evaluate code in JavaScript.

Evaluating Code Using eval()

The function call:

```
eval(str)
```

evaluates the JavaScript code in str. For example:

```
> var a = 12;
> eval('a + 5')
17
```

Note that `eval()` parses in statement context (see "Expressions Versus Statements" on page 54):

```
> eval('{ foo: 123 }')  // code block
123
> eval('({ foo: 123 })')  // object literal
{ foo: 123 }
```

Use eval() in strict mode

For `eval()`, you really should use strict mode (see "Strict Mode" on page 62). In sloppy mode, evaluated code can create local variables in the surrounding scope:

```
function sloppyFunc() {
    eval('var foo = 123');  // added to the scope of sloppyFunc
    console.log(foo);  // 123
}
```

That can't happen in strict mode:

```
function strictFunc() {
    'use strict';
    eval('var foo = 123');
    console.log(foo);  // ReferenceError: foo is not defined
}
```

However, even in strict mode, evaluated code still has read and write access to variables in surrounding scopes. To prevent such access, you need to call `eval()` indirectly.

Indirect eval() evaluates in global scope

There are two ways to invoke `eval()`:

- Directly (*http://ecma-international.org/ecma-262/5.1/#sec-15.1.2.1.1*). Via a direct call to a function whose name is "eval."

- Indirectly. In some other way (via `call()`, as a method of `window`, by storing it under a different name and calling it there, etc.).

As we have already seen, direct `eval()` executes code in the current scope:

```
var x = 'global';

function directEval() {
    'use strict';
    var x = 'local';

    console.log(eval('x')); // local
}
```

Conversely, indirect `eval()` executes it in global scope:

```
var x = 'global';

function indirectEval() {
    'use strict';
    var x = 'local';

    // Don't call eval directly
    console.log(eval.call(null, 'x')); // global
    console.log(window.eval('x')); // global
    console.log((1, eval)('x')); // global (1)

    // Change the name of eval
    var xeval = eval;
    console.log(xeval('x')); // global

    // Turn eval into a method
    var obj = { eval: eval };
    console.log(obj.eval('x')); // global
}
```

Explanation of (1): When you refer to a variable via its name, the initial result is a so-called *reference* (*http://ecma-international.org/ecma-262/5.1/#sec-8.7*), a data structure with two main fields:

- base points to the *environment*, the data structure in which the variable's value is stored.

- referencedName is the name of the variable.

During an eval() function call, the function call operator (the parentheses) encounters a reference to eval and can determine the name of the function to be called. Therefore, such a function call triggers a direct eval(). You can, however, force an indirect eval() by not giving the call operator a reference. That is achieved by retrieving the value of the reference before applying the operator. The comma operator does that for us in line (1). This operator evaluates the first operand and returns the result of evaluating the second operand. The evaluation always produces values, which means that references are resolved and function names are lost.

Indirectly evaluated code is always sloppy. That is a consequence of the code being evaluated independently of its current surroundings:

```
function strictFunc() {
    'use strict';

    var code = '(function () { return this }())';
    var result = eval.call(null, code);
    console.log(result !== undefined); // true, sloppy mode
}
```

Evaluating Code Using new Function()

The constructor `Function()` has the signature:

```
new Function(param1, ..., paramN, funcBody)
```

It creates a function whose zero or more parameters have the names `param1`, `parem2`, and so on, and whose body is `funcBody`; that is, the created function looks like this:

```
function («param1», ..., «paramN») {
    «funcBody»
}
```

Let's use `new Function()` to create a function `f` that returns the sum of its parameters:

```
> var f = new Function('x', 'y', 'return x+y');
> f(3, 4)
7
```

Similar to indirect `eval()`, `new Function()` creates functions whose scope is global:[1]

```
var x = 'global';

function strictFunc() {
    'use strict';
    var x = 'local';

    var f = new Function('return x');
    console.log(f()); // global
}
```

Such functions are also sloppy by default:

```
function strictFunc() {
    'use strict';

    var sl = new Function('return this');
    console.log(sl() !== undefined); // true, sloppy mode

    var st = new Function('"use strict"; return this');
    console.log(st() === undefined); // true, strict mode
}
```

eval() Versus new Function()

Normally, it is better to use `new Function()` than `eval()` in order to evaluate code: the function parameters provide a clear interface to the evaluated code and you don't need the slightly awkward syntax of indirect `eval()` to ensure that the evaluated code can access only global variables (in addition to its own).

---

1. Mariusz Nowak (@medikoo) told me that code evaluated by `Function` is sloppy by default, everywhere.

Best Practices

You should avoid `eval()` and `new Function()`. Dynamically evaluating code is slow and a potential security risk. It also prevents most tools (such as IDEs) that use static analysis from considering the code.

Often, there are better alternatives. For example, Brendan Eich recently tweeted (*http://bit.ly/1fwpWrB*) an antipattern used by programmers who want to access a property whose name is stored in a variable `propName`:

```
var value = eval('obj.'+propName);
```

The idea makes sense: the dot operator only supports fixed, statically provided property keys. In this case, the property key is only known at runtime, which is why `eval()` is needed in order to use that operator. Luckily, JavaScript also has the bracket operator, which does accept dynamic property keys. Therefore, the following is a better version of the preceding code:

```
var value = obj[propName];
```

You also shouldn't use `eval()` or `new Function()` to parse JSON data. That is unsafe. Either rely on ECMAScript 5's built-in support for JSON (see Chapter 22) or use a library.

Legitimate use cases

There are a few legitimate, albeit advanced, use cases for `eval()` and `new Function()`: configuration data with functions (which JSON does not allow), template libraries, interpreters, command lines, and module systems.

Conclusion

This was a relatively high-level overview of dynamically evaluating code in JavaScript. If you want to dig deeper, you can take a look at the article "Global eval. What are the options?" (*http://perfectionkills.com/global-eval-what-are-the-options/*) by kangax.

The Console API

In most JavaScript engines, there is a global object, `console`, with methods for logging and debugging. That object is not part of the language proper, but has become a de facto standard. Since their main purpose is debugging, the `console` methods will most frequently be used during development and rarely in deployed code.

This section provides an overview of the console API. It documents the status quo as of Chrome 32, Firebug 1.12, Firefox 25, Internet Explorer 11, Node.js 0.10.22, and Safari 7.0.

How Standardized Is the Console API Across Engines?

The implementations of the console API vary greatly and are constantly changing. If you want authoritative documentation, you have two options. First, you can look at standard-like overviews of the API:

- Firebug first implemented the console API, and the documentation (*http://bit.ly/1fwq1vk*) in its wiki is the closest thing to a standard there currently is.
- Additionally, Brian Kardell and Paul Irish are working on a specification (*http://bit.ly/1fwq7mX*) for the API, which should lead to more consistent behavior.

Second, you can look at the documentation of various engines:

- Chrome (*https://developers.google.com/chrome-developer-tools/docs/console-api/*)
- Firebug (*https://getfirebug.com/wiki/index.php/Console_API*)
- Firefox (*https://developer.mozilla.org/en-US/docs/Web/API/console*)
- Internet Explorer (*http://msdn.microsoft.com/en-us/library/ie/hh772183.aspx*)
- Node.js (*http://nodejs.org/api/stdio.html*)
- Safari (*http://bit.ly/1fwq9er*)

 There is a bug in Internet Explorer 9. In that browser, the console object exists only if the developer tools were open at least once. That means that you get a ReferenceError if you refer to console and the tools weren't open before. As a workaround, you can check whether console exists and create a dummy implementation if it doesn't.

Simple Logging

The console API includes the following logging methods:

console.clear()
> Clear the console.

console.debug(object1, object2?, ...)
> Prefer console.log(), which does the same as this method.

console.error(object1, object2?, ...)
> Log the parameters to the console. In browsers, the logged content may be marked by an "error" icon and/or include a stack trace or a link to the code.

console.exception(errorObject, object1?, ...]) *[Firebug-only]*
> Log object1 etc. and show an interactive stack trace.

```
console.info(object1?, object2?, ...)
```
Log the parameters to the console. In browsers, the logged content may be marked by an "info" icon and/or include a stack trace or a link to the code.

```
console.log(object1?, object2?, ...)
```
Log the parameters to the console. If the first parameter is a `printf`-style format string, use it to print the remaining parameters. For example (Node.js REPL):

```
> console.log('%s', { foo: 'bar' })
[object Object]
> console.log('%j', { foo: 'bar' })
{"foo":"bar"}
```

The only dependable cross-platform formatting directive is `%s`. Node.js supports `%j` to format data as JSON; browsers tend to support directives that log something interactive to the console.

```
console.trace()
```
Logs a stack trace (which is interactive in many browsers).

```
console.warn(object1?, object2?, ...)
```
Log the parameters to the console. In browsers, the logged content may be marked by a "warning" icon and/or include a stack trace or a link to the code.

Support on various platforms is indicated in the following table:

	Chrome	Firebug	Firefox	IE	Node.js	Safari
clear	✓	✓		✓		✓
debug	✓	✓	✓	✓		✓
error	✓	✓	✓	✓	✓	✓
exception		✓				
info	✓	✓	✓	✓	✓	✓
log	✓	✓	✓	✓	✓	✓
trace	✓	✓	✓	✓	✓	✓
warn	✓	✓	✓	✓	✓	✓

`exception` has been typeset in italics, because it is supported only on a single platform.

Checking and Counting

The console API includes the following checking and counting methods:

```
console.assert(expr, obj?)
```
If `expr` is `false`, log `obj` to the console and throw an exception. If it is `true`, do nothing.

```
console.count(label?)
```
Count how many times the line with this statement is executed with this label.

Support on various platforms is indicated in the following table:

	Chrome	Firebug	Firefox	IE	Node.js	Safari
assert	✓	✓		✓	✓	✓
count	✓	✓		✓		✓

Formatted Logging

The console API includes the following methods for formatted logging:

```
console.dir(object)
```
Print a representation of the object to the console. In browsers, that representation can be explored interactively.

```
console.dirxml(object)
```
Print the XML source tree of an HTML or XML element.

```
console.group(object1?, object2?, ...)
```
Log the objects to the console and open a nested block that contains all future logged content. Close the block by calling `console.groupEnd()`. The block is initially expanded, but can be collapsed.

```
console.groupCollapsed(object1?, object2?, ...)
```
Works like `console.group()`, but the block is initially collapsed.

```
console.groupEnd()
```
Close a group that has been opened by `console.group()` or `console.group Collapsed()`.

```
console.table(data, columns?)
```
Print an array as a table, one element per row. The optional parameter `columns` specifies which properties/array indices are shown in the columns. If that parameter is missing, all property keys are used as table columns. Missing properties and array elements show up as `undefined` in columns:

```
var persons = [
    { firstName: 'Jane', lastName: 'Bond' },
    { firstName: 'Lars', lastName: 'Croft', age: 72 }
];
// Equivalent:
console.table(persons);
console.table(persons, ['firstName', 'lastName', 'age']);
```

The resulting table is as follows:

(index)	firstName	lastName	age
0	"Jane"	"Bond"	undefined
1	"Lars"	"Croft"	72

Support on various platforms is indicated in the following table:

	Chrome	Firebug	Firefox	IE	Node.js	Safari
`dir`	✓	✓	✓	✓	✓	✓
`dirxml`	✓	✓		✓		✓
`group`	✓	✓	✓	✓		✓
`groupCollapsed`	✓	✓	✓	✓		✓
`groupEnd`	✓	✓	✓	✓		✓
`table`	✓	✓				

Profiling and Timing

The console API includes the following methods for profiling and timing:

`console.markTimeline(label)` *[Safari-only]*
    The same as `console.timeStamp`.

`console.profile(title?)`
    Turn on profiling. The optional `title` is used for the profile report.

`console.profileEnd()`
    Stop profiling and print the profile report.

`console.time(label)`
    Start a timer whose label is `label`.

`console.timeEnd(label)`
    Stop the timer whose label is `label` and print the time that has elapsed since starting it.

`console.timeStamp(label?)`
    Log a timestamp with the given `label`. May be logged to the console or a timeline.

Support on various platforms is indicated in the following table:

	Chrome	Firebug	Firefox	IE	Node.js	Safari
markTimeline						✓
`profile`	✓	✓	(devtools)	✓		✓
`profileEnd`	✓	✓	(devtools)	✓		✓

	Chrome	Firebug	Firefox	IE	Node.js	Safari
time	✓	✓	✓	✓ ✓		✓
timeEnd	✓	✓	✓	✓ ✓		✓
timeStamp	✓	✓				

markTimeline has been typeset in italics, because it is supported only on a single platform. The (devtools) designation means that the developer tools must be open in order for the method to work.[2]

Namespaces and Special Values

The following global variables serve as namespaces for functions. For details, see the material indicated in parentheses:

JSON
> JSON API functionality (Chapter 22)

Math
> Math API functionality (Chapter 21)

Object
> Metaprogramming functionality ("Cheat Sheet: Working with Objects" on page 270)

The following global variables contain special values. For more on them, review the material indicated in parentheses:

undefined
> A value expressing that something does not exist ("undefined and null" on page 71):
>
> ```
> > ({}.foo) === undefined
> true
> ```

NaN
> A value expressing that something is "not a number" ("NaN" on page 106):
>
> ```
> > 1 / 'abc'
> NaN
> ```

Infinity
> A value denoting numeric infinity ∞ ("Infinity" on page 107):
>
> ```
> > 1 / 0
> Infinity
> ```

---

2. Thanks to Matthias Reuter (@gweax) and Philipp Kyeck (@pkyeck), who contributed to this section.

CHAPTER 24

Unicode and JavaScript

This chapter is a brief introduction to Unicode and how it is handled in JavaScript.

Unicode History

Unicode was started in 1987, by Joe Becker (Xerox), Lee Collins (Apple), and Mark Davis (Apple). The idea was to create a universal character set, as there were many incompatible standards for encoding plain text at that time: numerous variations of 8-bit ASCII, Big Five (Traditional Chinese), GB 2312 (Simplified Chinese), and more. Before Unicode, no standard for multilingual plain text existed, but there were rich-text systems (such as Apple's WorldScript) that allowed you to combine multiple encodings.

The first Unicode draft proposal was published in 1988. Work continued afterward and the working group expanded. The *Unicode Consortium* (*http://www.unicode.org/consor tium/consort.html*) was incorporated on January 3, 1991:

> The Unicode Consortium is a non-profit corporation devoted to developing, maintaining, and promoting software internationalization standards and data, particularly the Unicode Standard [...]

The first volume of the Unicode 1.0 standard was published in October 1991, and the second in June 1992.

Important Unicode Concepts

The idea of a character may seem a simple one, but there are many aspects to it. That's why Unicode is such a complex standard. The following are important basic concepts:

Characters and graphemes
> These two terms mean something quite similar. Characters are digital entities, while graphemes are atomic units of written languages (alphabetic letters, typographic ligatures, Chinese characters, punctuation marks, etc.). Programmers think in

characters, but users think in graphemes. Sometimes several characters are used to represent a single grapheme. For example, we can produce the single grapheme ô by combining the character *o* and the character ^ (the circumflex accent).

Glyph
This is a concrete way of displaying a grapheme. Sometimes, the same grapheme is displayed differently, depending on its context or other factors. For example, the graphemes *f* and *i* can be presented as a glyph *f* and a glyph *i*, connected by a ligature glyph, or without a ligature.

Code points
Unicode represents the characters it supports via numbers called *code points*. The hexadecimal range of code points is 0x0 to 0x10FFFF (17 times 16 bits).

Code units
To store or transmit code points, we encode them as *code units*, pieces of data with a fixed length. The length is measured in bits and determined by an encoding scheme, of which Unicode has several—for example, UTF-8 and UTF-16. The number in the name indicates the length of the code unit, in bits. If a code point is too large to fit into a single code unit, it must be broken up into multiple units; that is, the number of code units needed to represent a single code point can vary.

BOM (byte order mark)
If a code unit is larger than a single byte, byte ordering matters. The BOM is a single pseudocharacter (possibly encoded as multiple code units) at the beginning of a text that indicates whether the code units are *big endian* (most significant bytes come first) or *little endian* (least significant bytes come first). The default for texts without a BOM is big endian. The BOM also indicates the encoding that is used; it is different for UTF-8, UTF-16, and so on. Additionally, it serves as a marker for Unicode if web browsers have no other information regarding the encoding of a text. However, the BOM is not used very often, for several reasons:

- UTF-8 is by far the most popular Unicode encoding and does not need a BOM, because there is only one way of ordering bytes.

- Several character encodings specify a fixed byte ordering. Then a BOM must not be used. Examples include UTF-16BE (UTF-16 big endian), UTF-16LE, UTF-32BE, and UTF-32LE. This is a safer way of handling byte ordering, because metadata and data stay separate and can't be mixed up.

Normalization
Sometimes the same grapheme can be represented in several ways. For example, the grapheme ö can be represented as a single code point or as an *o* followed by a combining character ¨ (diaeresis, double dot). Normalization is about translating a text to a canonical representation; equivalent code points and sequences of code points are all translated to the same code point (or sequence of code points). That

is useful for text processing (e.g., to search for text). Unicode specifies several normalizations.

Character properties

Each Unicode character is assigned several properties by the specification, some of which are listed here:

- *Name.* An English name, composed of uppercase letters A–Z, digits 0–9, hyphen (-), and <space>. Two examples:
  — "λ" has the name "GREEK SMALL LETTER LAMBDA."
  — "!" has the name "EXCLAMATION MARK."

- *General category* (*http://bit.ly/1fwsjL9*). Partitions characters into categories such as letter, uppercase letter, number, and punctuation.

- *Age.* With what version of Unicode was the character introduced (1.0, 1.1., 2.0, etc.)?

- *Deprecated.* Is the use of the character discouraged?

- *And many more.*

Code Points

The range of the code points was initially 16 bits. With Unicode version 2.0 (July 1996), it was expanded: it is now divided into 17 *planes*, numbered from 0 to 16. Each plane comprises 16 bits (in hexadecimal notation: 0x0000–0xFFFF). Thus, in the hexadecimal ranges that follow, digits beyond the four bottom ones contain the number of the plane.

- Plane 0, Basic Multilingual Plane (BMP): 0x0000–0xFFFF
- Plane 1, Supplementary Multilingual Plane (SMP): 0x10000–0x1FFFF
- Plane 2, Supplementary Ideographic Plane (SIP): 0x20000–0x2FFFF
- Planes 3–13, Unassigned
- Plane 14, Supplementary Special-Purpose Plane (SSP): 0xE0000–0xEFFFF
- Planes 15–16, Supplementary Private Use Area (S PUA A/B): 0x0F0000–0x10FFFF

Planes 1–16 are called *supplementary planes* or *astral planes*.

Unicode Encodings

UTF-32 (Unicode Transformation Format 32) is a format with 32-bit code units. Any code point can be encoded by a single code unit, making this the only fixed-length encoding; for other encodings, the number of units needed to encode a point varies.

UTF-16 is a format with 16-bit code units that needs one to two units to represent a code point. BMP code points can be represented by single code units. Higher code points are 20 bit (16 times 16 bits), after 0x10000 (the range of the BMP) is subtracted. These bits are encoded as two code units (a so-called *surrogate pair*):

Leading surrogate
> Most significant 10 bits: stored in the range 0xD800–0xDBFF. Also called *high-surrogate code unit*.

Trailing surrogate
> Least significant 10 bits: stored in the range 0xDC00–0xDFFF. Also called *low-surrogate code unit*.

The following table (adapted from Unicode Standard 6.2.0, Table 3-5) visualizes how the bits are distributed:

Code point	UTF-16 code unit(s)
xxxxxxxxxxxxxxxx (16 bits)	xxxxxxxxxxxxxxxx
pppppxxxxxxyyyyyyyyyy (21 bits = 5+6+10 bits)	110110qqqqxxxxxx 110111yyyyyyyyyy (qqqq = ppppp − 1)

To enable this encoding scheme, the BMP has a hole with unused code points whose range is 0xD800–0xDFFF. Therefore, the ranges of leading surrogates, trailing surrogates, and BMP code points are disjoint, making decoding robust in the face of errors. The following function encodes a code point as UTF-16 (later we'll see an example of using it):

```
function toUTF16(codePoint) {
    var TEN_BITS = parseInt('1111111111', 2);
    function u(codeUnit) {
        return '\\u'+codeUnit.toString(16).toUpperCase();
    }

    if (codePoint <= 0xFFFF) {
        return u(codePoint);
    }
    codePoint -= 0x10000;

    // Shift right to get to most significant 10 bits
    var leadingSurrogate = 0xD800 | (codePoint >> 10);

    // Mask to get least significant 10 bits
    var trailingSurrogate = 0xDC00 | (codePoint & TEN_BITS);

    return u(leadingSurrogate) + u(trailingSurrogate);
}
```

UCS-2, a deprecated format, uses 16-bit code units to represent (only!) the code points of the BMP. When the range of Unicode code points expanded beyond 16 bits, UTF-16 replaced UCS-2.

UTF-8 has 8-bit code units. It builds a bridge between the legacy ASCII encoding and Unicode. ASCII has only 128 characters, whose numbers are the same as the first 128 Unicode code points. UTF-8 is backward compatible, because all ASCII codes are valid code units. In other words, a single code unit in the range 0–127 encodes a single code point in the same range. Such code units are marked by their highest bit being zero. If, on the other hand, the highest bit is one, then more units will follow, to provide the additional bits for the higher code points. That leads to the following encoding scheme:

- 0000–007F: 0xxxxxxx (7 bits, stored in 1 byte)
- 0080–07FF: 110xxxxx, 10xxxxxx (5+6 bits = 11 bits, stored in 2 bytes)
- 0800–FFFF: 1110xxxx, 10xxxxxx, 10xxxxxx (4+6+6 bits = 16 bits, stored in 3 bytes)
- 10000–1FFFFF: 11110xxx, 10xxxxxx, 10xxxxxx, 10xxxxxx (3+6+6+6 bits = 21 bits, stored in 4 bytes). The highest code point is 10FFFF, so UTF-8 has some extra room.

If the highest bit is not 0, then the number of ones before the zero indicates how many code units there are in a sequence. All code units after the initial one have the bit prefix 10. Therefore, the ranges of initial code units and subsequent code units are disjoint, which helps with recovering from encoding errors.

UTF-8 has become the most popular Unicode format. Initially, its popularity was due to its backward compatibility with ASCII. Later, it gained traction because of its broad and consistent support across operating systems, programming environments, and applications.

JavaScript Source Code and Unicode

There are two ways in which JavaScript handles Unicode source code: internally (during parsing) and externally (while loading a file).

Source Code Internally

Internally, JavaScript source code is treated as a sequence of UTF-16 code units. According to Section 6 (*http://ecma-international.org/ecma-262/5.1/#sec-6*) of the EMCAScript specification:

> ECMAScript source text is represented as a sequence of characters in the Unicode character encoding, version 3.0 or later. [...] ECMAScript source text is assumed to be a sequence of 16-bit code units for the purposes of this specification. [...] If an actual source text is encoded in a form other than 16-bit code units, it must be processed as if it was first converted to UTF-16.

In identifiers, string literals, and regular expression literals, any code unit can also be expressed via a Unicode escape sequence \uHHHH, where HHHH are four hexadecimal digits. For example:

```
> var f\u006F\u006F = 'abc';
> foo
'abc'

> var λ = 123;
> \u03BB
123
```

That means that you can use Unicode characters in literals and variable names, without leaving the ASCII range in the source code.

In string literals, an additional kind of escape is available: *hexadecimal escape sequences* with two-digit hexadecimal numbers that represent code units in the range 0x00–0xFF. For example:

```
> '\xF6' === 'ö'
true
> '\xF6' === '\u00F6'
true
```

Source Code Externally

While UTF-16 is used internally, JavaScript source code is usually not stored in that format. When a web browser loads a source file via a `<script>` tag, it determines the encoding as follows (*http://bit.ly/1fwstC9*):

- If the file starts with a BOM, the encoding is a UTF variant, depending on what BOM is used.

- Otherwise, if the file is loaded via HTTP(S), then the `Content-Type` header can specify an encoding, via the `charset` parameter. For example:

    ```
    Content-Type: application/javascript; charset=utf-8
    ```

    The correct *media type* (formerly known as *MIME type*) for JavaScript files is `application/javascript`. However, older browsers (e.g., Internet Explorer 8 and earlier) work most reliably with `text/javascript`. Unfortunately, the default value (*http://bit.ly/1fwsvKe*) for the attribute `type` of `<script>` tags is `text/javascript`. At least you can omit that attribute for Java-Script; there is no benefit in including it.

- Otherwise, if the `<script>` tag has the attribute `charset`, then that encoding is used. Even though the attribute `type` holds a valid media type, that type must not have the parameter `charset` (like in the aforementioned `Content-Type` header). That ensures that the values of `charset` and `type` don't clash.

- Otherwise, the encoding of the document is used, in which the `<script>` tag resides. For example, this is the beginning of an HTML5 document, where a `<meta>` tag declares that the document is encoded as UTF-8:

```
<!doctype html>
<html>
<head>
    <meta charset="UTF-8">
...
```

It is highly recommended that you always specify an encoding. If you don't, a locale-specific default encoding (*http://bit.ly/1oODGWp*) is used. In other words, people will see the file differently in different countries. Only the lowest 7 bits are relatively stable across locales.

My recommendations can be summarized as follows:

- For your own application, you can use Unicode. But you must specify the encoding of the app's HTML page as UTF-8.
- For libraries, it's safest to release code that is ASCII (7 bit).

Some minification tools can translate source with Unicode code points beyond 7 bit to source that is "7-bit clean." They do so by replacing non-ASCII characters with Unicode escapes. For example, the following invocation of UglifyJS (*https://github.com/mishoo/UglifyJS2*) translates the file *test.js*:

```
uglifyjs -b beautify=false,ascii-only=true test.js
```

The file *test.js* looks like this:

```
var σ = 'Köln';
```

The output of UglifyJS looks like this:

```
var \u03c3="K\xf6ln";
```

Consider the following negative example. For a while, the library D3.js was published in UTF-8. That caused an error (*https://github.com/mbostock/d3/issues/1195*) when it was loaded from a page whose encoding was not UTF-8, because the code contained statements such as:

```
var π = Math.PI, ε = 1e-6;
```

The identifiers π and ε were not decoded correctly and not recognized as valid variable names. Additionally, some string literals with code points beyond 7 bit weren't decoded correctly either. As a workaround, you could load the code by adding the appropriate `charset` attribute to the `<script>` tag:

```
<script charset="utf-8" src="d3.js"></script>
```

JavaScript Strings and Unicode

A JavaScript string is a sequence of UTF-16 code units. According to the ECMAScript specification, Section 8.4 (*http://ecma-international.org/ecma-262/5.1/#sec-8.4*):

> When a String contains actual textual data, each element is considered to be a single UTF-16 code unit.

Escape Sequences

As mentioned before, you can use Unicode escape sequences and hexadecimal escape sequences in string literals. For example, you can produce the character ö by combining an *o* with a diaeresis (code point 0x0308):

```
> console.log('o\u0308')
ö
```

This works in JavaScript command lines, such as web browser consoles and the Node.js REPL. You can also insert this kind of string into the DOM of a web page.

Refering to Astral Plane Characters via Escapes

There are many nice Unicode symbol tables on the Web. Take a look at Tim Whitlock's "Emoji Unicode Tables" (*http://apps.timwhitlock.info/emoji/tables/unicode*) and be amazed by how many symbols there are in modern Unicode fonts. None of the symbols in the table are images; they are all font glyphs. Let's assume you want to display a Unicode character via JavaScript that is in an astral plane (obviously, there is a risk when doing so: not all fonts support all such characters). For example, consider a cow, code point 0x1F404: 🐄.

You can copy the character and paste it directly into your Unicode-encoded JavaScript source:

```
var str = '🐄';
```

JavaScript engines will decode the source (which is most often in UTF-8) and create a string with two UTF-16 code units. Alternatively, you can compute the two code units yourself and use Unicode escape sequences. There are web apps that perform this computation, such as:

- UTF Converter (*http://macchiato.com/unicode/convert.html*)
- "JavaScript escapes" (*http://mothereff.in/js-escapes*) by Mathias Bynens

The previously defined function toUTF16 performs it, too:

```
> toUTF16(0x1F404)
'\\uD83D\\uDC04'
```

The UTF-16 surrogate pair (0xD83D, 0xDC04) does indeed encode the cow:

```
> console.log('\uD83D\uDC04')
```

Counting Characters

If a string contains a surrogate pair (two code units encoding a single code point), then the `length` property doesn't count graphemes anymore. It counts code units:

```
> var str = '      ';
> str === '\uD83D\uDC04'
true
> str.length
2
```

This can be fixed via libraries, such as Mathias Bynens's Punycode.js (*https://github.com/ bestiejs/punycode.js*), which is bundled with Node.js:

```
> var puny = require('punycode');
> puny.ucs2.decode(str).length
1
```

Unicode Normalization

If you want to search in strings or compare them, then you need to normalize—for example, via the library unorm (*https://github.com/walling/unorm*) (by Bjarke Walling).

JavaScript Regular Expressions and Unicode

Support for Unicode in JavaScript's regular expressions (see Chapter 19) is very limited. For example, there is no way to match Unicode categories such as "uppercase letter."

Line terminators influence matching. A line terminator is one of four characters, specified in the following table:

Code unit	Name	Character escape sequence
\u000A	Line feed	\n
\u000D	Carriage return	\r
\u2028	Line separator	
\u2029	Paragraph separator	

The following regular expression constructs are based on Unicode:

- \s \S (whitespace, nonwhitespace) have Unicode-based definitions:

```
> /^\s$/.test('\uFEFF')
true
```

- . (dot) matches all code units (not code points!) except line terminators. See the next section to learn how to match any code point.
- Multiline mode /m: In multiline mode, the assertion ^ matches at the beginning of the input and after line terminators. The assertion $ matches before line terminators and at the end of the input. In nonmultiline mode, they match only at the beginning or the end of the input, respectively.

Other important character classes have definitions that are based on ASCII, not on Unicode:

- \d \D (digits, nondigits): A digit is equivalent to [0-9].
- \w \W (word characters, nonword characters): A word character is equivalent to [A-Za-z0-9_].
- \b \B (at word breaks, inside words): Words are sequences of word characters ([A-Za-z0-9_]). For example, in the string 'über', the character class escape \b sees the character *b* as starting a word:

```
> /\bb/.test('über')
true
```

Matching Any Code Unit and Any Code Point

To match any code unit, you can use [\s\S]; see "Atoms: General" on page 297.

To match any code point, you need to use:[1]

```
([\0-\uD7FF\uE000-\uFFFF]|[\uD800-\uDBFF][\uDC00-\uDFFF])
```

The preceding pattern works like this:

```
([BMP code point]|[leading surrogate][trailing surrogate])
```

As all of these ranges are disjoint, the pattern will correctly match code points in well-formed UTF-16 strings.

Libraries

A few libraries help with handling Unicode in JavaScript:

---

1. Strictly speaking, any Unicode scalar value (*http://www.unicode.org/glossary/#unicode_scalar_value*).

- Regenerate (*https://github.com/mathiasbynens/regenerate*) helps with generating ranges like the preceding one, for matching any code unit. It is meant to be used as part of a build tool, but also works dynamically, for trying out things.

- XRegExp (*http://xregexp.com*) is a regular expression library that has an official add-on (*http://xregexp.com/plugins/#unicode*) for matching Unicode categories, scripts, blocks, and properties via one of the following three constructs:

  \p{...} \p{^...} \P{...}

  For example, \p{Letter} matches letters in various alphabets while \p{^Letter} and \P{Letter} both match all other code points. Chapter 30 contains a brief overview of XRegExp.

- The ECMAScript Internationalization API (see "The ECMAScript Internationalization API" on page 406) provides Unicode-aware collation (sorting and searching of strings) and more.

Recommended Reading and Chapter Sources

For more information on Unicode, see the following:

- Wikipedia has several good entries on Unicode (*http://en.wikipedia.org/wiki/Unicode*) and its terminology.

- Unicode.org (*http://www.unicode.org/*), the official website of the Unicode Consortium, and its FAQ (*http://www.unicode.org/faq/*) are also good resources.

- Joel Spolsky's introductory article "The Absolute Minimum Every Software Developer Absolutely, Positively Must Know About Unicode and Character Sets (No Excuses!)" (*http://www.joelonsoftware.com/articles/Unicode.html*) is helpful.

For information on Unicode support in JavaScript, see:

- "JavaScript's internal character encoding: UCS-2 or UTF-16?" (*http://mathiasbynens.be/notes/javascript-encoding*) by Mathias Bynens

- "JavaScript, Regex, and Unicode" (*http://bit.ly/1oOE0oh*) by Steven Levithan

Acknowledgments

The following people contributed to this chapter: Mathias Bynens (@mathias), Anne van Kesteren (@annevk), and Calvin Metcalf (@CWMma).

CHAPTER 25

New in ECMAScript 5

This chapter lists features that are available only in ECMAScript 5. Should you have to work with older JavaScript engines, you should avoid these features or enable some of them via a library (how is described later). Note that normally, this book assumes that you are working with modern engines, which fully support ECMAScript 5.

The ECMAScript 5 specification contains the following description of its scope:

> The fifth edition of ECMAScript (published as ECMA-262 5th edition)
>
> - codifies de facto interpretations of the language specification that have become common among browser implementations and
> - adds support for new features that have emerged since the publication of the third edition. Such features include
>   — accessor properties,
>   — reflective creation and inspection of objects,
>   — program control of property attributes,
>   — additional array manipulation functions,
>   — support for the JSON object encoding format, and
>   — a strict mode that provides enhanced error checking and program security.

New Features

The new features included in ECMAScript 5 are as follows:

Strict mode (see "Strict Mode" on page 62)
Putting the following line first in a file or a function switches on the so-called *strict mode* that makes JavaScript a cleaner language by forbidding some features, performing more checks, and throwing more exceptions:

```
'use strict';
```

Accessors (see "Accessors (Getters and Setters)" on page 221)

Getters and setters allow you to implement the getting and setting of a property via methods. For example, the following object obj contains a getter for the property foo:

```
> var obj = { get foo() { return 'abc' } };
> obj.foo
'abc'
```

Syntactic Changes

ECMAScript 5 includes the following syntactic changes:

Reserved words as property keys

You can use reserved words (such as new and function) after the dot operator and as unquoted property keys in object literals:

```
> var obj = { new: 'abc' };
> obj.new
'abc'
```

Legal trailing commas

Trailing commas in object literals and array literals are legal.

Multiline string literals

String literals can span multiple lines if you escape the end of the line via a backslash.

New Functionality in the Standard Library

ECMAScript 5 brought several additions to JavaScript's standard library. This section lists them by category.

Metaprogramming

Getting and setting prototypes (see "Getting and Setting the Prototype" on page 214):

- Object.create()
- Object.getPrototypeOf()

Managing property attributes via property descriptors (see "Property Descriptors" on page 223):

- Object.defineProperty()
- Object.defineProperties()

- `Object.create()`
- `Object.getOwnPropertyDescriptor()`

Listing properties (see "Iteration and Detection of Properties" on page 217):

- `Object.keys()`
- `Object.getOwnPropertyNames()`

Protecting objects (see "Protecting Objects" on page 229):

- `Object.preventExtensions()`
- `Object.isExtensible()`
- `Object.seal()`
- `Object.isSealed()`
- `Object.freeze()`
- `Object.isFrozen()`

New `Function` method (see "Function.prototype.bind(thisValue, arg1?, ..., argN?)" on page 205):

- `Function.prototype.bind()`

New Methods

Strings (see Chapter 12):

- New method `String.prototype.trim()`
- Access characters via the bracket operator `[ ... ]`

New `Array` methods (see "Array Prototype Methods" on page 286):

- `Array.isArray()`
- `Array.prototype.every()`
- `Array.prototype.filter()`
- `Array.prototype.forEach()`
- `Array.prototype.indexOf()`
- `Array.prototype.lastIndexOf()`
- `Array.prototype.map()`

- `Array.prototype.reduce()`
- `Array.prototype.some()`

New `Date` methods (see "Date Prototype Methods" on page 319):

- `Date.now()`
- `Date.prototype.toISOString()`

JSON

Support for JSON (see Chapter 22):

- `JSON.parse()` (see "JSON.parse(text, reviver?)" on page 340)
- `JSON.stringify()` (see "JSON.stringify(value, replacer?, space?)" on page 337)
- Some built-in objects have special `toJSON()` methods:
  — `Boolean.prototype.toJSON()`
  — `Number.prototype.toJSON()`
  — `String.prototype.toJSON()`
  — `Date.prototype.toJSON()`

Tips for Working with Legacy Browsers

The following resources will be useful if you need to work with legacy browsers:

- A compatibility table (*http://kangax.github.io/es5-compat-table/*) by Juriy Zaytsev ("kangax") shows how much of ECMAScript 5 is supported by various versions of various browsers.
- es5-shim (*https://github.com/kriskowal/es5-shim/*) brings most (but not all) of ECMAScript 5's functionality to browsers that support only ECMAScript 3.

PART IV

Tips, Tools, and Libraries

This part gives tips for using JavaScript (best practices, advanced techniques, and learning resources) and describes a few important tools and libraries.

CHAPTER 26

A Meta Code Style Guide

JavaScript has many great style guides. Thus, there is no need to write yet another one. Instead, this chapter describes meta style rules and surveys existing style guides and established best practices. It also mentions practices I like that are more controversial. The idea is to complement existing style guides rather than to replace them.

Existing Style Guides

These are style guides that I like:

- Idiomatic.js: Principles of Writing Consistent, Idiomatic JavaScript (*https://github.com/rwaldron/idiomatic.js/*)
- Google JavaScript Style Guide (*http://bit.ly/1oOEfQ7*)
- jQuery JavaScript Style Guide (*http://contribute.jquery.org/style-guide/js/*)
- Airbnb JavaScript Style Guide (*https://github.com/airbnb/javascript*)

Additionally, there are two style guides that go meta:

- Popular Conventions on GitHub (*http://sideeffect.kr/popularconvention/*) analyzes GitHub code to find out which coding conventions are most frequently used.
- JavaScript, the winning style (*http://seravo.fi/2013/javascript-the-winning-style*) examines what the majority of several popular style guides recommend.

General Tips

This section will cover some general code writing tips.

Code Should Be Consistent

There are two important rules for writing consistent code. The first rule is that, if you start a new project, you should come up with a style, document it, and follow it everywhere. The larger the team, the more important it is to check for adherence to the style automatically, via tools such as JSHint. When it comes to style, there are many decisions to make. Most of them have generally agreed-upon answers. Others have to be defined per project. For example:

- How much whitespace (after parentheses, between statements, etc.)
- Indentation (e.g., how many spaces per level of indentation)
- How and where to write `var` statements

The second rule is that, if you are joining an existing project, you should follow its rules rigorously (even if you don't agree with them).

Code Should Be Easy to Understand

> Everyone knows that debugging is twice as hard as writing a program in the first place. So if you are as clever as you can be when you write it, how will you ever debug it?
> —Brian Kernighan

For most code, the time used for reading it is much greater than the time used for writing it. It is thus important to make the former as easy as possible. Here are some guidelines for doing that:

Shorter isn't always better
Sometimes writing *more* means that things are actually faster to read. Let's consider two examples. First, familiar things are easier to understand. That can mean that using familiar, slightly more verbose, constructs can be preferable. Second, humans read tokens, not characters. Therefore, `redBalloon` is easier to read than `rdBlln`.

Good code is like a textbook
Most code bases are filled with new ideas and concepts. That means that if you want to work with a code base, you need to learn those ideas and concepts. In contrast to textbooks, the added challenge with code is that people will not read it linearly. They will jump in anywhere and should be able to roughly understand what is going on. Three parts of a code base help:

- *Code* should explain *what* is happening; it should be self-explanatory. To write such code, use descriptive identifiers and break up long functions (or methods) into smaller subfunctions. If those functions are small enough and have meaningful names, you can often avoid comments.
- *Comments* should explain *why* things are happening. If you need to know a concept to understand the code, you can either include the name of the concept

in an identifier or mention it in a comment. Someone reading the code can then turn to the documentation to find out more about the concept.

- *Documentation* should fill in the blanks left by the code and the comments. It should tell you how to get started with the code base and provide you with the big picture. It should also contain a glossary for all important concepts.

Don't be clever; don't make me think

There is a lot of clever code out there that uses in-depth knowledge of the language to achieve impressive terseness. Such code is usually like a puzzle and difficult to figure out. You will encounter the opinion that if people don't understand such code, maybe they should really learn JavaScript first. But that's not what this is about. No matter how clever you are, entering other people's mental universes is always challenging. So simple code is not stupid, it's code where most of the effort went into making everything easy to understand. Note that "other people" includes your future selves. I often find that clever thoughts I had in the past don't make sense to my present self.

Avoid optimizing for speed or code size

Much cleverness is directed at these optimizations. However, you normally don't need them. On one hand, JavaScript engines are becoming increasingly smart and automatically optimize the speed of code that follows established patterns. On the other hand, minification tools (Chapter 32) rewrite your code so that it is as small as possible. In both cases, tools are clever for you, so that you don't have to be.

Sometimes you have no choice but to optimize the performance of your code. If you do, be sure to measure and optimize the right pieces. In browsers, the problems are often related to DOM and HTML and not the language proper.

Commonly Accepted Best Practices

A majority of JavaScript programmers agree on the following best practices:

- Use strict mode. It makes JavaScript a cleaner language (see "Strict Mode" on page 62).

- Always use semicolons. Avoid the pitfalls of automatic semicolon insertion (see "Automatic Semicolon Insertion" on page 59).

- Always use strict equality (===) and strict inequality (!==). I recommend never deviating from this rule. I even prefer the first of the following two conditions, even though they are equivalent:

    ```
    if (x !== undefined && x !== null) ... // my choice
    if (x != null) ... // equivalent
    ```

- Either use only spaces or only tabs for indentation, but don't mix them.

- Quoting strings: You can write string literals with either single quotes or double quotes in JavaScript. Single quotes are more common. They make it easier to work with HTML code (which normally has attribute values in double quotes). Other considerations are mentioned in "String Literals" on page 133.
- Avoid global variables ("Best Practice: Avoid Creating Global Variables" on page 187).

Brace Styles

In languages where braces delimit blocks of code, a brace style determines where you put those braces. Two brace styles are most common in C-like languages (such as Java and JavaScript): Allman style and 1TBS.

Allman style

If a statement contains a block, that block is considered as somewhat separate from the head of the statement: its opening brace is in a line of its own, at the same indentation level as the head. For example:

```
// Allman brace style
function foo(x, y, z)
{
    if (x)
    {
        a();
    }
    else
    {
        b();
        c();
    }
}
```

1TBS (One True Brace Style)

Here, a block is more closely associated with the header of its statement; it starts after it, in the same line. The bodies of control flow statements are always put in braces, even if there is only a single statement. For example:

```
// One True Brace Style
function foo(x, y, z) {
    if (x) {
        a();
    } else {
        b();
        c();
    }
}
```

1TBS is a variant of the (older) K&R (Kernighan and Ritchie) style.[1] In K&R style, functions are written in Allman style and braces are omitted where they are not necessary—for example, around single-statement then cases:

```javascript
// K&R brace style
function foo(x, y, z)
{
    if (x)
        a();
    else {
        b();
        c();
    }
}
```

JavaScript

The de facto standard in the JavaScript world is 1TBS. It has been inherited from Java and most style guides recommend it. One reason for that is objective. If you return an object literal, you must put the opening brace in the same line as the keyword `return`, like this (otherwise, automatic semicolon insertion inserts a semicolon after `return`, meaning that nothing is returned; see "Pitfall: ASI can unexpectedly break up statements" on page 60):

```javascript
return {
    name: 'Jane'
};
```

Obviously, an object literal is not a code block, but things look more consistent and you are less likely to make mistakes if both are formatted the same way.

My personal style and preference is:

- 1TBS (which implies that you use braces whenever possible).
- As an exception, I omit braces if a statement can be written in a single line. For example:
  ```javascript
  if (x) return x;
  ```

Prefer Literals to Constructors

Several literals produce objects that can also be created by constructors. However, the latter is normally the better choice:

```javascript
var obj = new Object(); // no
var obj = {}; // yes
```

---

1. Some people even say that they are synonyms, that 1TBS is a way to jokingly refer to K&R.

```
var arr = new Array(); // no
var arr = []; // yes

var regex = new RegExp('abc'); // avoid if possible
var regex = /abc/; // yes
```

Don't ever use the constructor Array to create an array with given elements. "Initializing an array with elements (avoid!)" on page 275 explains why:

```
var arr = new Array('a', 'b', 'c'); // never ever
var arr = [ 'a', 'b', 'c' ]; // yes
```

Don't Be Clever

This section collects examples of unrecommended cleverness.

Conditional operator

Don't nest the conditional operator:

```
// Don't:
return x === 0 ? 'red' : x === 1 ? 'green' : 'blue';

// Better:
if (x === 0) {
    return 'red';
} else if (x === 1) {
    return 'green';
} else {
    return 'blue';
}

// Best:
switch (x) {
    case 0:
        return 'red';
    case 1:
        return 'green';
    default:
        return 'blue';
}
```

Abbreviating if statements

Don't abbreviate if statements via logical operators:

```
foo && bar(); // no
if (foo) bar(); // yes

foo || bar(); // no
if (!foo) bar(); // yes
```

Increment operator

If possible, use the increment operator (++) and the decrement operator (--) as statements; don't use them as expressions. In the latter case, they return a value and while there is a mnemonic, you still need to think to figure out what is going on:

```
// Unsure: what is happening?
return ++foo;

// Easy to understand
++foo;
return foo;
```

Checking for undefined

```
if (x === void 0) x = 0; // not necessary in ES5
if (x === undefined) x = 0; // preferable
```

Starting with ECMAScript 5, the second way of checking is better. "Changing undefined" on page 75 explains why.

Converting a number to an integer

```
return x >> 0; // no
return Math.round(x); // yes
```

The shift operator can be used to convert a number to an integer. However, it is usually better to use a more explicit alternative such as Math.round(). "Converting to Integer" on page 117 gives an overview of all ways of converting to integer.

Acceptable Cleverness

Sometimes you can be clever in JavaScript—if the cleverness has become an established pattern.

Default values

Using the Or (||) operator to provide default values is a common pattern—for example, for parameters:

```
function f(x) {
    x = x || 0;
    ...
}
```

For details and more examples, consult "Pattern: providing a default value" on page 100.

Generic methods

If you use methods generically, you can abbreviate Object.prototype as {}. The following two expressions are equivalent:

```
Object.prototype.hasOwnProperty.call(obj, propKey)
{}.hasOwnProperty.call(obj, propKey)
```

And `Array.prototype` can be abbreviated as `[]`:

```
Array.prototype.slice.call(arguments)
[].slice.call(arguments)
```

I'm ambivalent about this one. It is a hack (you are accessing a prototype property via an instance). But it reduces clutter, and I expect engines to eventually optimize this pattern.

ECMAScript 5: trailing commas

Trailing commas in object literals are legal in ECMAScript 5:

```
var obj = {
    first: 'Jane',
    last: 'Doe', // legal: trailing comma
};
```

ECMAScript 5: reserved words

ECMAScript 5 also allows you to use reserved words (such as `new`) as property keys:

```
> var obj = { new: 'abc' };
> obj.new
'abc'
```

Controversial Rules

Let's look at some conventions I like that are a bit more controversial.

Syntax

We'll start with syntactic conventions:

Tight whitespace

I like *relatively* tight whitespace. The model is written English: there are no spaces after an opening parenthesis and before a closing parenthesis. And there are spaces after commas:

```
var result = foo('a', 'b');
var arr = [ 1, 2, 3 ];
if (flag) {
    ...
}
```

For anonymous functions, I follow Douglas Crockford's rule of having a space after the keyword `function`. The rationale is that this is what a named function expression looks like if you remove the name:

```
function foo(arg) { ... }   // named function expression
function (arg) { ... }      // anonymous function expression
```

Four spaces per indentation level

Most code I am seeing uses spaces for indentation, because tabs are displayed so differently between applications and operating systems. I prefer four spaces per level of indentation, because that makes the indentation more visible.

Put the conditional operator in parentheses

This helps with reading, because it is easier to make out the scope of the operator:

```
return result ? result : theDefault;   // no
return (result ? result : theDefault); // yes
```

Variables

Next, I'll cover conventions for variables:

One variable declaration per line

I don't declare multiple variables with a single declaration:

```
// no
var foo = 3,
    bar = 2,
    baz;

// yes
var foo = 3;
var bar = 2;
var baz;
```

The advantages of this approach are that deleting, inserting, and rearranging lines is simpler and the lines are automatically indented correctly.

Keep variable declarations local

If your function isn't too long (which it shouldn't be, anyway), then you can afford to be less careful with regard to hoisting and pretend that var declarations are block-scoped. In other words, you can declare a variable in the context in which it is used (inside a loop, inside a then block or an else block, etc.). This kind of local encapsulation makes a code fragment easier to understand in isolation. It is also easier to remove the code fragment or to move it somewhere else.

If you are inside a block, stay inside that block

As an addendum to the previous rule: don't declare the same variable twice, in two different blocks. For example:

```
// Don't do this
if (v) {
    var x = v;
} else {
    var x = 10;
```

```
    }
    doSomethingWith(x);
```

The preceding code has the same effect and intention as the following code, which is why it should be written that way:

```
    var x;
    if (v) {
        x = v;
    } else {
        x = 10;
    }
    doSomethingWith(x);
```

Object Orientation

Now we'll cover conventions relating to object orientation.

Prefer constructors over other instance creation patterns
I recommend that you:

- Always use constructors.
- Always use new when creating an instance.

The main advantages of doing so are:

- Your code better fits into the JavaScript mainstream and is more likely to be portable between frameworks.
- In modern engines, using instances of constructors is very fast (e.g., via hidden classes (*http://bit.ly/1oOEAlZ*)).
- Classes, the default inheritance construct in the upcoming ECMAScript 6, will be based on constructors.

For constructors, it is important to use strict mode, because it protects you against forgetting the new operator for instantiation. And you should be aware that you can return any object in a constructor. More tips for using constructors are mentioned in "Tips for Implementing Constructors" on page 239.

Avoid closures for private data
If you want an object's private data to be completely safe, you have to use closures. Otherwise, you can use normal properties. One common practice is to prefix the names of private properties with underscores. The problem with closures is that code becomes more complicated (unless you put all methods in the instance, which is unidiomatic and slow) and slower (accessing data in closures is currently slower than accessing properties). "Keeping Data Private" on page 244 covers this topic in more detail.

Write parens if a constructor has no arguments

I find that such a constructor invocation looks cleaner with parentheses:

```
var foo = new Foo;    // no
var foo = new Foo();  // yes
```

Be careful about operator precedence

Use parens so that two operators don't compete with each other—the result is not always what you might expect:

```
> false && true || true
true
> false && (true || true)
false
> (false && true) || true
true
```

`instanceof` is especially tricky:

```
> ! {} instanceof Array
false
> (!{}) instanceof Array
false
> !({} instanceof Array)
true
```

However, I find method calls after a constructor unproblematic:

```
new Foo().bar().baz();    // ok
(new Foo()).bar().baz();  // not necessary
```

Miscellaneous

This section collects various tips:

Coercing

Coerce a value to a type via `Boolean`, `Number`, `String()`, `Object()` (used as functions —never use those functions as constructors). The rationale is that this convention is more descriptive:

```
> +'123'  // no
123
> Number('123')  // yes
123

> ''+true  // no
'true'
> String(true)  // yes
'true'
```

Avoid `this` *as an implicit parameter*

    `this` should refer only to the receiver of the current method invocation; it should not be abused as an implicit parameter. The rationale is that such functions are easier to call and understand. I also like to keep object-oriented and functional mechanisms separate:

```
// Avoid:
function handler() {
    this.logError(...);
}

// Prefer:
function handler(context) {
    context.logError(...);
}
```

Check for the existence of a property via `in` *and* `hasOwnProperty` *(see "Iteration and Detection of Properties" on page 217)*

    This is more self-explanatory and safer than comparing with `undefined` or checking for truthiness:

```
// All properties:
if (obj.foo) // no
if (obj.foo !== undefined)  // no
if ('foo' in obj) ... // yes

// Own properties:
if (obj.hasOwnProperty('foo')) ... // risky for arbitrary objects
if (Object.prototype.hasOwnProperty.call(obj, 'foo')) ... // safe
```

Fail fast

    If you can, it's best to fail fast and to not fail silently. JavaScript is only so forgiving (e.g., division by zero), because the first version of ECMAScript did not have exceptions. For example, don't coerce values; throw an exception. However, you have to find ways to recover gracefully from failure when your code is in production.

Conclusion

Whenever you are considering a style question, ask yourself: what makes my code easier to understand? Resist the temptation to be clever and leave most of the mechanical cleverness to JavaScript engines and minifiers (see Chapter 32).

CHAPTER 27

Language Mechanisms for Debugging

The following three language constructs help with debugging. They should obviously be complemented by a proper debugger:

- The `debugger` statement behaves like a breakpoint and launches the debugger.
- `console.log(x)` logs the value x to the console of the JavaScript engine.
- `console.trace()` prints a stack trace to the engine's console.

The console API provides more debugging help and is documented in more detail in "The Console API" on page 351. Exception handling is explained in Chapter 14.

CHAPTER 28

Subclassing Built-ins

JavaScript's built-in constructors are difficult to subclass. This chapter explains why and presents solutions.

Terminology

We use the phrase *subclass a built-in* and avoid the term *extend*, because it is taken in JavaScript:

Subclassing a built-in A

> Creating a subconstructor B of a given built-in constructor A. B's instances are also instances of A.

Extending an object obj

> Copying one object's properties to another one. Underscore.js uses this term (*http://underscorejs.org/#extend*), continuing a tradition established by the Prototype framework.

There are two obstacles to subclassing a built-in: instances with internal properties and a constructor that can't be called as a function.

Obstacle 1: Instances with Internal Properties

Most built-in constructors have instances with so-called *internal properties* (see "Kinds of Properties" on page 197), whose names are written in double square brackets, like this: [[PrimitiveValue]]. Internal properties are managed by the JavaScript engine and usually not directly accessible in JavaScript. The normal subclassing technique in JavaScript is to call a superconstructor as a function with the this of the subconstructor (see "Layer 4: Inheritance Between Constructors" on page 251):

```
function Super(x, y) {
    this.x = x;  // (1)
    this.y = y;  // (1)
}
function Sub(x, y, z) {
    // Add superproperties to subinstance
    Super.call(this, x, y);  // (2)
    // Add subproperty
    this.z = z;
}
```

Most built-ins ignore the subinstance passed in as this (2), an obstacle that is described in the next section. Furthermore, adding internal properties to an existing instance (1) is in general impossible, because they tend to fundamentally change the instance's nature. Hence, the call at (2) can't be used to add internal properties. The following constructors have instances with internal properties:

Wrapper constructors

Instances of Boolean, Number, and String wrap primitives. They all have the internal property [[PrimitiveValue]] whose value is returned by valueOf(); String has two additional instance properties:

- Boolean: Internal instance property [[PrimitiveValue]].

- Number: Internal instance property [[PrimitiveValue]].

- String: Internal instance property [[PrimitiveValue]], custom internal instance method [[GetOwnProperty]], normal instance property length. [[GetOwnProperty]] enables indexed access of characters by reading from the wrapped string when an array index is used.

Array

The custom internal instance method [[DefineOwnProperty]] intercepts properties being set. It ensures that the length property works correctly, by keeping length up-to-date when array elements are added and by removing excess elements when length is made smaller.

Date

The internal instance property [[PrimitiveValue]] stores the time represented by a date instance (as the number of milliseconds since 1 January 1970 00:00:00 UTC).

Function

The internal instance property [[Call]] (the code to execute when an instance is called) and possibly others.

RegExp

The internal instance property [[Match]], plus two noninternal instance properties. From the ECMAScript specification:

> The value of the [[Match]] internal property is an implementation dependent representation of the Pattern of the RegExp object.

The only built-in constructors that don't have internal properties are Error and Object.

Workaround for Obstacle 1

MyArray is a subclass of of Array. It has a getter size that returns the actual elements in an array, ignoring holes (where length considers holes). The trick used to implement MyArray is that it creates an array instance and copies its methods into it:[1]

```
function MyArray(/*arguments*/) {
    var arr = [];
    // Don't use Array constructor to set up elements (doesn't always work)
    Array.prototype.push.apply(arr, arguments);  // (1)
    copyOwnPropertiesFrom(arr, MyArray.methods);
    return arr;
}
MyArray.methods = {
    get size() {
        var size = 0;
        for (var i=0; i < this.length; i++) {
            if (i in this) size++;
        }
        return size;
    }
}
```

This code uses the helper function copyOwnPropertiesFrom(), which is shown and explained in "Copying an Object" on page 226.

We do not call the Array constructor in line (1), because of a quirk: if it is called with a single parameter that is a number, the number does not become an element, but determines the length of an empty array (see "Initializing an array with elements (avoid!)" on page 275).

Here is the interaction:

```
> var a = new MyArray('a', 'b')
> a.length = 4;
> a.length
4
```

---

1. Inspired by a blog post by Ben Nadel (*http://bit.ly/1oOERFo*).

```
> a.size
2
```

Caveats

Copying methods to an instance leads to redundancies that could be avoided with a prototype (if we had the option to use one). Additionally, `MyArray` creates objects that are not its instances:

```
> a instanceof MyArray
false
> a instanceof Array
true
```

Obstacle 2: A Constructor That Can't Be Called as a Function

Even though `Error` and subclasses don't have instances with internal properties, you still can't subclass them easily, because the standard pattern for subclassing won't work (repeated from earlier):

```
function Super(x, y) {
    this.x = x;
    this.y = y;
}
function Sub(x, y, z) {
    // Add superproperties to subinstance
    Super.call(this, x, y);  // (1)
    // Add subproperty
    this.z = z;
}
```

The problem is that `Error` always produces a new instance, even if called as a function (1); that is, it ignores the parameter `this` handed to it via `call()`:

```
> var e = {};
> Object.getOwnPropertyNames(Error.call(e)) // new instance
[ 'stack', 'arguments', 'type' ]
> Object.getOwnPropertyNames(e) // unchanged
[]
```

In the preceding interaction, `Error` returns an instance with own properties, but it's a new instance, not `e`. The subclassing pattern would only work if `Error` added the own properties to `this` (`e`, in the preceding case).

Workaround for Obstacle 2

Inside the subconstructor, create a new superinstance and copy its own properties to the subinstance:

```
function MyError() {
    // Use Error as a function
    var superInstance = Error.apply(null, arguments);
    copyOwnPropertiesFrom(this, superInstance);
}
MyError.prototype = Object.create(Error.prototype);
MyError.prototype.constructor = MyError;
```

The helper function copyOwnPropertiesFrom() is shown in "Copying an Object" on page 226. Trying out MyError:

```
try {
    throw new MyError('Something happened');
} catch (e) {
    console.log('Properties: '+Object.getOwnPropertyNames(e));
}
```

here is the output on Node.js:

```
Properties: stack,arguments,message,type
```

The instanceof relationship is as it should be:

```
> new MyError() instanceof Error
true
> new MyError() instanceof MyError
true
```

Another Solution: Delegation

Delegation is a very clean alternative to subclassing. For example, to create your own array constructor, you keep an array in a property:

```
function MyArray(/*arguments*/) {
    this.array = [];
    Array.prototype.push.apply(this.array, arguments);
}
Object.defineProperties(MyArray.prototype, {
    size: {
        get: function () {
            var size = 0;
            for (var i=0; i < this.array.length; i++) {
                if (i in this.array) size++;
            }
            return size;
        }
    },
    length: {
        get: function () {
            return this.array.length;
        },
        set: function (value) {
            return this.array.length = value;
```

```
        }
    }
});
```

The obvious limitation is that you can't access elements of MyArray via square brackets; you must use methods to do so:

```
MyArray.prototype.get = function (index) {
    return this.array[index];
}
MyArray.prototype.set = function (index, value) {
    return this.array[index] = value;
}
```

Normal methods of Array.prototype can be transferred via the following bit of metaprogramming:

```
[ 'toString', 'push', 'pop' ].forEach(function (key) {
    MyArray.prototype[key] = function () {
        return Array.prototype[key].apply(this.array, arguments);
    }
});
```

We derive MyArray methods from Array methods by invoking them on the array this.array that is stored in instances of MyArray.

Using MyArray:

```
> var a = new MyArray('a', 'b');
> a.length = 4;
> a.push('c')
5
> a.length
5
> a.size
3
> a.set(0, 'x');
> a.toString()
'x,b,,,c'
```

CHAPTER 29

JSDoc: Generating API Documentation

It is a common development problem: you have written JavaScript code that is to be used by others and need a nice-looking HTML documentation of its API. The de facto standard tool in the JavaScript world for generating API documentation is *JSDoc* (*http://usejsdoc.org*).[1] It is modeled after its Java analog, JavaDoc.

JSDoc takes JavaScript code with **/** */** comments (normal block comments that start with an asterisk) and produces HTML documentation for it. For example, given the following code:

```
/** @namespace */
var util = {
    /**
     * Repeat <tt>str</tt> several times.
     * @param {string} str The string to repeat.
     * @param {number} [times=1] How many times to repeat the string.
     * @returns {string}
     */
    repeat: function(str, times) {
        if (times === undefined || times < 1) {
            times = 1;
        }
        return new Array(times+1).join(str);
    }
};
```

the generated HTML looks as shown in Figure 29-1 in a web browser.

---

1. The JSDoc website is the main source of this chapter; some examples are borrowed from it.

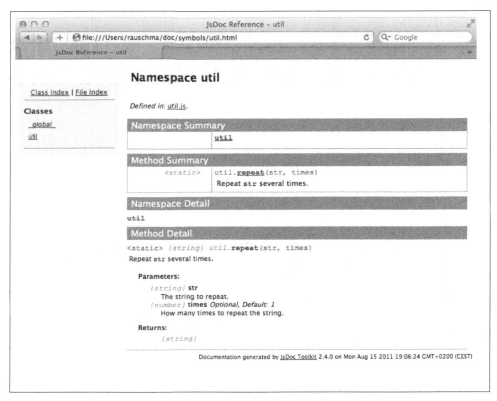

Figure 29-1. HTML output produced by JSDoc.

The Readme (*http://usejsdoc.org/about-jsdoc3.html*) on the JSDoc website explains how to install and call this tool.

The Basics of JSDoc

JSDoc is all about documenting *entities* (functions, methods, constructors, etc.). That is achieved via comments that precede the entities and start with /**.

Syntax

Let's review the comment shown at the beginning:

```
/**
 * Repeat <tt>str</tt> several times.
 * @param {string} str The string to repeat.
 * @param {number} [times=1] How many times to repeat the string.
 * @returns {string}
 */
```

This demonstrates some of the JSDoc syntax, which consists of the following pieces:

JSDoc comment
> This is a JavaScript block comment whose first character is an asterisk. This creates the illusion that the token /** starts such a comment.

Tags
> You structure comments by starting lines with *tags*, keywords that are prefixed with an @ symbol. @param is an example in the preceding code.

HTML
> You can freely use HTML in JSDoc comments. For example, <tt> displays a word in a monospaced font.

Type annotations
> You can document the type of an entity via a type name in braces. Variations include:
> - Single type: @param {string} name
> - Multiple types: @param {string|number} idCode
> - Arrays of a type: @param {string[]} names

Namepaths
> Inside JSDoc comments, so-called *namepaths* are used to refer to entities. The syntax of such paths is as follows:
> ```
> myFunction
> MyClass
> MyClass.staticMember
> MyClass#instanceMember
> ```

Classes are usually (implemented by) constructors. Static members are, for example, properties of constructors. JSDoc has a broad definition of *instance member*. It means everything that can be accessed via an instance. Therefore, instance members include instance properties and prototype properties.

Naming Types

The types of entities are either primitive types or classes. The names of the former always start with lowercase letters; the names of the latter always start with uppercase letters. In other words, the type names of primitives are boolean, number, and string, just like the results returned by the typeof operator. That way, you cannot confuse strings (primitives) with instances of the constructor String (objects).

Basic Tags

Following are the basic metadata tags:

@fileOverview description

Marks a JSDoc comment that describes the whole file. For example:

```
/**
 * @fileOverview Various tool functions.
 * @author <a href="mailto:jd@example.com">John Doe</a>
 * @version 3.1.2
 */
```

@author

Refers to who has written the entity being documented.

@deprecated

Indicates that the entity is not supported anymore. It is a good practice to document what to use instead.

@example

Contains a code example illustrating how the given entity should be used:

```
/**
 * @example
 * var str = 'abc';
 * console.log(repeat(str, 3)); // abcabcabc
 */
```

Basic tags for linking are as follows:

@see

Points to a related resource:

```
/**
 * @see MyConstructor#myMethod
 * @see The <a href="http://example.com">Example Project</a>.
 */
```

{@link ...}

Works like **@see**, but can be used inside other tags.

@requires resourceDescription

Indicates a resource that the documented entity needs. The resource description is either a namepath or a natural language description.

Versioning tags include the following:

@version versionNumber

Indicates the version of the documented entity. For example:

```
@version 10.3.1
```

`@since versionNumber`
> Indicates since which version the documented entity has been available. For
> example:
>
> ```
> @since 10.2.0
> ```

Documenting Functions and Methods

For functions and methods, you can document parameters, return values, and exceptions they may throw:

`@param {paramType} paramName description`
> Describes the parameter whose name is `paramName`. Type and description are optional. Here are some examples:
>
> ```
> @param str The string to repeat.
> @param {string} str
> @param {string} str The string to repeat.
> ```
>
> Advanced features:
>
> - Optional parameter:
>
>   ```
>   @param {number} [times] The number of times is optional.
>   ```
>
> - Optional parameter with default value:
>
>   ```
>   @param {number} [times=1] The number of times is optional.
>   ```

`@returns {returnType} description`
> Describes the return value of the function or method. Either type or description can be omitted.

`@throws {exceptionType} description`
> Describes an exception that might be thrown during the execution of the function or method. Either type or description can be omitted.

Inline Type Information ("Inline Doc Comments")

There are two ways of providing type information for parameters and return values. First, you can add type annotations to `@param` and `@returns`:

```
/**
 * @param {String} name
 * @returns {Object}
 */
function getPerson(name) {
}
```

Second, you can inline the type information:

```
function getPerson(/**String*/ name) /**Object*/ {
}
```

Documenting Variables, Parameters, and Instance Properties

The following tags are used for documenting variables, parameters, and instance properties:

@type {typeName}

What type does the documented variable have? For example:

```
/** @type {number} */
var carCounter = 0;
```

This tag can also be used to document the return type of functions, but @returns is preferable in this case.

@constant

A flag that indicates that the documented variable has a constant value.

```
/** @constant */
var FORD = 'Ford';
```

@property {propType} propKey description

Document an instance property in the constructor comment. For example:

```
/**
 * @constructor
 * @property {string} name The name of the person.
 */
function Person(name) {
    this.name = name;
}
```

Alternatively, instance properties can be documented as follows:

```
/**
 * @class
 */
function Person(name) {
    /**
     * The name of the person.
     * @type {string}
     */
    this.name = name;
}
```

Which one of those styles to use is a matter of personal preference.

`@default defaultValue`
What is the default value of a parameter or instance property? For example:

```
/** @constructor */
function Page(title) {
    /**
     * @default 'Untitled'
     */
    this.title = title || 'Untitled';
}
```

Documenting Classes

JSDoc distinguishes between classes and constructors. The former concept is more like a type, while a constructor is one way of implementing a class. JavaScript's built-in means for defining classes are limited, which is why there are many APIs that help with this task. These APIs differ, often radically, so you have to help JSDoc with figuring out what is going on. The following tags let you do that:

`@constructor`
Marks a function as a constructor.

`@class`
Marks a variable or a function as a class. In the latter case, `@class` is a synonym for `@constructor`.

`@constructs`
Records that a method sets up the instance data. If such a method exists, the class is documented there.

`@lends namePath`
Specifies to which class the following object literal contributes. There are two ways of contributing.

- `@lends Person#`: The object literal contributes instance members to `Person`.
- `@lends Person`: The object literal contributes static members to `Person`.

`@memberof parentNamePath`
The documented entity is a member of the specified object. `@lends MyClass#`, applied to an object literal, has the same effect as marking each property of that literal with `@memberof MyClass#`.

The most common ways of defining a class are: via a constructor function, via an object literal, and via an object literal that has an `@constructs` method.

Defining a Class via a Constructor Function

To define a class via a constructor function, you must mark the constructor function; otherwise, it will not be documented as a class. Capitalization alone does not mark a function as a constructor:

```
/**
 * A class for managing persons.
 * @constructor
 */
function Person(name) {
}
```

Defining a Class via an Object Literal

To define a class via an object literal, you need two markers. First, you need to tell JSDoc that a given variable holds a class. Second, you need to mark an object literal as defining a class. You do the latter via the @lends tag:

```
/**
 * A class for managing persons.
 * @class
 */
var Person = makeClass(
    /** @lends Person# */
    {
        say: function(message) {
            return 'This person says: ' + message;
        }
    }
);
```

Defining a Class via an Object Literal with an @constructs Method

If an object literal has an @constructs method, you need to tell JSDoc about it, so that it can find the documentation for the instance properties. The documentation of the class moves to that method:

```
var Person = makeClass(
    /** @lends Person# */
    {
        /**
         * A class for managing persons.
         * @constructs
         */
        initialize: function(name) {
            this.name = name;
        },
        say: function(message) {
            return this.name + ' says: ' + message;
        }
```

```
        }
    );
```

If you omit the `@lends`, you must specify which class the methods belong to:

```
var Person = makeClass({
    /**
     * A class for managing persons.
     * @constructs Person
     */
    initialize: function(name) {
        this.name = name;
    },
    /** @memberof Person# */
    say: function(message) {
        return this.name + ' says: ' + message;
    }
    }
);
```

Subclassing

JavaScript has no built-in support for subclassing. When you subclass in your code (be it manually, be it via a library), you have to tell JSDoc what is going on:

`@extends namePath`
> Indicates that the documented class is the subclass of another one. For example:

```
/**
 * @constructor
 * @extends Person
 */
function Programmer(name) {
    Person.call(this, name);
    ...
}
// Remaining code for subclassing omitted
```

Other Useful Tags

All of these tags are documented at the JSDoc website (*http://usejsdoc.org/*):

- Modularity: `@module`, `@exports`, `@namespace`
- Custom types (for virtual entities such as callbacks, whose signature you can document): `@typedef`, `@callback`
- Legal matters: `@copyright`, `@license`
- Various kinds of objects: `@mixin`, `@enum`

CHAPTER 30

Libraries

This chapter covers JavaScript libraries. It first explains what shims and polyfills are, two special kinds of libraries. Then it lists a few core libraries. Lastly, it points to additional library-related resources.

Shims Versus Polyfills

Shims and polyfills are libraries that retrofit newer functionality on older JavaScript engines:

- A *shim* is a library that brings a new API to an older environment, using only the means of that environment.
- A *polyfill* is a shim for a browser API. It typically checks if a browser supports an API. If it doesn't, the polyfill installs its own implementation. That allows you to use the API in either case. The term *polyfill* comes from a home improvement product; according to Remy Sharp (*http://bit.ly/MmZZmZ*):

  > Polyfilla is a UK product known as Spackling Paste in the US. With that in mind: think of the browsers as a wall with cracks in it. These [polyfills] help smooth out the cracks and give us a nice smooth wall of browsers to work with.

Examples include:

- "HTML5 Cross Browser Polyfills" (*http://bit.ly/1oOGuTE*): A list compiled by Paul Irish.
- es5-shim (*http://bit.ly/1oOGxi4*) is a (nonpolyfill) shim that retrofits ECMAScript 5 features on ECMAScript 3 engines. It is purely language-related and makes just as much sense on Node.js as it does on browsers.

Four Language Libraries

The following libraries are quite established and close to the language. It is useful to be aware of them:

- The ECMAScript Internationalization API helps with tasks related to internationalization: collation (sorting and searching strings), number formatting, and date and time formatting. The next section explains this API in more detail.

- Underscore.js (*http://underscorejs.org*) complements JavaScript's relatively sparse standard library with tool functions for arrays, objects, functions, and more. As Underscore predates ECMAScript 5, there is some overlap with the standard library. That is, however, a feature: on older browsers, you get functionality that is normally ECMAScript-5-only; on ECMAScript 5, the relevant functions simply forward to the standard library.

- Lo-Dash (*http://lodash.com*) is an alternative implementation of the Underscore.js API, with a few additional features. Check out the website to find out if it suits you better than Underscore.js.

- XRegExp (*http://xregexp.com*) is a regular expression library with several advanced features such as named captures and free-spacing (which allows you to spread out a regular expression across multiple lines and document per line). Behind the scenes, enhanced regular expressions are translated to normal regular expressions, meaning that you don't pay a performance penalty for using XRegExp.

The ECMAScript Internationalization API

The ECMAScript Internationalization API is a standard JavaScript API that helps with tasks related to internationalization: collation (sorting and searching strings), number formatting, and date and time formatting. This section gives a brief overview and points you to more reading material.

The ECMAScript Internationalization API, Edition 1

The first edition of the API provides the following services:

- *Collation* supports two scenarios: sorting a set of strings and searching within a set of strings. Collation is parameterized by locale and aware of Unicode.

- *Number formatting.* Parameters include:
  - Style of formatting: decimal, currency (which one and how to refer to it is determined by other parameters), percent
  - Locale (directly specified or best fit, searched for via a matcher object)

— Numbering system (Western digits, Arabic digits, Thai digits, etc.)

— Precision: number of integer digits, fraction digits, significant digits

— Grouping separators on or off

- *Date and time formatting.* Parameters include:

— What information to format and in which style (short, long, numeric, etc.)

— A locale

— A time zone

Most of the functionality is accessed via an object in the global variable `Intl`, but the API also augments the following methods:

- `String.prototype.localeCompare`
- `Number.prototype.toLocaleString`
- `Date.prototype.toLocaleString`
- `Date.prototype.toLocaleDateString`
- `Date.prototype.toLocaleTimeString`

What Kind of Standard Is It?

The number of the standard "ECMAScript Internationalization API" (EIA) is ECMA-402. It is hosted by Ecma International, the association that also hosts EMCA-262, the ECMAScript language specification. Both standards are maintained by TC39. Therefore, EIA is as close to the language as you can get without being part of ECMA-262. The API has been designed to work with both ECMAScript 5 and ECMA-Script 6. A set of conformance tests complements the standard and ensures that the various implementations of the API are compatible (ECMA-262 has a similar test suite).

When Can I Use It?

Most modern browsers already support it or are in the process of supporting it. David Storey has created a detailed compatibility table (*http://bit.ly/1oOGIdo*) (indicating which browsers support which locales and more).

Further Reading

The specification (*http://bit.ly/1oOGQth*) of the ECMAScript Internationalization API is edited by Norbert Lindenberg. It is available in PDF, HTML, and EPUB format. Additionally, there are several comprehensive introductory articles:

- "The ECMAScript Internationalization API" (*http://bit.ly/1oOGT8C*) by Norbert Lindenberg
- "ECMAScript Internationalization API" (*http://bit.ly/1oOGYcc*) by David Storey
- "Using the JavaScript Internationalization API" (*http://bit.ly/1oOH2sz*) by Marcos Caceres

Directories for JavaScript Resources

This section describes sites that collect information on JavaScript resources. There are several kinds of such directories.

Following is a list of general directories for JavaScript:

- "JavaScriptOO: Every JavaScript project you should be looking into" (*http://www.javascriptoo.com/*)
- JSDB (*http://www.jsdb.io/*): A collection of the best JavaScript libraries
- JSter (*http://jster.net/*): A catalog of JavaScript libraries and tools for development
- "Master List of HTML5, JavaScript, and CSS Resources" (*http://bit.ly/1oOH7MW*)

Specialized directories include:

- "Microjs: Fantastic Micro-Frameworks and Micro-libraries for Fun and Profit" (*http://microjs.com/*)
- "Unheap: A tidy repository of jQuery plugins" (*http://www.unheap.com/*)

Obviously, you can always directly browse the registries of package managers:

- npm (*https://npmjs.org/*) (Node Packaged Modules)
- Bower (*http://bower.io/*)

Directories for CDNs (content delivery networks) and CDN content include:

- jsDelivr (*http://www.jsdelivr.com/*): Free CDNs for JavaScript libraries, jQuery plug-ins, CSS frameworks, fonts, and more
- "cdnjs: The missing CDN for JavaScript and CSS" (*http://cdnjs.com/*) (hosts less popular libraries)

Acknowledgments

The following people contributed to this section: Kyle Simpson (@getify), Gildas Lormeau (@check_ca), Fredrik Sogaard (@fredrik_sogaard), Gene Loparco (@gloparco), Manuel Strehl (@m_strehl), and Elijah Manor (@elijahmanor).

CHAPTER 31

Module Systems and Package Managers

JavaScript does not have built-in support for modules, but the community has created impressive workarounds. To manage modules, you can use so-called *package managers*, which handle discovery, installation, dependency management, and more.

Module Systems

The two most important (and unfortunately incompatible) standards for JavaScript modules are:

CommonJS Modules (CJS)

> The dominant incarnation of this standard is Node.js modules (*http://nodejs.org/api/modules.html*) (Node.js modules have a few features that go beyond CJS). Its characteristics include:
>
> - Compact syntax
> - Designed for synchronous loading
> - Main use: server

Asynchronous Module Definition (AMD)

> The most popular implementation of this standard is RequireJS (*http://requirejs.org/*). Its characteristics include:
>
> - Slightly more complicated syntax, enabling AMD to work without `eval()` or a static compilation step
> - Designed for asynchronous loading
> - Main use: browsers

Package Managers

When it comes to package managers, npm (*https://npmjs.org*) (Node Packaged Modules) is the canonical choice for Node.js. For browsers, two options are popular (among others):

- Bower (*http://bower.io*) is a package manager for the Web that supports both AMD and CJS.
- Browserify (*http://browserify.org*) is a tool based on npm that compiles npm packages to something you can use in a browser.

Quick and Dirty Modules

For normal web development, you should use a module system such as RequireJS or Browserify. However, sometimes you just want to put together a quick hack. Then the following simple module pattern can help:

```javascript
var moduleName = function () {
    function privateFunction () { ... }
    function publicFunction(...) {
        privateFunction();
        otherModule.doSomething(); // implicit import
    }
    return { // exports
        publicFunction: publicFunction
    };
}();
```

The preceding is a module that is stored in the global variable `moduleName`. It does the following:

- Implicitly imports a dependency (the module `otherModule`)
- Has a private function, `privateFunction`
- Exports `publicFunction`

To use the module on a web page, simply load its file and the files of its dependencies via `<script>` tags:

```html
<script src="modules/otherModule.js"></script>
<script src="modules/moduleName.js"></script>
<script type="text/javascript">
    moduleName.publicFunction(...);
</script>
```

If no other module is accessed while a module is loaded (which is the case for `module Name`), then the order in which modules are loaded does not matter.

Here are my comments and recommendations:

- I've used this module pattern for a while, until I found out that I hadn't invented it and that it had an official name. Christian Heilmann popularized it and called it the "revealing module pattern" (*http://bit.ly/1c1InUg*).
- If you use this pattern, keep it simple. Feel free to pollute the global scope with module names, but do try to find unique names. It's only for hacks, so there is no need to get fancy (nested namespaces, modules split across multiple files, etc.).

CHAPTER 32

More Tools

Module systems and package managers are covered in Chapter 31. But there are additional important categories of tools:

Linting

Lint tools analyze source code and report potential problems and style violations. Three popular ones are:

- JSLint (*http://www.jslint.com*) by Douglas Crockford
- JSHint (*http://www.jshint.com*) by Anton Kovalyov
- ESLint (*https://github.com/nzakas/eslint*) by Nicholas Zakas

Unit testing

Ideally, a unit test framework runs on both of the two large JavaScript platforms—the browser and Node.js. Two important frameworks that do are:

- Jasmine (*http://pivotal.github.io/jasmine/*)
- mocha (*http://visionmedia.github.io/mocha/*)

Minification

JavaScript source code usually wastes space—variable names are longer than need be, there are comments, extra whitespace, and so on. A minification tool removes the waste and compiles code to smaller code. Some parts of the removal process are relatively complex (e.g., the renaming of variables to short names). Three popular minification tools are:

- UglifyJS (*https://github.com/mishoo/UglifyJS2/*)
- YUI Compressor (*https://github.com/yui/yuicompressor*)
- Closure Compiler (*https://developers.google.com/closure/compiler/*)

Building

For most projects, there are many operations that you need to apply to their artifacts: lint the code, compile code (compilation happens even in web projects—for example, to compile a CSS language such as LESS or Sass to plain CSS), minify code, and more. Build tools help you do that. Two classic examples are make for Unix and Ant for Java. Two popular build tools for JavaScript are Grunt (*http://gruntjs.com*) and Gulp (*http://gulpjs.com/*). One of their most intriguing features is that you can stay in JavaScript while working with them; they are both based on Node.js.

Scaffolding

A scaffolding tool sets up an empty project, preconfigures build files, and more. Yo (*https://github.com/yeoman/yo*) is one such tool. It is part of the Yeoman (*http://yeoman.io*) suite of tools for web development, which bundles yo, Bower, and Grunt.

CHAPTER 33

What to Do Next

Now that you know the JavaScript language, how do you proceed? What is the best way to get to know the whole ecosystem? Here are some suggestions:

- Frontend Rescue (*http://uptodate.frontendrescue.org*) is a site with tips to get you started with browser development.

- JSbooks (*http://jsbooks.revolunet.com*) links to a variety of free books on JavaScript and related technologies.

- Twitter is a good tool for staying up-to-date with web development. Start with famous JavaScript people you know (e.g., the creator of your framework of choice) and continue from there; sooner or later, you will get plenty of ideas for who to follow next.

- JSMentors (*https://groups.google.com/forum/#!forum/jsmentors*) is a forum dedicated to "helping developers become better JavaScript coders in a professional & non-confrontational environment."

- Apart from Twitter, there are many other interesting news sources to explore. The following are a few examples:

  — Echo JS (*http://www.echojs.com*) is a community-driven news site focused on JavaScript and HTML5.

  — Cooper Press (*https://cooperpress.com*) publishes several web-development-related email newsletters (disclaimer: I'm editor of the "JavaScript Weekly" newsletter).

  — Open Web Platform Daily Digest (*http://webplatformdaily.org/*) contains daily lists of newsworthy links.

  — Best of JavaScript, HTML & CSS (*http://flippinawesome.org/category/news/best-of/*) is a weekly list of links.

- JavaScript user groups (*http://communityjs.org*) are a fun and educational way of meeting like-minded people. Most of them assemble regularly, with talks and more.
- JavaScript conferences (*http://lanyrd.com/topics/javascript/*) are another good source of information. Many of them publish freely accessible videos of their talks online.

Finally, you can also take a look at the book's companion website, SpeakingJS.com (*http://speakingjs.com/*), where I'll occasionally publish material related to this book.

Index

Symbols

! (exclamation mark)
   != (inequality) operator, 14, 83, 84
   !== (strict inequality) operator, 14, 83, 84, 377
      checking for NaN, 107
   logical NOT operator, 89, 101
" " (quotation marks, double)
   best practice in JavaScript, 378
   for string literals, 15, 133
$ (dollar sign)
   in a replacement string, 143
% (percent sign)
   %= compound assignment operator, 82
   remainder operator, 15, 122, 124
& (ampersand)
   & (bitwise AND) operator, 89, 126
   && (logical AND) operator, 13, 89, 99, 100
   &= (bitwise AND and assignment) operator, 82
' ' (quotation marks, single)
   best practice in JavaScript, 378
   for string literals, 15, 133
* (asterisk)
   *= compound assignment operator, 82
   multiplication operator, 15, 122
+ (plus sign)
   ++ (increment) operator, 15, 123, 381
   += compound assignment operator, 6

+= operator, concatenating strings, 16
addition operator, 15, 122
string concatenation operator, 16, 134, 137
   performance of, 138
, (comma) operator, 90
- (minus sign)
   -- (decrement operator), 381
   -- (decrement) operator, 15, 123
   -= compound assignment operator, 82
   negation operator, 15, 123
   subtraction operator, 15, 122
. (comma), trailing commas in object literals and array literals, 370
. (dot operator), 8
   calling methods with, 199
   using to access properties, 67, 199
   working with objects, 271
/ (slash)
   /* and */ delimiting multiline comments, 6
   // delimiting single-line comments, 6
   /= compound assignment operator, 82
   division operator, 15, 122
0 (zero), positive and negative, 109–111
1TBS (One True Brace Style), 378
32-bit integers, 114
   signed, 125
   via bitwise operators, 119
64-bit precision, JavaScript numbers, 111

We'd like to hear your suggestions for improving our indexes. Send email to index@oreilly.com.

value to properties using dot operator, 8
assignment operator (=), 4, 54, 81
assignment operators, compound, 82
Asynchronous Module Definition (AMD), 411
attributes (property), 217, 222
    common to all properties, 223
    default values, 223
    getting and setting via property descriptors, 225
    managing via property descriptors, 370
    sealing to prevent change in, 230
automatic semicolon insertion (see ASI)

B

backreferences in regular expressions, 300
best practices (coding style), 377
binary logical operators, 13, 99
binary numbers, inputting and outputting, 125
binary representation of numbers, 111
bind() method, 26, 170
    creating constructor via, 207
    preventing shadowing of this, 210
bitwise operators, 89, 114, 124
    binary, 126
    bitwise shift operators, 127
    converting numbers to integers, 119–120
block scoping, 181
    simulating via IIFEs, 183
blocks
    replacing statements with, 57
    semicolon (;) terminating, 5
    statements ending in, no semicolon, 58
    using for bodies of loops, 145
BOM (byte order mark), 358
Boolean() function, 78, 97
booleans, 12, 53, 69, 97–102
    conversions to, and lenient equality, 85
    converting values to, 78, 97, 97
    invoking Boolean() as constructor, 98
    logical NOT (!) operator, 101
    operators for, 89
    truthy and falsy values, 98
    wrapper object for, 75
        unwrapping, 77
Bower (package manager), 412
brace styles, 378
bracket operator ([]), 201, 271
    accessing properties via, 202
    calling methods via, 202

deleting properties via, 202
    setting properties via, 202
break statements in loops, 18, 146
browser as operating system, 50
Browserify, 412
browsers
    consoles for entering JavaScript, xiii
    global object, window, 188
    javascript: URLs and, 91
    legacy, tips for working with, 372
    package managers for, 412
build tools, 416
byte order mark (BOM), 358

C

call() method (see Function.prototype.call() method)
callbacks and extracted methods, 209
case
    converting strings to lowercase, 141
    converting strings to uppercase, 141
case clause in switch statements, 17, 151
catch clause
    in try-catch statement, 21, 235
    in try-catch-finally statement, 159
character class escapes in regular expressions, 298
character classes in regular expressions, 298
character escape sequences, 134
character escapes in regular expressions, 298
character properties, 359
characters
    accessing in strings, 135
    and graphemes, 357
Chrome OS, 50
CJS (CommonJS Modules), 411
clases, documenting (JSDoc)
    subclassing, 403
classes, documenting (JSDoc), 397, 401
    defining a class via constructor function, 402
    defining a class via object literal, 402
    defining a class via object literal with @constructs method
        object literal with @constructs method, 402
Closure Compiler, 415
closures, 23, 193
    avoiding for private data, 384
    defined, 193

logical operators, 89, 99
    abbreviating if statements, 380
    logical NOT (!), 101
lookbehind, manually implementing, 313
loops, 17, 146–150
    bodies of, 145
    do-while loop, 147
    for each-in loop, 150
    for loop, 147
    for-in loop, 148
    mechanisms to be used with, 146
        exiting loops, 146
    while loop, 146, 146
low-surrogate code unit, 360

M

machine epsilon, 113
map() method
    creating new array from existing array, 31
    parseInt() function passed as argument to, 175
maps
    arrays as, 274
    using objects as, pitfalls in, 266
marked property keys, 247
Math object, 327–331
    arithmetic functions, 31
    numerical functions, 328
    other functions, 330
    properties, 327
    trigonometric functions, 329
Math.abs() function, 328
Math.acos() function, 330
Math.asin() function, 330
Math.atan() function, 330
Math.atan2() function, 110, 330
Math.ceil() function, 118, 328
Math.cos() function, 330
Math.exp() function, 328
Math.floor() function, 118, 328
Math.log() function, 328
Math.max() function, 330
Math.min() function, 330
Math.pow() function, 110, 328
Math.random() function, 331
Math.round() function, 118, 329
Math.sin() function, 330
Math.sqrt() function, 329
MDN (Mozilla Developer Network), xv

media type for JavaScript files, 362
metadata tags in JSDoc, 397
methods, 25, 166, 198
    attaching global data via IIFE, 250
    calling, 4
    calling using bracket operator, 202
    calling using dot operator, 199
    common to all objects, 257, 272
    documenting (JSDoc), 399
    extracting, 26
        callbacks and, 209
        losing this, 208
    functions inside, 27
        shadowing this, 209
    generic (see generic methods)
    invoking on number literals, 62, 104
    invoking with dot operator, 8
    new, in ECMAScript 5, 371
    overriding, 254
    privileged, 245, 246
    supercalling, 254
    this as implicit parameter, 204
minification, 39
    tools for, 363, 415
mocha (unit test frameworks), 415
module systems, 411
    keeping global data private, 250
    leading to fewer globals, 187
    quick and dirty modules, 412
Mozilla Developer Network (MDN), xv
multidimensional arrays, 276
multiline comments, 6, 54

N

named accessor properties, 198
named data properties, 198
named function expressions, 167, 169
named parameters, 176–177
    as descriptions, 176
    optional, 176
    optional parameters as, 174
    simulating in JavaScript, 176
NaN (not a number), 14, 106, 356
    comparing via strict equality, 84
    isNaN() function, 131
    pitfall, checking whether a value is NaN, 107
Netscape, 43

About the Author

Dr. Axel Rauschmayer specializes in JavaScript and web development. He blogs at 2ality.com, is a trainer for Ecmanauten, edits JavaScript Weekly, and organizes the MunichJS user group. He also frequently holds talks and workshops at conferences.

Axel has been programming since 1985 and developing web applications since 1995. In 1999, he was technical manager at a German Internet startup that later expanded internationally. In 2006, he held his first talk on Ajax.

Axel has done extensive research into programming language design and has followed the state and future of JavaScript since its creation.

Colophon

The animal on the cover of *Speaking JavaScript* is a Papuan Hornbill (*Rhyticeros plicatus*), a large bird inhabiting the forest canopy in Eastern Indonesia and New Guinea. This species is also known as Blyth's hornbill after Edward Blyth (1810–1873), an English zoologist and Curator of the Museum of the Asiatic Society of Bengal.

The male hornbill is quite unusual in appearance due to its reddish-orange or golden-yellow plumage that surrounds the head and neck. Females differ by having a black head and neck. Both sexes have a largely black body, except for the contrasting short, white tail, and the bare, bluish-white skin around the eyes and throat. Hornbills also have red eyes, although those of the male are far brighter.

The variety of honking and grunting calls of the Papuan hornbill are believed to have led to reports of this bird laughing. In flight, the sound of its wings is loud and distinctive, a rushing noise that has been compared to the sound of steam escaping from a steam locomotive. Unsurprisingly, considering its rather large size and striking appearance, the Papuan hornbill is said to be a conspicuous bird, which can be seen flying high over the forest, frequently emitting its distinctive call.

These impressive birds are hunted on their native islands for food and as a trophy, and their skulls are sometimes worn as ornaments. Like other hornbills, its diet consists mainly of fruits—especially figs—occasionally supplemented with insects and other small animals.

The cover image is from Braukhaus Lexicon. The cover fonts are URW Typewriter and Guardian Sans. The text font is Adobe Minion Pro; the heading font is Adobe Myriad Condensed; and the code font is Dalton Maag's Ubuntu Mono.

Get even more
for your money.

Join the O'Reilly Community, and register the O'Reilly books you own. It's free, and you'll get:

- $4.99 ebook upgrade offer
- 40% upgrade offer on O'Reilly print books
- Membership discounts on books and events
- Free lifetime updates to ebooks and videos
- Multiple ebook formats, DRM FREE
- Participation in the O'Reilly community
- Newsletters
- Account management
- 100% Satisfaction Guarantee

Signing up is easy:

1. Go to: oreilly.com/go/register
2. Create an O'Reilly login.
3. Provide your address.
4. Register your books.

Note: English-language books only

To order books online:
oreilly.com/store

For questions about products or an order:
orders@oreilly.com

To sign up to get topic-specific email announcements and/or news about upcoming books, conferences, special offers, and new technologies:
elists@oreilly.com

For technical questions about book content:
booktech@oreilly.com

To submit new book proposals to our editors:
proposals@oreilly.com

O'Reilly books are available in multiple DRM-free ebook formats. For more information:
oreilly.com/ebooks

O'REILLY®

Spreading the knowledge of innovators

oreilly.com

DISCARD

CPSIA information can be obtained at www.ICGtesting.com
Printed in the USA
BVOW10s1430070314

346984BV00006B/18/P